ARCHAEOLOGICAL STUDIES
IN SZECHWAN

CHÊNG TÊ-K'UN

ARCHAEOLOGICAL STUDIES
IN SZECHWAN

CONDUCTED UNDER THE AUSPICES OF
THE HARVARD-YENCHING INSTITUTE AND
THE WEST CHINA UNION
UNIVERSITY

CAMBRIDGE
PUBLISHED ON BEHALF OF THE
FACULTY OF ORIENTAL STUDIES
AT THE UNIVERSITY PRESS
1957

PUBLISHED BY

THE SYNDICS OF THE CAMBRIDGE UNIVERSITY PRESS

Bentley House, 200 Euston Road, London, N.W. 1
American Branch: 32 East 57th Street, New York 22, N.Y.

Printed in Great Britain at the University Press, Cambridge
(Brooke Crutchley, University Printer)

CONTENTS

CONTENTS

PART II. HAN BURIAL REMAINS IN SZECHWAN.
THE KILN SITES OF CH'IUNG-LAI AND LIU-LI-CH'ANG.
SUNG BURIAL REMAINS IN SZECHWAN

LIST OF ILLUSTRATIONS

PLATES

MAPS

LIST OF ABBREVIATIONS

ALL references in the text are placed in parentheses, for example, '(**25**, 125)'. The number in bold face refers to the book or article under that number in the Bibliography which appears on pp. 178–96. The number following is the page reference. Where two numbers follow the bold face numerals, '(**58**, 11. 15)', the first number refers to chapter, unless otherwise indicated.

Other abbreviations are as follows:

AA	*American Anthropologist*, Lancaster.
AMNH	American Museum of Natural History, New York.
AO	*Archaeologia Orientalis*, Tōkyō.
AS	Academia Sinica, Nanking.
ASAG	*Archives Suisses d'anthropologie*, Geneva.
BGSC	*Bulletin of the Geological Society of China*, Peking.
BMFEA	*Bulletin of the Museum of Far Eastern Antiquities*, Stockholm.
BRM	*Bulletin of the Raffles Museum*, Singapore.
BSGI	*Bulletin du Service Géologique de L'Indo-Chine*, Hanoi.
BSPF	*Bulletin de la Société préhistorique française*, Paris.
CCPF	*Congrès préhistorique de France, Compte-rendu*, Paris.
CYYY	*Bulletin of the National Research Institute of History and Philology, Academia Sinica*, Peking. 中央研究院歷史語言研究所集刊.
GSC	Geological Survey of China, Peking.
HJAS	*Harvard Journal of Asiatic Studies*, Cambridge, U.S.A.
HN	*Hongkong Naturalist*, Hongkong.
HP	*L'Homme Préhistorique*, Paris.
JARS	*Journal of the Archaeological Research Society*, Kyotō. 考古學論叢.
JAST	*Journal of the Anthropological Society of Tokyo*, Tōkyō. 人類學雜誌.
JFMSM	*Journal of the Federated Malay States Museums*, Singapore.
JMRAS	*Journal of the Malayan Branch of the Royal Asiatic Society*, Singapore.

JWCBRS	*Journal of the West China Border Research Society*, Chengtu.
KZ	*Kôkogaku Zasshi*, Tōkyō. 考古學雜誌.
M	Many
MAGW	*Mitteilungen der Anthropologischen Gesellschaft in Wien*, Vienna.
MGSC	*Memoirs of the Geological Survey of China*, Peking.
MSGI	*Mémoires du Service Géologique de L'Indo-Chine*, Hanoi.
MUT	*Memoirs of the Science Department, University of Tokyo*, Tōkyō.
ND	*Nanpō Dozoku* 南方土俗, Taihoku.
NH	*Natural History*, New York.
NHCA	*Natural History of Central Asia*, Vol. One, New York, 1932.
PAI	*Papers of the Anthropological Institute, Faculty of Science, Imperial University of Tokyo*, Tōkyō.
PAO	*Praehistoria Asiae Orientalis*, Vol. One, Premier Congrès des Préhistoriens d'Éxtrême-Orient, Hanoi, 1932.
PS	*Paleontologia Sinica*, Peking.
RA	*Revue Anthropologique*, Paris.
RARKU	*Reports upon Archaeological Research in the Department of Literature, Kyoto Imperial University*, Kyotō.
RFSEM	*Reports of the First Scientific Expedition to Manchoukou*, Tōkyō.
RV	*Reallexikon der Vorgeschichte*, Berlin.
S	Several
SWYK	*Shuo-wên yüeh-k'an* 説文月刊, Chungking.
SZ	*Shizengaku Zasshi*, Tōkyō. 史前學雜誌.
TYKP	*Tien yeh k'ao ku pao kao*, AS, Shanghai, 1936. 田野考古報告.
YCHP	*Yenching Journal of Chinese Studies* 燕京學報, Peking.
ZFE	*Zeitschrift für Ethnologie*, Berlin.

ACKNOWLEDGEMENTS

I⊤ is a very pleasant duty to record my indebtedness to those who have helped me in the preparation of this book. I must first and foremost address myself to the Trustees and Director, Dr Serge Elisséeff, of the Harvard-Yenching Institute. To them I owe a great and deep debt of gratitude, not only for the opportunity of pursuing three years of study in the Graduate School of Arts and Sciences at Harvard University, but also for their continual support of our museum programme at the West China Union University. They have also made a generous subsidy towards the publication of this volume.

In the preparation of Part I of this book, I should like to express my deep gratitude to Dr N. C. Nelson, the curator of prehistoric archaeology in the American Museum of Natural History, for his generosity in making his Szechwan and Yünnan collection and his invaluable unpublished journals available for my study and in allowing me to make an unlimited use of the materials, without which this study would never have been possible. The thoroughness of his investigation in the field, his exactness in documentation and his excellent classification and cataloguing of the material make his work unrivalled among those of the archaeologists who have devoted their attention to this region. With his profound experience in the archaeology of Eastern Asia he proved a rich source of information. I enjoyed perfect hospitality in his laboratory.

It is also pleasant to acknowledge my indebtedness to other members of the staff of the American Museum of Natural History, especially Dr Clark Wissler, Miss Bella Weitzner, Dr Robert von Heine-Geldern, Mr Ernest A. Neilson and Mr Chris E. Olsen, who helped me in every way possible.

I find it difficult to express the gratitude I feel for the privilege of working for three years under Mr Lauriston Ward, Lecturer in Anthropology and Curator of Asiatic Archaeology of the Peabody Museum, Harvard University. To the problems of Far Eastern prehistory he brought a wide familiarity with Near Eastern and European Archaeology, but even more valuable to me have been the general critical methods he applied to any body of archaeological data, whatever the geographical location. Under his tutelage, stone and bone and pottery became actual languages. Like a Chinese scholar of the old school, he gives freely to his students of his time, his interest and of the fruits of his own researches. In supervising the writing on prehistoric Szechwan he has not only given critical comments at any number of points but he undertook to read and discuss with the writer the entire manuscript with a view to remedying faults in English expression.

In the preparation of the other parts of this book, I am particularly indebted to my distinguished predecessors, Professor Daniel Sheets Dye, Rev. Thomas Torrance and Dr David Crocket Graham, who have devoted much time and energy in putting the West China Museum collection on a scientific basis.

For information and help of one kind or another, I should like to thank the following: Dr Fêng Han-yi, Curator of the Szechwan Museum; Mr Huang Hsi-ch'eng, owner of the Hsi-ch'eng Museum; Dr Laurence Picken of Cambridge; Dr Ch'iu K'ai-ming of Harvard; and past and present members of the Museum staff, Lin Ming-chun, Michael Sullivan, Sung Shu-ch'ing, Ch'êng En-yüan, Liu Sheng-yü and Chou Lo-hsing.

Finally, I wish to express my deep appreciation of the kindness and patience of Messrs Gabriel W. Lasker, Lin Yüeh-hwa, John H. Cox, and J. L. Cranmer-Byng, and Professor E. G. Pulleyblank, in reading the manuscript. It has not always been an easy task to convert the text into clear and readable English. I must not forget to thank Dr Serge Polevoy, who has so kindly helped me with the Russian reports.

CHÊNG TÊ-K'UN

INTRODUCTION

SZECHWAN ARCHAEOLOGY

THE present volume comprises four archaeological studies which I had the opportunity of making in Szechwan between 1940 and 1948. They represent some of the results of the research programme which I had undertaken as the curator of the West China Union University Museum in Chengtu.

For more than thirty years the University Museum has been accumulating local archaeological specimens and data, and my main task in recent years has been the co-ordination of this material in order to formulate an archaeological chronology for the province. I have tried to trace the development of culture in this western part of China and to find how this province was linked up with the rest of the world.

This was of course no easy task, because very little work had been done on Szechwan archaeology, and research had to be combined with field work and adding to the Museum collection. During the period several excavations and many extensive reconnaissance and collecting trips in the province and its neighbouring areas were made. The result was fruitful and encouraging, and it now seems possible to describe the development of culture in Szechwan purely from the archaeological point of view.

The archaeology of Szechwan may be divided into eleven stages, and this volume touches on only some of these. It therefore seems worth while to present here a brief summary of the general sequence, so that the reader will see how the work described here fits into a study of Szechwan archaeology as a whole.

In the autumn of 1940 I had the privilege of studying, in the American Museum of Natural History in New York, the Szechwan collection which Dr N. C. Nelson collected along the Yangtse in 1925–6. I came to the conclusion that the prehistory of this province may be divided into four stages, and in going over the collection of stone artifacts in the West China Union University Museum I found that this chronology could also be applied to them. The stages are:

Stage I: Mesolithic period (probably 5000 B.C. to 3000 B.C.), characterized by some chipped stone tools.

Stage II: Early neolithic period (3000 B.C. to 2000 B.C.), represented by some chipped-and-polished stone tools.

Stage III: Late neolithic period (2000 B.C. to 1200 B.C.), represented by some chipped-pecked-and-polished and some polished stone tools which were found associated with a series of pottery, consisting of cord-marked, red, black, white and grey wares.

Stage IV: Aeneolithic period (1200 B.C. to 700 B.C.), represented by some highly finished stone tools which were found associated with grey and black pottery in coarse or fine paste.

A detailed study of these four stages appears as Part I of this book.

The aeneolithic period of Szechwan may be best illustrated by the cultural deposit of Han-chou, which Dr D. C. Graham excavated in 1934 (**1**). A closer study of the excavation revealed the fact that the cultural stratum had been cut by a ceremonial pit which may be dated between 700 B.C. and 500 B.C. The pottery unearthed from the pit was similar to those found in the cultural stratum, but the pit yielded also a series of jade and stone artifacts which might have been interred by an ancient governor of Szechwan after offering sacrifice to the god of the Min Mountain 岷 山. It was an old belief and practice that jade was a food of the gods and that it should be buried in the ground after the sacrificial ceremony. The Han-chou excavation serves to link the prehistory of Szechwan with early historic times, and the ceremonial pit may be taken to represent Stage V in the development of the province. A study of this particular excavation has been published under the title 'The T'ai-p'ing-ch'ang 太 平 塲 Culture', in the *Hsieh-ta Journal of Chinese Studies* 協 大 學 報 (Foochow, 1949).

It was probably at this stage that megalithic culture made its appearance in this province. Some of these big stone remains in the form of dolmens, menhirs and alignments are still in existence in Szechwan, and they are, no doubt, some of the most important archaeological remains in western China. I have given a list of some of the megalithic remains in Chapter III of my book, *A History of Ancient Szechwan* (**2**). I am inclined to think that the ceremonial pit of Han-chou was probably part of some megalithic remains.

Stage VI of Szechwan archaeology may be represented by three types of remains. A rich collection of bronze objects, said to have been unearthed in the vicinity of Pai-ma-ssŭ temple 白 馬 寺 in the northern suburbs of Chengtu, is preserved in the Hsi-ch'êng Museum in Chengtu, and Mr Wei Chu-hsien published a detailed report on bronzes of this type in his collection in Chung-king (3). I kept a close watch on the site, from which clay was being taken by a brick factory, but I did not have the good fortune to see any bronzes un-earthed *in situ*. The origin of this group of Szechwan bronze vessels and weapons has yet to be investigated.

In 1942 Dr Wu Gin-ding 吳金鼎 of the Academia Sinica conducted an excavation of the cemetery site at P'êng-shan 彭山, opening hundreds of ancient tombs. Although he did not find a single burial that had not been rifled, yet some of the tombs were said to have yielded fragments of bronze mirrors which were definitely in the Late Chou tradition. Dr Wu's report on his excavation at P'eng-shan will furnish us with some material for Stage VI of Szechwan archaeology.

For the present, this stage of development is represented by the remains of the slate tombs which were found in large numbers in the Li-fan 理番 region in the north-western part of the province. The slate tombs of Li-fan yielded a grey or black pottery which may be regarded as a descendant of the T'ai-p'ing-ch'ang ware, but the shape was strongly influenced by the Ch'i-chia industry of Kansu. The bronze objects unearthed showed close affiliations with the Ordos Bronze found in the region of the Great Wall, as well as with the metal industry of the Chengtu plain. It was also in these tombs that glass beads of Near Eastern origin were discovered, together with various imitations of stone and shell, and *pan-liang* and *wu-chu* coins. The discovery of these slate tombs links Szechwan with the great Northern Nomadic culture that flourished in the steppe regions of central and western Asia and eastern Europe. A survey of the Li-fan slate tombs has appeared in the *Harvard Journal of Asiatic Studies* (**9**. 63–180). The contents of the tombs included fragments of iron implements which seemed to indicate that the slate tombs were approximately 500 B.C. to 1 B.C. in date.

Stage VII of Szechwan archaeology is represented by a rich collection of funerary objects found in brick or cave tombs which can definitely be dated from A.D. 1 to A.D. 500. The ceramic industry of this stage produced grey ware in many varieties, and the shape varied from daily utensils, bricks, tiles, and coffins to models of human beings, animals, houses, rockeries and so forth. The tombs were usually decorated with pictures executed in bas-relief on stone or brick and with sculpture in the round. The art resembled closely that found in Shantung and Honan. The Szechwan tombs also yielded large quantities of bronze and iron vessels, utensils, tools and implements, ornaments of various descriptions, mirrors, coins and some vases made of pewter. Shell and lacquer articles were also found. The University Museum has preserved a rich collection of objects from this period and the important specimens are described in Chapter VI below.

The present Curator of the University Museum, Professor Wên Yu 聞宥, has collaborated with Professor Richard C. Rudolph of California in publishing 100 examples of the pictorial art of Szechwan as represented in stone and clay reliefs of this stage (4). A recent communication from Chengtu gives an enthusiastic report of a joint expedition to the district of Lo-shan 樂山 by the University and Provincial Museums. The party found no less than 1000 cave tombs of the Later Han period. At Shih-tzǔ-wan 柿子灣 alone more than 130 caves were studied.

The ceramic art of Szechwan shows a very flourishing development in Stage VIII, covering a period of no less than 400 years, from about A.D. 500 to A.D. 900. Professor Yang Hsiao-ku 楊獻谷 of the University Museum is inclined to classify the Szechwan ceramics of this stage into five traditions (5). The first is the famous Ta-yi 大邑 ware, mentioned by Tu Fu 杜甫, the celebrated poet of T'ang period. Professor Yang reports a figurine unearthed at Tung-kuan-ch'ang 東關壩, in Ta-yi, bearing the following inscription:

大唐天寶三載六月四日唐安郡晋原縣德信里永昌窯敬造窯王像

which may be translated as:

On the fourth day of the sixth moon, in the third year of T'ien-pao in the Great T'ang Dynasty, the Yung-ch'ang Kiln of Tê-hsin- li, in Chin-yüan hsien, T'ang-an chün respectfully manufactures the Image of the King of the Kiln.

The figurine was made of white paste and covered with a white glaze. It verifies the poem of Tu Fu often quoted in this connexion, and the kiln was known as Yung-ch'ang-yao. Fragments of this type of white ware have often been found in other parts of the province, but the paste was not translucent and the ware did not have the fine texture of later imperial products. The site of the Yung-ch'ang kiln, however, has yet to be located.

Another kiln site has been located at P'ang-tzǔ-tien 胖子店, 180 li to the south of Chung-chiang-hsien 中江縣. The kiln, known as Fu-ch'êng-yao 涪城窯, produced a type of ware similar to the ch'ing-pai ware of eastern China. The paste was white while the glaze was slightly bluish. The shape varied from the *p'ing*-vase 瓶, *kuan*-jar 罐, *p'an*-dish 盤 and *wan*-bowl 盌 to the *tsun*-cup 尊 and other bronze shapes. The design on the vessel was either impressed or incised and the glaze was occasionally crackled like the *ko* ware 哥. Some of the vessels were decorated with designs in spots of brown, achieved by the use of ferric oxide. Professor Yang is inclined to think that the Fu-ch'êng industry was established earlier than the Yüeh ware 越 by several decades. In the Chengtu market the Fu-ch'êng ware is popularly known as Shu ware 蜀.

The third kiln site has been found in the compound of the P'u-chao-ssŭ 普照寺, at Tz'ŭ-fêng-hsiang 磁峯鄉 in P'êng-hsien 彭縣. Professor Yang maintains that the P'êng-hsien kiln was in operation in the Han and T'ang times, when it produced only bricks and other earthenwares. From the time of the Five Dynasties, it made vessels with greenish-grey or whitish-grey glaze. Some of the bowls and dishes were stamped with square seals, reading 'Ho-pin yi fan' 河濱遺範 or 'Chin yü man t'ang' 金玉滿堂. The ware was fired at high temperature, but the paste was a purified grey clay.

The other two kilns were known as the Ch'iung-lai-yao 邛崍 and the Liu-li-ch'ang-yao 琉璃廠. The former was located at Ch'iung-lai-hsien. The kiln was developed out of an earthenware industry established probably as early as the Han dynasty. With improvements in the preparation of paste and the introduction of slip and glaze, the industry produced not only daily utensils, but also excellent art objects. It continued to operate in the Sung dynasty.

The Liu-li-ch'ang kiln, situated to the east of Chengtu, was first established in the T'ang dynasty. In many respects the tradition was similar to that of the Ch'iung ware, but the potters at Liu-li-ch'ang seemed to have taken a great fancy to imitating the famous wares from other provinces. The kiln reached its full development in the Sung period, so the majority of its products should be dated from A.D. 901 to A.D. 1300.

These two kilns have been investigated by Dr David C. Graham (6) and myself, and the results of this investigation appear in Chapter VII below.

Buddhism was introduced into Szechwan probably at the end of Stage VII, but in Stage VIII it exerted great influence in the province. Many Buddhist cave monasteries and temples of this period still decorate the countryside of the Szechwan basin. Dated sculptures from the Six Dynasties and the T'ang period have been found and reported in large numbers notably from Chengtu,

Ta-tsu 大足 and Kuang-yüan 廣元. The Szechwan Provincial Museum and the Hsi-ch'êng Museum in Chengtu contain fine collections of Buddhist remains from this period.

In the autumn of 1947, the ruin of the Ta-fo-yüan 大佛院 at Ch'iung-lai was brought to light by a flood in the preceding summer. Mr Ch'êng Ên-yüan 成恩元 of the University Museum set out immediately to investigate the site. Fragments of Buddhist stone carvings were acquired by the hundred and Mr Ch'êng identifies the Ta-fo-yüan as the Lung-hsing Ssŭ 龍興寺 of the T'ang dynasty (7). It is hoped that Mr Ch'êng will incorporate most of the important Buddhist relics of the province in his report on the Lung-hsing Ssŭ site.

Stage IX of Szechwan archaeology was first represented by the contents of the Royal Tomb of Wang Chien 王建. The excavation was undertaken under the auspices of the Provincial Museum and several members of the University Museum were invited to help in the field work. The tomb produced a rich collection of valuable remains, namely wall paintings, bas-reliefs, sculptures, bronze and silver works, iron sacrificial animals, jade carvings, pottery vessels from the Liu-li-ch'ang kiln and others. They are indeed the cream of Szechwan art objects. My account of the tomb has been published (8).

Besides the Wang Chien tomb and several kiln sites, Stage IX of Szechwan archaeology may also be represented by a series of brick and stone tombs found in and around Chengtu. They contained rich varieties of pottery mortuary objects usually accompanied by a bronze mirror and a tombstone inscribing the deed of the ground for the burial. The stone and brick burials of the Sung dynasty are described in Chapter VIII below.

The ceramic art in Stage X of Szechwan archaeology may be represented by two series of grave objects, usually found associated with dated tombstones from A.D. 1301 to A.D. 1600. The first series was probably produced by the Liu-li-ch'ang kiln, which continued in operation in this period. It consisted of mono-glazed, painted or poly-glazed wares. The blue-on-white porcelain was found in large quantity. The other series was a later development of the appliqué design.

Taoist religion was at its height in Szechwan during the Ming period. Many of these tombs seemed to have been made according to the Taoist ritual, as manifested by a large quantity of tombstones bearing inscriptions and diagrams of Taoist origin. Sculptures and paintings which survived from this period also show this tendency, though Buddhist tradition was the foundation of its artistic expression.

The ceramic art of Szechwan was at its lowest ebb in the last stage of its development, A.D. 1601 to A.D. 1900. The devastation brought about by Chang Hsien-chung 張獻忠, the notorious rebel of the seventeenth century, may have been responsible for the destruction of most of the industrial centres in this province. The factories that were built after this were probably not in a position to compete with the products of eastern China, and the vessels they produced were limited to daily utensils, mostly earthen- or stone-wares. The Shao-chiu-fang 燒酒房 factory at Jung-ch'ang 榮昌 is a typical example, and it is still producing a large quantity of common pottery for daily consumption.

In the formulation of this chronology, one interesting fact about the development of the province has been revealed. Szechwan is fundamentally a marginal area, and the culture of this province has never been a result of independent development. It has always been under the influence of some neighbouring culture.

In prehistoric days, this region was a wooded area, and the first human being came probably by boat from eastern China and engaged in forest-clearing and in slash-and-burn agriculture.

Classical Chinese culture penetrated into this province definitely from the north. It was introduced by the Ch'in people who began to dominate the modern provinces of Kansu and Shensi in the sixth century B.C. The sinification of ancient Szechwan began in earnest about the beginning of the fourth century B.C.

The discovery of the Li-fan slate tombs brought to light another influence from the north-west and made the province a link in the famous culture of the Northern Nomads. It was also in these tombs that bronze and iron tools were found existing side by side. So far we have no archaeological material prior to this to indicate that bronze tools existed in Szechwan before iron implements, and it seems safe to conclude that Szechwan, like many marginal areas in Asia, did not pass through a true bronze age.

The construction of brick and cave tombs in the Han-Chin period followed closely the North China tradition. The medium was different, but the ideas and the way of expression and technique were fundamentally the same. The rich collection of archaeological remains from this period should be studied as a western branch of the great artistic achievement of the Han Chinese.

Buddhism also came into Szechwan from the north. Buddhist sculptures found in this area in the round or in bas-relief were mostly in the Lung-men 龍門 and the Yün-kang 雲岡 style. Influence from Tibet was also felt, though slightly, during the T'ang period, as indicated by a printed charm found in a grave of this period excavated by the Provincial Museum.

The great culture that flourished in China during the T'ang dynasty became the fashion in Szechwan at this period and in the succeeding dynasties. The kilns of Szechwan took particular interest in imitating masterpieces produced by other kilns in northern and eastern China, including the famous tri-coloured glazed wares, a chief characteristic of T'ang ceramic art.

The fashion reached its climax in the tenth century. The Royal Tomb of Wang Chien has yielded a series of excellent pieces of sculpture. The carving of jade, the execution of the decoration in high and low relief, and the chiselling of the figures in the round all follow closely the North China technique. The warriors supporting the platform of the royal coffin did not appear strange to those who had visited a Buddhist site of this period in the northern provinces. The orchestra was but a replica of those which decorated the altar of the Stone Cave Monastery in Kung-hsien 鞏縣 Honan.

The famous Taoist paintings from a temple on Mt Omei 峨嵋, now preserved in the Provincial and University Museums, were dated from A.D. 1693. These pictures were painted not in the style of the Tibetan *thankas*, but rather in that of the Tunhüang wall painting.

Szechwan has also been open to influence from the south. The famous bronze drum, popularly known as an invention of Chu-ko Liang 諸葛亮, was but one example of a non-classical Chinese art which enjoyed a wide distribution in southern China as well as in Indo-China, Burma, Siam and some islands off the China coast. The specimens unearthed in Szechwan may be as late as the T'ang period. Furthermore, some of the bronze implements included in the Pai-ma-ssŭ series show close similarities to the Yünnan and D'ong Son bronze art.

The highly appliqué grave-jars of the Sung and Ming periods were also related to a non-classical Chinese culture in the south. The industry was limited to a smaller area than that of the bronze drum. It was distributed only in the south-western provinces of China.

The archaeology of Szechwan is summarized in Table 1.

Proposed Stage and Dating	Type of Remains / Type of Site	Stone Artifacts	Pottery Ware	Metal Objects	Other Materials
XI A.D. 1601–A.D. 1900	Kiln sites: Shao-chiu-fang, P'êng-hsien Tombs: Brick and stone Temples: Fu-hu-ssŭ and others	Sculpture: Buddhist, Taoist and tomb Tomb-stones	Shao-Chiu-fang ware P'êng-hsien ware	Mortuary objects and ornaments Religious objects and idols Coins: K'ang-hsi and others	Paintings of Fu-hu-ssŭ
X A.D. 1301–A.D. 1600	Kiln site: Liu-li-ch'ang Tombs: Brick and stone Temples: Lung-chü-ssŭ and others	Sculpture: Buddhist, Taoist and tomb Tomb-stones	Liu-li-ch'ang ware Appliqué glazed pottery Blue-on-white porcelain	Mortuary objects and ornaments Religious objects and idols Coins: Hung-wu and others	Wall-paintings of Lung-chü-ssŭ Ming paper currencies
IX A.D. 901–A.D. 1300	Kiln sites: Ch'iung-lai, Liu-li-ch'ang, Fu-ch'êng, Tz'ŭ-fêng, Huang-ko-ya Royal tomb: the Yung-ling Tombs: Brick and stone Temples	Sculpture: Buddhist Jade book and sculpture of Yung-ling Stone classics Tomb-stones	Liu-Li-ch'ang ware Ch'iung-lai ware Huang-ko-ya ware 'Shu' ware	Silver and other metal objects of Yung-ling Mortuary objects and ornaments Coins: Ts'ung-ning and others	Paintings of Yung-ling
VIII A.D. 501–A.D. 900	Kiln sites: Ch'iung-lai, Yung-ch'ang, Fu-ch'êng Tz'ŭ-fêng Tombs: Brick and stone Temples: Cave, Ta-fo-yüan and others	Sculpture: Buddhist Buddhist Sutra Tomb-stones	Ch'iung-lai ware Yung-ch'ang ware	Mortuary objects Bronze drum Coins: K'ai-yüan and others	Printed matter
VII A.D. 1–A.D. 500	Tombs: Brick and cave Temples: Cave	Sculpture: Gates, pillars, coffins, animal and human figures Mortuary stone and jade	Coarse grey ware Fine grey ware Painted grey ware	Mortuary objects Coins: Wu-shu, Ho-ch'uan, Ho-pu and others	Lacquer objects Shell ornaments
VI 500 B.C.–1 B.C.	Li-fan slate tombs P'êng-hsien cemetery Pai-ma-ssŭ site (?)	Slate tombs Marble beads Mortuary stone and jade	Coarse grey ware Fine grey ware Painted grey ware	Mortuary objects and artifacts Coins: Pan-Liang, Wu-shu, Yo-hsin and others Sacrificial vessels and mirrors	Lacquer objects Glass beads Wooden vessels Shell ornaments
V 700 B.C.–500 B.C.	T'ai-p'ing-ch'ang ceremonial pit Megalithic remains	Polished tools Ceremonial stone and jade Turquoise beads and flakes Dolmens, menhirs, alignments	Coarse grey ware Fine grey ware		
IV 1200 B.C.–700 B.C.	T'ai-p'ing-ch'ang dwelling site	Polished tools	Coarse grey ware Fine greyish-black ware		
III 2000 B.C.–1200 B.C.	Late Neolithic dwelling sites	Chipped-pecked-and-polished tools Polished tools	Cord-marked coarse and fine grey ware Fine red ware Fine black ware Fine white ware Hard grey ware		
II 3000 B.C.–2000 B.C.	Early Neolithic dwelling sites	Chipped-and-polished tools			
I 5000 B.C.–3000 B.C.	Mesolithic dwelling sites	Chipped pebble tools Chipped flake implements			

PART I

PREHISTORIC ARCHAEOLOGY OF SZECHWAN

CHAPTER I

OUTLINE OF THE STUDY: GEOGRAPHICAL AND HISTORICAL BACKGROUND

OUTLINE OF THE STUDY

IN the last half-century many prehistoric remains have been discovered in the province of Szechwan. No less than 90 prehistoric sites have been investigated either by zealous individuals or by organized expeditions. Some of the material collected has been described, but for the most part, the materials housed in museums both in China and abroad have not. The need is apparent for gathering together the evidence and undertaking a systematic study of this material. Through analysing and synthesizing these collected surface finds, and through comparisons with related materials from other areas, it may be possible to reconstruct a picture of the prehistory of Szechwan.

The study of the prehistoric archaeology of Szechwan has, however, a more ambitious purpose than the mere solving of its own problem. Our knowledge of the prehistoric archaeology of eastern Asia, which has its centre in northern China, is still in its infancy. A few palaeolithic and several neolithic sites have been excavated with gratifying results. But there lies a gap between the upper palaeolithic and the late neolithic ages. Dr Pei Wên-chung 裴文中, the discoverer of *Sinanthropus*, has attempted to fill this gap with the deposits of northern Manchuria and of the Kwangsi caves in southern China. Geographically, Szechwan lies at the edge of the North China Plain, and materials recovered from this marginal area may throw some light on the problem. In other words, it is one of the main purposes of this study to see what bearing the early culture of Szechwan has on the prehistory of eastern Asia as a whole and of northern China in particular.

The sources I have at hand comprise three groups: (1) sixteen published reports consisting of books and articles appearing in various journals; (2) a set of photographs of the stone artifacts preserved in the West China Union University Museum of Archaeology; and (3) the Nelson collection in the American Museum of Natural History, New York, and Dr Nelson's unpublished journals. The last group forms the backbone of this study.

It must be borne in mind that the major portion of the archaeological material from Szechwan consists of surface finds. Therefore, in the present investigation it has been necessary to concentrate largely on typology and geographical distribution. I have first studied the various types of stone artifacts and potsherds, and compared them, and also instituted comparisons with materials found in other parts of eastern Asia. I have also divided the types of stone artifacts into four major industries or techniques, and the potsherds similarly into six classes. And, finally, with the help of the evidence given by geographical distribution, I have proposed a tentative chronological sequence for the stone industries.

I have divided my study into five chapters:

The first chapter deals with the geographical and historical background of Szechwan. It gives a general description of the region and a brief account of its early history with special emphasis on the native population and the communications with the outside world.

Chapter II includes a narrative account of the reconnaissances and excavations which have been made in Szechwan, and continues with a detailed description of the prehistoric sites according to their geographical location, each with a full list of artifacts discovered. This forms the basis for the study of the geographical distribution of the archaeological materials in this region.

Chapter III is devoted to the study of the stone artifacts. This covers typology, comparison with materials from other parts of eastern Asia, geographical distribution not only of typical artifacts but also of various industries, and a proposed chronological sequence for these stone industries.

The study of the pottery is reported in Chapter IV, with consideration of typology, comparison with pottery outside Szechwan, geographical distribution and association with the stone industries.

The final chapter is a summary of our present knowledge of the prehistoric archaeology of Szechwan and its bearing on the prehistory of eastern Asia.

The illustrations (Pls. 1–15) represent stone objects and pottery. A very limited number of these are copies of illustrations in various published reports, but the majority are pictures of unpublished specimens, reproduced through the courtesy of the American Museum of Natural History, New York.

GEOGRAPHICAL AND HISTORICAL BACKGROUND

The province of Szechwan, situated in the very heart of China, was once the largest province in the country. It derives its name 'Four Streams' 四川 from the four tributaries Chia-ling 嘉陵, T'o 沱, Min 岷, and Ya-lung 鴉礱, which flow through the province from north to south into the Yangtse river. Between the last two streams flows the mighty Ta-tu 大渡 river, which runs almost parallel to the course of the Ya-lung, but turns sharply eastward at Han-yüan hsien 漢源縣 to join the Min river at Chia-ting 嘉定. Since the establishment of Hsikang as a province in 1928, the western part of Szechwan, including the Ya-lung valley and a part of the Ta-tu valley, has been incorporated under the jurisdiction of the new province.

The region under investigation in this book covers the present province of Szechwan and its adjoining areas. In the east, it extends to I-tu hsien 宜都縣 in Hupei province (111° E.). In the south, it reaches the most southern curve of the Yangtse at Yüan-mou hsien 元謀縣, in Yünnan (26° N.). In the west, it stretches to Li-hua 理化, in Hsikang (101° E.). And in the north, it extends as far as Li-fan 理番 in north-western Szechwan (32° N.).

The area of this region is about 167,000 sq. miles. Topographically, it may be divided into two areas with the city of Ya-chou 雅州 (103° E., 30° N.) as the dividing point.

The western part of the region consists of the mountainous areas of western Szechwan and eastern Hsikang. It is the eastern extremity of the tremendous crescentic continuation of the great Himalaya range. The high mountains lift the general level to over 10,000 ft. above the sea. To the west of these ranges lie the grasslands which form the bulk of the Tibetan plateau, and below to the east stretches the fertile plain of Chengtu, which is green with vegetation all the year round. Across these ranges, the two mighty rivers, Ya-lung and Ta-tu, with their tributaries, force their way through treacherous and narrow gorges. The valleys are of two kinds: the deserted valleys, in which roll the rapid streams, and the wooded valleys that lead up to the high passes over which one can reach the grasslands.

In spite of the fact that most of the mountains are ice- and snow-capped nearly all the year, this border region is now peopled, though sparsely, by aboriginal tribes. Cultivation is practised only in the wooded valleys by the Chinese who have penetrated into the region with their agricultural and industrial pursuits.

5

These wooded valleys had probably been peopled before the arrival of the Chinese. Evidence has been found on the terraces which are abundant in the grasslands, generally above 12,000 ft., and under the rock shelters, between 6000 and 12,000 ft. above sea level.

The landscape changes when we turn to the eastern part of Szechwan. This half has been called the 'Red Basin', because the surface is generally covered with a thick layer of red and grey or yellow sandstone. The basin is surrounded by high mountain ranges, including those of western Szechwan described above, and is drained by the Min, the T'o, the Chia-ling and the Yangtse rivers. The three former run from north to south and enter the Yangtse at Suifu 叙府, Lu-chou 瀘州 and Chungking 重慶 respectively. The main valley of the Yangtse itself runs generally in a west-south-west to east-north-east direction and the river has forced an outlet through the eastern ranges. The magnificent gorges, which constitute the most attractive scenery to the traveller who passes through this region, begin in the east of the province, a little below Wan-hsien 萬縣, and continue for about 100 miles into Hupei.

With the exception of the Chengtu plain, which is a little less than 5000 sq. miles in area, there is very little level ground in this basin. The elevation is high in many places and some of the river beds lie at an altitude of 1000 ft. above sea level. The basin itself has been broken up by foldings of the earth's crust, forming ranges of hills which are being eroded while the plain is being actively aggraded.

There are no extremes of climate in the plain of Chengtu. The fact that the swallow does not find it necessary to migrate is sufficient guarantee of the mildness of the climate in winter. In the summer, the temperature rarely exceeds 100° F. in the shade. The humidity is high and there is usually a bank of mist hanging over the plain. Sunshine is rare in winter and it is a popular saying that the dogs of Chengtu would all bark at the sight of the sun. But on the hilltops, in the basin and on the surrounding mountains snow lies for a time every winter and huge séracs decorate the mountain passes. The Chengtu plain did not become an important centre of agriculture until the installation of the irrigation system, reputedly at the end of the fourth century B.C.

In earlier days, eastern Szechwan was probably a wooded area, as is the western part of the region at present. The swiftness of the streams and the ruggedness of the country probably contributed to its impenetrability. The forbidding character of this environment might have kept the true primitive hunter out of the scene, but should not have constituted a barrier to the woodsman or agriculturist who also knew the art of boating. This marginal area would not be habitable unless there were means of clearing the forest. The first settlers were probably woodsmen and agriculturists, as aboriginal tribes are mostly agriculturists and live along river valleys. Owing to its remoteness and to the difficulty of reaching it, Szechwan must always have produced its own food. The expansion of the population would naturally have followed the line of soil fertility. The distribution of the prehistoric remains along the river banks suggests that the people might have come by boat.

A brief account of the early history (see Map 1) of Szechwan and the communication of this border area with the outside world may help to give us a better understanding of the situation in prehistoric times. For geographical reasons the Chinese expansion into Szechwan came first into the Red Basin, which was then dominated by the Shu 蜀 and the Pa 巴 peoples and then into the mountainous areas beyond on the west and the south, which were populated by the so-called south-western Barbarians 西南夷.

Many myths and legends dealing with the origin of the Szechwan people still survive (**65,** 1, 1–3a; 3, 1–4a; **2,** 14–19). These stories are probably of late origin as they are connected with Chinese mythology and legendary emperors. The earliest date we have at present in the Chinese records, which may be considered reasonably reliable, goes back to the last quarter of the twelfth century before the Christian era. In the year 1122 B.C., King Wu of Chou 周武王 conducted an expedition against the Shang people. In reviewing his troops at Mu 牧, he made a declaration of his epoch-making campaign, which was recorded in the *Shu-ching* (**58,** 11, 15b–16a). There he addressed not only his own followers and his allies, but also the men of Yung 庸, Shu 蜀, Ch'iang 羌, Mou 髳, Wei 微, Lu 盧, P'êng 彭 and P'u 濮. According to the commentaries of the Classic, these eight foreign tribes or states were all located beyond the south-western part of the kingdom, which covered the Wei 渭 valley in the modern province of Shensi, and they acknowledged the supremacy of the Chou king. The capital of Shu is said to have been situated at modern Chengtu, but the chief cities of the other seven states are unknown. However, their general location can probably be identified. Yung and P'u are said to have occupied the region south of the Yangtse and the Han 漢 river in the modern province of Hupei. The other five states are said to be all located in Szechwan: Ch'iang, to the west of Chengtu; Mou and Wei, between the Shu capital and

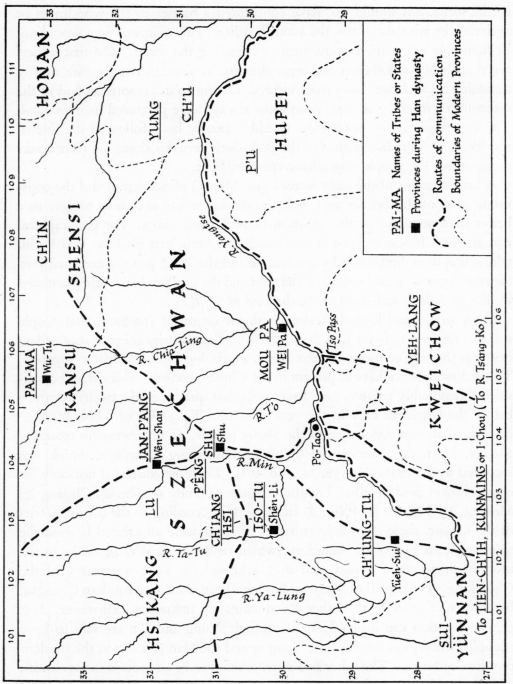

MAP I. Szechwan, 1122–122 B.C.

modern Chungking; and Lu and P'êng, to the north-west of Chengtu (cf. 61, 3, 5, 301–2).

Among these eight states, Shu was probably the greatest and in the next few hundred years that followed, this state played the leading rôle in this outlying region. But at the end of the eighth century B.C., the situation changed and Shu found a great rival state, Pa, rising to the south-east, with its capital in modern Chungking. The state was first mentioned in the *Ch'un-ch'iu* 春秋 in the year 711 B.C. (59, 7, 5a) and after that it maintained a close relationship with Shu to the north-west and with Ch'u 楚, the great kingdom on the lower Yangtse.

At times Shu and Pa were on friendly terms. Their friendship was occasionally strengthened by intermarriage of their ruling houses. But the rivalry between them was always present and sometimes they were bitter enemies. This rivalry paved the way for the intervention of Ch'in 秦, their strong northern neighbour, which for years had planned a military conquest of this south-western region. The troops of the ambitious Ch'in widened the old road which ran through the mountainous region, leading from the modern city of Ning-ch'iang 甯羌 in Shensi, into the Red Basin, by way of the modern cities of Kuang-yüan 廣元, Chao-hua 昭化 and Chien-ko 劍閣 in Szechwan. They finally invaded Shu and Pa while the two states were at war with each other. Under the able command of Chang Yi 張儀 and Ssŭ-ma Ts'o 司馬錯, two of Ch'in's best generals, the conquest was completed in 316 B.C. (62, 5, 25a; 65, 3, 3a).

Thus ended the native kingdoms of the Red Basin and an active penetration of Chinese culture began. Organized migration of the Ch'in people into Szechwan took place and the Chinese political system, economic organization and educational institutions were introduced (65, 3, 3a–5a). In order to carry out his ambitious programme, Chang Yi built Chengtu, the first city Szechwan had ever seen. It had a wall twelve *li* long and seventy feet high. Unfortunately, not a trace of this important structure has survived to the present day.

Chang Yi was not satisfied with the conquest of Shu alone. Ssŭ-ma Ts'o's armies marched into the country of Tsu, as well as the state of Pa. The whole territory of Szechwan was incorporated into the Ch'in domain in the same year, becoming three separate provinces.

Ch'in was not the only state that sought to expand into Szechwan. The kings of Ch'u, the powerful neighbour of Pa and Shu on the east, had been no less ambitious than the Ch'in monarchs. Before the fall of the Szechwan states,

King Wei of Ch'u (339–329 B.C.) 楚威王 had sent General Chuang Ch'iao 莊蹻 (62, 116, 2a–b) with his troops up the Yangtse to subdue Pa, Shu and other states that were on the south of the great river. He did not challenge the forces of Pa and Shu, but proceeded south-westward until he reached T'ien-ch'ih 滇池 (now Kunming, in northern Yünnan). The people there were very much impressed by his military power and he succeeded in putting the country under the rule of Ch'u. But when he was planning to return to report on his mission, the Ch'in troops had already overrun Pa and Shu and were on their way to invade Ch'u. The homeward route was blocked, so the Ch'u general returned with his men to T'ien-ch'ih and proclaimed himself king of the country. In this expedition we have an example which shows that the great Yangtse has probably been the main route of communication in this region ever since prehistoric days.

Ch'u was probably the first state to seek expansion into the distant south-west beyond Pa and Shu. This policy was followed by the Ch'in people. It is said that during the Ch'in dynasty, Ch'ang An 常頞 (62, 116, 2b), probably a Ch'in general, constructed a road (which was five feet wide) into the south-west, and appointed officials there. The course of the road was not recorded, yet this status of dominion continued for more than ten years until the fall of the dynasty.

At the beginning of the Han dynasty, Pa and Shu continued to be Han provinces, but the mountainous areas beyond them were completely disregarded. Only some Pa and Shu people went over the border as private traders and profited greatly (62, 116, 2b).

It is well known that the first emperor of the Han dynasty took refuge in Szechwan before he succeeded in establishing his dynasty. The region furnished him with supplies of grain and manpower as it did for other ambitious leaders in the centuries that followed. His armies were supplied by a fleet of ten thousand boats which carried Szechwan grain down the Yangtse, and his position was greatly strengthened by the shock troops raised in the province. In his campaign against Hsiang Yü 項羽, his greatest rival, men living along the Chia-ling river served as Han vanguards. They were noted for the songs and dances they indulged in as they went into battle; these latter were famous as the 'dances of the Pa guerillas'. Because Emperor Kao-tsu 漢高祖 controlled the valuable land of Szechwan behind his lines, he was able to accomplish the general unification of China, as the Ch'in emperor previously had done.

With the enthronement of the ambitious monarch, Emperor Wu-ti 武帝 (140–87 B.C.), Chinese expansion into the land of the South-western Barbarians began in earnest. The relative locations of the tribes were for the first time clearly recorded. Ssŭ-ma Ch'ien 司馬遷, the great historian who served at the emperor's court, writes (**62,** 1a–2a; **64,** 2, 1–4) as follows:

Among the south-western Barbarians, the chieftains may be counted by tens. The Yeh-lang 夜郎 [capital at present T'ung-tzŭ hsien 桐梓縣, Kueichou] is the greatest among these tribes. To the west of the Yeh-lang, among the tribes of the Mi-mo 靡莫 people [the chieftains] may be counted by tens and T'ien 滇 [or T'ien-ch'ih] is the greatest among them. From T'ien northward, the chieftains there may be counted by tens and among them the Ch'iung-tu 邛都 [covering the region around modern Hsi-ch'ang 西昌, Szechwan] is the greatest. All these people entwine their hair in the shape of a club. They practise agriculture and live in villages.

To the west of this region, from T'ung-shih 同師 [probably modern Lung-ling hsien 龍陵縣, Yünnan] eastward and north to Yeh-yü 楪楡 [modern Yün-nan hsien 雲南縣, Yünnan], there are the lands of Sui 嶲 and K'un-ming 昆明 [modern Yung-ch'ang 永昌, T'êng-yüeh 騰越 and Shun-ning 順甯, Yünnan]. All these people braid their hair and move about with their herds. They have no definite dwelling places and no chieftains among them. This district covers an area of possibly several thousand *li*.

To the north-east of Sui, the chieftains there may be counted by tens. The Hsi 徙 [modern T'ien-ch'uan-hsien 天全縣, Szechwan] and the Tso-tu 筰都 [modern Han-yüan hsien 漢源縣, Szechwan] are the greatest among these tribes.

To the north-east of Tso, the chieftains there may be counted by tens. The Jan-p'ang 冉駹 [modern Mao-hsien 茂縣, Szechwan] are the greatest of these tribes. As to their customs, some live in permanent quarters and some move about.

To the west of Shu and from Jan-p'ang north-eastward, the chieftains there may be counted by tens, Pai-ma 白馬 [modern Ch'êng-hsien 成縣, Kansu] being the greatest among the tribes. They all belong to the Ti 氐 people.

—All these are the barbarians living to the south-west outside of the Pa and the Shu borders.

In the year 135 B.C. (**62,** 116, 2b–3b; 117, 28b) T'ang Mêng 唐蒙, a Han official, discovered the trade route through which the relish of Shu, betel pepper, was shipped to Nan-yüeh 南越, a southern tributary state with its capital at modern Canton. The road started out from the Pass of Tso 筰關, south of modern Ho-chiang hsien 合江縣, Szechwan, and ran through into the land of Yeh-lang until it reached the great navigable river, Ts'ang-k'o 牂柯 (modern Nan-p'an-chiang 南盤江 in southern Kweichow). Here the Shu cargoes could float down the river into the southern state. Therefore he advised the emperor to construct a road from P'o-tao 僰道 (modern Suifu) to the river for military adventures in the future. This proposal was promptly approved by the emperor, Wu-ti, and the construction programme was actually carried on for several years.

T'ang Mêng was not the only person advocating the expansion into the south-west. Ssŭ-ma Hsiang-ju 司馬相如, one of the greatest poets of the day and native of Shu (62, 116, 3b; 117, 28b–29b) was also a strong exponent of the aggressive programme. He was appointed by the emperor to work on the subjugation of the Ch'iung and the Tso barbarians on the west of Shu. His mission was very successful.

The Han expansion into the south-west received a fresh stimulus in 122 B.C. (62, 116, 4; 63, 61, 3b) when Chang Ch'ien 張騫, the famous Han delegate, returned from his mission to Ta-hsia 大夏 (Bactria) in central Asia. When he was in the west, he saw Shu cloths and bamboo canes from Ch'iung. After inquiring into the origin of these products, he found that they had come from a country to the south-east of Ta-hsia, called Shên-tu 身毒 (modern India). He was also informed that there were trade relations between Shên-tu and Han's south-west regions. So the famous explorer advised the emperor to trace this important route of international communication. His proposal was immediately put into effect by the emperor, who sent out four exploration parties to Szechwan to find the way to India. The parties started out from Jan-p'ang (modern Mao-hsien), Tso and Hsi (modern Ya-chou 雅州), Ch'iung (modern Hsi-ch'ang) and P'o-tao respectively and proceeded westward. They journeyed for several years but all their attempts ended in failure, which may have been due to lack of co-operation by the inhabitants of the regions. But it is clear that these four directions constituted the four possible routes across the mountainous areas beyond the Red Basin, which were not at all impenetrable at the dawn of Chinese history. So it may be safe to assume that communications on these mountain paths were probably possible in prehistoric days. It is also interesting to note that these four routes comprise the four highways leading out of Szechwan to the south-west to-day.

After long years of political penetration and military campaigns, the territories of the South-western Barbarians finally came under the domain of the Emperor Wu (62, 116, 5a–b). With the exception of the lord of Yeh-lang, who was created king of his land by the emperor, all the other chieftainships were abolished and their lands became Han provinces. Ch'iung-tu was made the province of Yüeh-sui 越巂 (now Hsi-ch'ang hsien, Szechwan); Tso-tu, the province of Shên-li 沈犁 (now Han-yüan hsien, Szechwan); Jan-p'ang, the province of Wên-shan 汶 山 (north of Mao-hsien, Szechwan); Pai-ma, the province of Wu-tu 武 都 (now the south-eastern part of Kansu) and, finally, T'ien, the province of I-chou 益 州 (now K'un-ming, Yünnan).

The development of this south-western hinterland into Chinese provinces was a slow process. It took several centuries and involved several of the most capable figures of the Ch'in and Han dynasties. An account of this achievement in bringing Chinese civilization to the region will provide the necessary background for the understanding of the archaeological remains discussed in Part II.

The political pacification of Pa and Shu was achieved under a capable young administrator named Chang Jo 張 若. It was the policy of Ch'in at first to hand back the political power to the native princes, but they revolted and proved of no help in carrying out the conqueror's programme. Chang Jo was sent to the province in 314 B.C., two years after the conquest, and he stayed there as governor for over half a century. Under his wise administration, tens of thousands of Ch'in families emigrated into this region and helped the governor to subdue most of the minor rebellions.

We have no way of knowing how large the population of Szechwan was in ancient times. Besides the ten thousand families transferred from Ch'in by Governor Chang to colonize this region, many criminals and their families and retainers were exiled into this south-western province. After Ch'in completed the conquest of all the feudal states, the newly-established dynasty forced many distinguished families from the conquered states to migrate to Szechwan. As a result the population increased rapidly at that time.

The earliest population statistics are for A.D. 2, giving the total for the districts within modern Szechwan as around 4,000,000 persons. Although this figure is less than one-tenth of the present population, when it is compared with the total population of China at that time, the number is fairly large, for the entire empire contained only 60,000,000 individuals—one-eighth of the present population.

At that time Ch'eng-tu hsien was second in size only to the imperial capital of Ch'ang-an. Chengtu in the first century had a population of about 380,000, which is not much smaller than the present city. We can readily imagine how prosperous Chengtu was in the first century A.D.

Governor Chang stayed at Chengtu. For other districts he built walled cities, large granaries and other public buildings. He also introduced a new system of civil service, public markets and village administration, based mostly on the Ch'in systems. But the economic development of the province was perfected by the succeeding governor, Li Ping 李 冰. The wealth of Szechwan was gradually increased and the agricultural, industrial and commercial enterprises reached their height in the Han dynasty. This also accounted for the rapid increase of population during this period.

Among the governors of Szechwan, none was better known than Governor Li Ping, one of the greatest engineers that China has ever produced. He was appointed in 250 B.C. and devoted all his time and energy to the improvement of the economic and agricultural condition of the province. The water resources of Szechwan were an important source of wealth and an aid to its economic development in the Ch'in-Han times. The four rivers and the Yangtse supplied adequate water power for transportation and economic enterprise. Before Ch'in conquered Shu, the people of Shu had already attempted to exploit their water resources. With the help of some Ch'in experts, they had tried in 361 B.C. to divert the course of the Ch'ing-i river 青 衣 水 into the Yangtse, but this was nothing in comparison with the great project completed by Governor Li. He redirected the waters of the Min river and opened two waterways near Chengtu, providing irrigation for more than one million *mou* of rice lands. He also supervised the construction of a dam at Lo-shan in order to control the current. After the completion of these two great projects, boat-travel in the province was easy, and irrigation convenient. The amount of water could be controlled by the dam according to need, and there never was a famine year. This great irrigation system made the province the granary of the empire. For more than two thousand years this system has been in constant use, and to-day the Min river still flows across the Chengtu plain to bear witness to the remarkable achievement of Governor Li Ping.

The richness of the Chengtu plain brought prosperity to every field of activity. Metallurgy was developed and the weaving industry well established. Gold, silver, iron, steel and a kind of stone used in refining iron were among the important natural resources. Silk and wool were abundant, and the production of blankets of bear and fox hair, and of clothing made from the hides of these animals, was notable.

In the beginning of the Han dynasty, in the second century B.C., the imperial government controlled the iron mines of four cities, three of which were located in Szechwan at Ch'iung-lai 邛 崍, at P'êng-hsien 彭 縣 and at Chia-chiang 夾 江, the other being in Shensi. The imperial government also had a superintendent of lumber in Hsikang and superintendents of orange cultivation at Yün-yang 雲 陽 and Fêng-chieh 奉 節 in the eastern part of the province.

Besides the products controlled by the imperial government, there were many others that were not controlled and could be freely exploited. Among these were silver, copper and jade. There is a story about Têng T'ung 鄧 通, a favourite eunuch in Emperor Wên-ti's 文 帝 palace, in this connexion. Têng T'ung had his fortune told one day, and the fortune-teller predicted that he would die of poverty and starvation. Whereupon the emperor bestowed upon him a copper mine in Szechwan and gave him permission to mint coins privately. Têng's coins enjoyed a wide circulation throughout the empire, but he did not escape the fate predicted by the fortune-teller.

Millionaires were common in Szechwan at that time. Among them the Cho family was the best known. Father Cho Wang-sun 卓 王 孫 was originally a native of Chao 趙, in modern Shansi and Hopei. When Ch'in conquered his country, many of his compatriots were ordered to migrate to Szechwan. Pushing a wheelbarrow, Father Cho and his wife accompanied other emigrants going west. All the others, afraid to travel so far away, bribed the guards to let them stop at places closer to their homes. Only the Cho family reached its destination. Father Cho was a blacksmith. When the family arrived at Ch'iung-lai and saw iron produced, they settled there and soon were engaged in iron-casting. They soon became prosperous, and before long Ch'iung-lai became a great industrial centre, attracting workers not only from other parts of Szechwan but also from Yunnan. History records that the Chos had around a thousand servants, and their extravagance resembled that of the royal family.

It is a common saying that Szechwan girls are sentimental and enjoy love-making and romance. This generalization dates back to the days of the Cho family. Daughter Cho Wên-chün 卓 文 君 was a famous beauty who fell in love with a lute-player named Ssŭ-ma Hsiang-ju. He was poor, however, and Father Cho would not give his consent to their marriage. At last, Wên-chün decided to elope with her lover and live in poverty. Father Cho was enraged and disowned her. After his friends had urged him to reconsider his attitude toward his daughter, he relented and gave her one hundred servants and one million in cash. Thus, the poor Ssŭ-ma Hsiang-ju was able to devote all his energy to literary achievement. He later became one of the greatest poets and scholars that Szechwan has ever produced.

Side by side with the development of various industries was the rapid growth of foreign trade. Szechwan rice was shipped into many famine districts, and Szechwan copper coins circulated throughout the empire. By means of the Yangtse, Szechwan salt was shipped to the provinces in the east. Silk fabrics and brocades from Chengtu were the fashion of the day, its gold and silver articles were the pride of the imperial court and its fine bronze mirrors were the precious belongings of many a court lady. Its lacquer work was exported to Korea and became the treasures of Korean Han tombs.

The history of Szechwan would not be complete without mention of Governor Wên Wêng 文翁. This famous administrator and educator was a native of modern Anhwei. As soon as he assumed his new position in western China, he gave his earnest attention to the promotion of education. At first he selected unimportant but capable civil servants from his territory and sent them to Ch'ang-an, the capital, where they studied under imperial scholars or read and practised law. When their training was finished, they returned to Szechwan and were given better positions than they had formerly held. They were gradually promoted, and some even reached high positions in the imperial administration.

Governor Wên also provided schools for the children, one of which supposedly occupied the site of the present Temple of Confucius inside the Old South Gate in Chengtu. It was he who set the stage in this remote region for the future literary figures who rank among the greatest that China has ever produced.

When Emperor Wu-ti saw what Wên Wêng was accomplishing, he ordered every province of the empire to follow his example and establish schools. When Wên Wêng died, the people of Shu built a temple as a memorial to him, just as they had done for Governor Li Ping. Even to-day, whenever capable officials of Szechwan are mentioned, Wên Wêng and Li Ping are always included.

It seems probable that Szechwan had a local culture of its own before the Ch'in-Han conquest. The enforced migrations from other parts of China were so extensive, however, that the colonists soon outnumbered the native-born. The immigrants naturally had brought with them the culture of central and northern China, but before long a new culture appeared in the province and began to influence the entire population. The people of Szechwan became very prosperous and consequently very extravagant, a condition deplored by scholars like Ch'ang Chü 常 璩. Disapproving of the results of such a rapid development, he wrote, in the third century:

When Emperor Ch'in-shih-huang conquered the Six States, he would from time to time send some of their influential people off to Shu. As it was a rich land, some families made a fortune from salt and copper, others from lumber, so abundant in the forests on the hills and along the rivers. Houses were plentiful, the people well satisfied, and they competed with each other in accumulating wealth. Hence, a labourer and a merchant were able to have a number of horses for their chariots, and members of any influential family dressed as beautifully as princes. Sacrificial oxen were prepared and served at weddings, and the bride might arrive with a hundred carts. Burials required a large grave with pottery tomb-chambers, pigs and other sacrificial animals being offered at the altar. Funerary gifts of silk clothes were freely given and presents of money exceeded the amount prescribed by the established rituals. This is all wrong and one can trace its origin back to Ch'in culture (65, 3, 8).

This account by Ch'ang Chü was no doubt correct, as Han burial remains to be discussed in Part II, consisting of hand-hewn caves, burial mounds, brick chambers, stone coffins, steles, animals, gate-towers and mortuary objects, exist to-day and are proof of the great influence exerted by the Ch'in-Han Chinese in western China.

CHAPTER II

PREHISTORIC SITES

PREHISTORIC remains in Szechwan were first reported by E. Colborne Baber. During his travels and researches in the interior of China, in 1882, he came upon two polished stone celts in Chungking which he described in his reports (9).

J. Hutson Edgar was probably the first to make extensive investigations in this region. Since 1913 he had found dozens of prehistoric sites along the Yangtse and the Min rivers and in the mountainous areas of Hsikang. The publication of his discoveries (10, 11, 12) has attracted wide attention in China and abroad.

With the exception of a small collection of stone implements which Edgar presented to the Museum of the Royal Asiatic Society in Shanghai, practically all of his collection is in the Museum of Archaeology of West China Union University. This enabled Mr Daniel S. Dye, who is himself an enthusiastic investigator in the field, to publish some data about a few of these implements and others collected by various residents in the province (13, 14). A red pot-sherd was found in association with some of these stone artifacts.

It is rather unfortunate that Edgar was interested only in the stone implements and did not report any other kind of relics which might have been associated with them. Moreover, his account of the implements is very cursory, although we can get a general impression of his finds from the pictures of the fourteen specimens which accompanied his first article. Dye gives a more detailed description of the artifacts, but the terms he uses are not standardized and so fail to present a clear picture of these tools. However, the drawings of the specimens by Mrs J. Kitchen, which are published in his article, are quite faithful.

In the winter seasons of 1921–2, 1922–3 and 1925–6, Dr Walter Granger, of the American Central Asiatic Expedition, made his palaeontological explorations in eastern Szechwan. He collected a large quantity of fossils at Yen-ching-kou, a little village located about ten miles up the river from Wan-hsien. A careful watch was kept by him for any trace of contemporary life in the fossil pits. Granger obtained a small perforated disc of stone which was well encrusted with calcareous deposit. He also found a deer antler, some of the prongs of which appeared to have been cut off with some crude implement. The antler was fossilized, but the incisions were thought to have been done while the antler was still fresh. Therefore, he assumed that the human beings were contemporaries of the Yen-ching-kou fauna, which was determined to be Pliocene and Pleistocene in date (15).

Granger's discoveries attracted Dr N. C. Nelson, also of the American Central Asiatic Expedition, to the scene. He made a most thorough investigation of the caves along the Yangtse. He navigated the river between Ku-lao-pei 古 老 背 some 15 miles below I-ch'ang and Pai-shui-hsi 白 水 溪, a few miles above Wan-hsien, a distance of some 230 statute miles, and made excursions on foot up the various tributaries and into the back country totalling at least an equal distance. He examined 367 caves and shelters, of which 139 were, or had lately been, inhabited. He also noted the presence and position of 316 additional caves and shelters, many of which likewise gave proof of modern occupation. As a result of his careful investigation, he concluded that evidence of palaeolithic man was completely absent, and that there were only very scanty traces of neolithic man in this region.

However, Nelson's reconnaissance did not confine itself entirely to the caves. He found several neolithic workshops or settlement sites along the banks of the river. Stone implements of various types as well as a considerable amount of broken pottery and some human bones were collected. Some of the materials were found on the river banks, others in cultivated fields above. Only a small number was dug out of actual cultural deposits. With the exception of a representative series of specimens which was left with the Museum of the Geological Survey of China in Peking, this collection of archaeological material from the Yangtse gorges is now preserved in the American Museum of Natural History in New York. The objects are all numbered and catalogued. Dr Nelson's invaluable unpublished journals, as well as the material itself, were made available for study through his great kindness (16, 17, 18, 19).

Following up their work in Szechwan, Granger and Nelson conducted another trip of investigation to Yünnan in 1926–7. Most of their work was concentrated along the northern border of Yünnan at the southernmost bend of the Yangtse. Nelson examined 16 archaeological sites and 20 caves, but the results were largely negative. The only neolithic site worthy of attention was found at Lung-kai 龍 街 on the Yangtse, which yielded stone tools similar to those from eastern Szechwan (20, 21, 22, 23).

In the summer of 1930, Dr Arnold Heim of the National Chung-san University, Canton, led an expedition into the Hsikang region. The party was accompanied by Edgar, and they succeeded in finding two stone scrapers of alleged Mousterian technique in a loess deposit in the Tao-fu 道孚 valley. These two implements were first described in the report of this expedition (24).

In 1931, Dr Gordon T. Bowles, a fellow of the Harvard-Yenching Institute, engaged in an ethnological and anthropological research in western Szechwan. With the help of Edgar, he made four successive trips in the mountainous areas of this region, visited the cultural sites in the loess deposit at Tao-fu and K'ang-ting and found prehistoric remains scattered at random along the main routes, along valley bottoms, and more especially at points of juncture of rivers, streams, and roads. He distinguishes the artifacts found associated with loess deposits from those collected at random from other localities. The implements of the former group were found embedded in the loess deposit in association with pottery, red ochre, bone utensils and human remains. He has succeeded in drawing a clear picture of prehistoric times in this outlying region (25).

Another enthusiastic worker in this field is Dr David C. Graham of the West China Union University. Besides familiarizing himself with the Edgar collections and other materials in the University Museum, he travelled extensively in the province and made a large collection himself, which is also preserved in the museum. He classified these materials into two groups: chipped tools, which he described as palaeolithic implements, and polished ones, which he calls neolithic (26, 27).

Most of the stone artifacts in the University Museum have not been published. Graham has taken photographs of the outstanding specimens there and an album of the collections has been made (28). It consists of two parts: (1) neolithic stone implements from southern Szechwan, collected by D. C. Graham; and (2) neolithic and palaeolithic stone implements from west China, collected by J. Hutson Edgar. Unfortunately, some of the photographs are far from being satisfactory and the labels are too summary to be of use.

Graham has made an even better contribution to the prehistoric archaeology of Szechwan by excavating a prehistoric site at Han-chou 漢州. The site was first discovered in 1931 by the owner of the land, and Graham's excavation was done three years later. The work is very important since it is the only excavation of a site in this whole region as yet reported (29, 30, 31). It has attracted wide attention both in China and abroad (see p. xiv).

In the summer of 1937, the Swedish geologist and archaeologist, Dr J. G. Andersson, visited the Hsikang region. With the help of Dr Ch'i Yen-p'ei 祁 延 霈 of the Academia Sinica, Professor Chou Hsiao-ho 周 曉 和 of the National Szechwan University and Dr Graham of the West China Union University, a party was organized, and they made extensive glaciological and archaeological researches in the mountainous region. They looked for prehistoric remains on the Malan terraces that are abundant in this country. They investigated some of Edgar's sites with negative results, and they did not find a single specimen that could be accepted as a palaeolith (**32, 33**).

However, many neolithic sites were investigated. Andersson says that there are not less than seventeen sites in the Tao-fu valley which are very important. Some red and grey pottery was found together with slate implements. We are looking forward to the detailed report of Ch'i Yen-p'ei, who supervised the excavation.

The region investigated by the scientists mentioned above covers the province of Szechwan and its immediate vicinity. No less than ninety prehistoric sites have been visited or excavated by them. These sites are distributed in thirty different districts (or *hsien*), which are located along five main river valleys, namely, Yangtse, T'o, Min, Ta-tu and Ya-lung. No report of prehistoric sites has yet been made in the Chia-ling valley, which occupies a large portion of the Red Basin. Of the thirty districts, four are in the province of Hupei, one in the province of Yünnan, five in Hsikang and the remaining twenty districts are all in Szechwan (Map 2).

The purpose of this chapter is to give a detailed description of all the prehistoric sites found in the thirty districts mentioned above. The exact location of each site will be given whenever the record is available. The artifacts found in each locality will be classified and, if possible, the number of specimens obtained will also be given. Typical artifacts will be described in the next chapter.

In cataloguing the archaeological material from the Yangtse Gorges and from Yünnan, Nelson has made a splendid classification of the stone tools (**19 and 22**). But in order to standardize the typology for the whole region under investigation I venture to propose a more detailed classification, based primarily on the technique by which an artifact was manufactured, secondarily on its function, in so far as that can be determined from its appearance, and finally on its shape. A more detailed discussion of my system of typology will

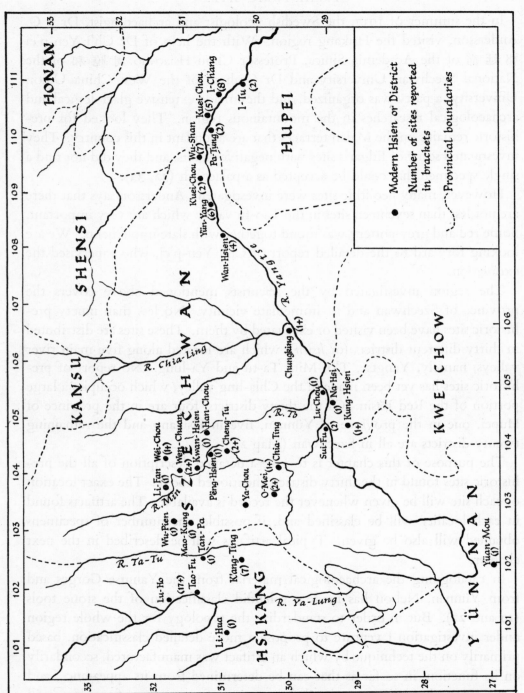

MAP 2. Prehistoric sites in Szechwan.

Modern Hsien or District
Number of sites reported in brackets
Provincial boundaries

22

be given in Chapter III. For the present purpose, I list only the types of implements found, using Nelson's terms as much as possible. In the cases where a new name for a type is given, Nelson's original name will be attached in parenthesis. The number of specimens of each type of artifact found will also be listed whenever possible. In the recording of stone tools found in other sites, this same method will be followed.

The prehistoric pottery of Szechwan has not been classified so far. I venture to divide the sherds into twenty-four types, based on the colour, the paste and the surface treatment of the ware. This will be discussed in full in Chapter IV. In this chapter, I name only the types in connexion with the site in which they were found.

In reporting on these sites and the material that has been found, we shall start in the east and, working westward, we shall follow up each of the five rivers, treating the sites in their geographical order.

THE YANGTSE VALLEY

There are fourteen districts along the Yangtse river in which prehistoric sites have been reported. Of these, four districts lie in Hupei, nine in Szechwan and one in Yünnan.

I. I-TU 宜都 (16, 17, 18, 19)

In I-tu hsien, Hupei, two prehistoric sites were investigated by Nelson. One was situated at a town named Ku-lao-pei on the left bank of the Yangtse and the other in the valley of Hsien-jên-ch'iao 仙 人 橋 (or the Fairy Bridge).

KU-LAO-PEI SITE. The Ku-lao-pei site was a settlement site of neolithic date. It was found at the base of a nearly thirty-foot bluff, on a gently sloping foreshore, and was about 100 yards wide by 600 yards long (16, 547). The artifacts occurred not only on the surface, but for a foot down into a lime concretionary deposit. This deposit rested on a greenish-yellow sandy clay of which the bluff also appeared to be composed. Digging in the artifact-bearing layer indicated that while the stone implements and possibly primitive pottery occurred deep down, so also did brickbats and bits of porcelain, so that undisturbed stratigraphy evidently did not exist at this site, except probably in the bluff itself (9, 32).

On this foreshore, Nelson collected 226 stone implements and 26 potsherds.

These constituted only a small proportion of the material found on the site. It was estimated that about 50 whole axes, 500 broken axes, 500 discs and 200 hammerstones were left on the beach (**17**, 33).

It is interesting to note that stone artifacts, which occurred in large numbers on the beach, did not occur on the field around the village above the bluff. The bluff has doubtless been washed back, giving rise to the specimens now found on the sloping bank. Nelson is inclined to think that the beach had not altered much since neolithic times and that the makers of these implements had their workshops here, using as raw material the fine quartzite pebbles which weathered out of the conglomerate just below (**17**, 32).

Stone implements

The stone implements of Ku-lao-pei may be classified as follows:

CHIPPED TOOLS

Discoidal choppers (flaked discs or ovals)	42	Picks (pointed implements)	2
Curved-bit axes (celts)	27	Discoidal scrapers (scrapers or flaked discs)	26
Rectangular axes (celts)	2	Pebble hammerstones (hammerstones)	4
Stemmed axes (hoes)	5	Hammerstones	17
Curved-bit adzes	2	Cores	2
Chisel (adze)	1		

CHIPPED-AND-POLISHED TOOLS

Straight-bit axe (celt)	1	Straight-bit adzes	2
Curved-bit axes (celts)	8	Curved-bit adzes	2
Stemmed axes (hoes)	2	Chisels	4

CHIPPED-PECKED-AND-POLISHED TOOLS

Curved-bit axes (celts)	67	Chisels	3
Broad axes (celts)	2		

POLISHED TOOLS

Axe (celt)	1	Mealing stones	2
Straight-bit chisel	2		

Pottery

Broken sherds of pottery were found with the stone tools on the foreshore of Ku-lao-pei. Several potsherds were also collected from a heap of rocks picked up by the farmer in his field. These were all associated with modern debris, so were difficult to distinguish from the modern fragments. Nelson has succeeded in pointing out the historic or modern potsherds, but he did not try to classify the prehistoric wares (**19**). I venture to classify the Ku-lao-pei pottery as follows:

Cord-marked coarse red ware	Plain or slipped fine red ware
Grooved coarse red ware	Painted fine red ware
Cord-marked coarse brown ware	Plain fine black ware

HSIEN-JÊN-CH'IAO SITE. The Hsien-jên-ch'iao site is situated in the valley of the tributary which joins the Yangtse at the Fairy bridge. A piece of rubbing stone was found on the right bank, but on the left, cultural remains were found in large quantities. In the fields high up on the east face of the adjacent gorge, about 300 yd. back from the stream, pottery and stone implements were found (**17**, 26). Near the fields, a rock shelter is situated in the face of a pyramidal shaped hill, and here, in a place about 50 ft. long by 7 or 8 ft. wide, Nelson found, at a depth of about 2 ft., two potsherds and some broken animal bones, which he maintains to be undoubtedly pre-Chinese and probably of neolithic origin (**17**, 11).

Stone implements

The forty-three specimens of stone tools from the Hsien-jên-ch'iao site may be classified as follows:

CHIPPED TOOLS

Discoidal choppers	2	Pebble scraper (scraper)	1
Short axe	1	End scrapers (flaked core)	2
Point (raw flake)	1	Raw flakes	19

POLISHED TOOLS

Axes	2	Curved-bit chisels	3
Broad axes	2	Spear point	1
Narrow-bit chisels	4	Rubbing stone	1
Straight-bit chisels	4		

Pottery

Six hundred and fifty-one pieces of potsherd were collected from the Hsien-jên-ch'iao site. These include some modern fragments and three pottery spindle whorls. They were found associated with stone implements as well as modern debris. A large proportion of them may be regarded as prehistoric and may be classified as follows:

Plain coarse grey ware	Plain fine black ware
Plain or slipped fine grey ware	Comb-marked fine grey ware
Appliqué fine grey ware	Stamped fine grey ware
Plain or appliqué fine brown ware	Incised fine brown ware
Plain or slipped fine red ware	

2. I-CH'ANG 宜昌 (17, 18, 19)

Prehistoric remains were found by Nelson at eight different sites in I-ch'ang. They are mostly situated on the foreshore along the Yangtse.

SITE I. This is situated on the right bank, 14 miles below the city of I-ch'ang. 29 stone tools were recorded and may be classified as below:

CHIPPED TOOLS

Curved-bit axes	3	Hammerstone	1
Stemmed axe (celt)	1	Reject flakes	14
Discoidal scrapers (flaked cores)	3		

CHIPPED-PECKED-AND-POLISHED TOOLS

Curved-bit axes	4	Rubbing stones (whetstones)	2
Adze (celt)	1		

SITE II. From a site on the left bank, three miles below the city, seven stone tools were recorded:

CHIPPED TOOLS

Discoidal chopper	1	Stemmed axe	1
Curved-bit axe	2	Curved-bit adze	1
Rectangular axe	1		

CHIPPED-PECKED-AND-POLISHED TOOL

Axe	1

SITE III. This is situated on the right bank, opposite the upper end of the city of I-ch'ang. Eight stone celts were reported:

CHIPPED TOOLS

Curved-bit axe	3	Stemmed axe	1

CHIPPED-AND-POLISHED TOOL

Curved-bit axe	1

CHIPPED-PECKED-AND-POLISHED TOOLS

Curved-bit axe	1	Broad axe	2

SITE IV. This is a site on the right bank, opposite the city at the extreme lower end of the I-ch'ang gorge. Four stone tools were reported. They were:

CHIPPED TOOLS

Rectangular axe	1	Stemmed axe	1

CHIPPED-AND-POLISHED TOOL

Curved-bit axe	1

CHIPPED-PECKED-AND-POLISHED TOOL

Grooved axe (celt)	1

SITE V. This is situated on the left bank just opposite Site IV. Here, on the foreshore, a polished curved bit axe and a polished curved-bit chisel were found associated with several potsherds. The latter may be grouped as:

Cord-marked coarse red ware	Stamped fine white ware

SITE VI. This is located on the left bank opposite to the P'ing-shan-pa 平山壩 customs station in the I-ch'ang gorge. 12 stone implements were reported:

CHIPPED TOOLS

Rectangular axe	1	Chisel	1
Stemmed axes	2	Discoidal scrapers	2

CHIPPED-AND-POLISHED TOOL

Curved bit axe	1

CHIPPED-PECKED-AND-POLISHED TOOL

Grooved axe	1

POLISHED TOOLS

Axe	1	Flat adze	1
Straight-bit adze	1	Straight-bit chisel	1

Nelson also found nine flint blocks of no definite shape on the right bank of the Yangtse at the big bend of the river above the P'ing-shan-pa site.

HUANG-LING-MIAO SITE. This is on the right bank of the Yangtse near the village of Huang-ling-miao 黃 陵 廟. Thirteen worked stones were reported from this site:

CHIPPED TOOLS

Rectangular axe	1	Core scraper (flint block)	1
Rectangular scraper (flint block)	1	Flint blocks	8
Side scraper (flint block)	1		

CHIPPED-AND-POLISHED TOOL

Stemmed axe (hoe)	1

TATUNG RAPIDS SITE. On the left bank of the Yangtse at the Tatung rapids, 28 miles above the city of I-ch'ang, one polished axe (celt) and one pebble polishing stone were found.

3. KUEI-CHOU 歸 州 (17, 18, 19)

In the district of Kuei-chou, Nelson found prehistoric implements from five different sites. They are located at Miao-ho 廟河, Hsin-t'an 新 灘, Hsiang-hsia 香 峽, the New Kuei-chou and the Old Kuei-chou.

MIAO-HO SITE. On the right bank of the Yangtse at Miao-ho, at the lower end of the Lushan gorge, two axes were found on the foreshore and three other implements were obtained from a rock shelter near by.

CHIPPED TOOLS

Pebble axes (scrapers)	2	Flake	1
Broad axe (celt)	1		

CHIPPED-AND-POLISHED TOOL

Curved-bit axe (celt)	1

HSIN-T'AN SITE. This is situated on the right bank of the Yangtse at the Plant monument. Nelson found two chipped axes of the curved-bit type associated with some potsherds, partly modern. Prehistoric pottery is represented by three types:

Cord-marked coarse brown ware	Plain or slipped fine red ware
Stamped coarse brown ware	

HSIANG-HSIA SITE. This is situated on the right bank of the Yangtse above the village of Hsiang-hsi 香 溪. Nine specimens of stone tools were reported to have been associated with some pottery, some of which is modern. The stone implements were:

CHIPPED TOOLS

Curved-bit axe	1	Straight-bit adze	1
Stemmed axe	1		

CHIPPED-AND-POLISHED TOOL

Curved-bit axe	1

CHIPPED-PECKED-AND-POLISHED TOOL

Curved-bit axe	1

POLISHED TOOLS

Axes	2	Polishing stone	1
Straight-bit chisel	1		

Among the fragments of pottery, a cord-marked coarse black ware may be considered prehistoric.

NEW KUEI-CHOU SITE. This is situated on the right bank of the Yangtse at the modern city of Kuei-chou. 25 specimens of worked stone were reported by Nelson:

CHIPPED TOOLS

Rectangular axes	2	Pebble scraper	1
Stemmed axes	2	Discoidal scraper	1
Chisel	1	Flakes	7

CHIPPED-AND-POLISHED TOOLS

Curved-bit axe	2	Curved-bit adze	1
Straight-bit adzes	2	Chisel	1

CHIPPED-PECKED-AND-POLISHED TOOL

Adze	1

POLISHED TOOLS

Axe	2	Rubbing stone	1

OLD KUEI-CHOU SITE. This is on the right bank of the Yangtse opposite the modern city of Kuei-chou. Two chipped pebble scrapers were found by Nelson.

4. PA-TUNG 巴 東 (17, 18, 19)

In the district of Pa-tung, Hupei, Nelson investigated two prehistoric sites. One is located at Kuan-tu-k'ou 官 督 口 and the other at Huo-yen-shih 火 餤 石.

KUAN-TU K'OU SITE. This is situated on the right bank of the Yangtse at the lower entrance to the Wushan gorge. A hammerstone was found on the foreshore and 14 worked stones were discovered in a rock shelter:

CHIPPED TOOLS

Pebble axe (unfinished celt)	1	Curved-bit axes	4
Discoidal choppers (hammerstone,		Straight-bit adze	1
scraper)	2	Curved-bit adze	1

CHIPPED-AND-POLISHED TOOLS

Curved-bit axes	3	Chisel	1
Curved-bit adze	1		

CHIPPED-PECKED-AND-POLISHED TOOL

Curved-bit axe	1

HUO-YEN-SHIH SITE. This site is on the right bank of the Yangtse at the village of the same name, in the Wushan gorge. Nelson found a chipped curved-bit axe and a chipped-and-polished chisel here.

5. WU-SHAN 巫 山 (13, 17, 18, 19)

In the district of Wu-shan, which covers the whole stretch of the Wushan gorge, Nelson discovered seven prehistoric sites. They are located at the lower Wushan gorge, P'ei-shih 培 石, T'iao-shih 跳 石, the upper Wushan gorge, Wu-shan, Hsia-ma-t'an 下 馬 灘 and Tai-hsi 代 (帶) 溪. The last is the most important site among those of eastern Szechwan, because it represents a cultural deposit with possible stratigraphic evidence. Edgar also found some chipped implements near the city of Wu-shan (13, 68–9).

LOWER WUSHAN GORGE SITES. These are situated on both banks at the lower end of the gorge. Nelson found 27 specimens of worked stone, some of which were in association with prehistoric potsherds.

Stone implements

CHIPPED TOOLS

Discoidal chopper (scraper)	2	Curved-bit adze	1
Curved-bit axes	6	Chisel	1
Broad axe	1	Ordinary flakes	8

CHIPPED-AND-POLISHED TOOLS

Curved-bit axes	2	Chisel	1

CHIPPED-PECKED-AND-POLISHED TOOLS

Curved-bit axes	3

POLISHED TOOLS

Axes	1	Straight-bit adze	1

Pottery

Plain coarse red ware	Stamped coarse red ware
Cord-marked coarse red ware	Stamped fine black ware

P'EI-SHIH SITE. This is a cave, situated on the right bank of the Yangtse, and is high up in the main cliff escarpment, with a small field below it. It measures about 30 ft. wide, 50 ft. deep and 12 ft. high. The floor is mostly stone. It had been occupied some time ago and the stone implements found were evidently brought in. These implements, seven in number, may be classified as follows:

CHIPPED TOOLS

Broad axe	1	Discoidal scraper (flaked disc)	1
Short axe	1	Single blade knives (unfinished celts)	2
Chisel	1		

POLISHED TOOL

Axe	1

T'IAO-SHIH SITE. This is situated on the right bank of the Yangtse at T'iao-shih-t'an 跳石灘. Nelson found 11 specimens of stone artifacts: one chipped stemmed axe, two polished axes and seven ordinary flakes some of which are probably end scrapers.

UPPER WUSHAN GORGE SITE. This is on the left bank of the Yangtse at the upper end of the gorge. Nelson found in this place three flakes, which consisted of a side scraper and two points. Some sherds of the incised fine grey ware and the plain or appliqué fine brown ware were also found, but they seem to have no association with the flakes.

WU-SHAN SITE. This is situated on the left bank of the Yangtse on the beach fronting the city of Wu-shan. Nelson found 59 specimens of worked stones. Edgar did not mention where he found his stone artifacts, but we may presume that he found them on the beach, too. On his walk along the beach, Nelson discovered some incised grey potsherds several miles above the town. They were found together with some modern debris. At another point on the beach, he gathered three stone artifacts. The stone tools of Wu-shan may be classified as follows:

CHIPPED TOOLS

Pebble axes (unfinished celts)	2	Straight-bit adzes	2
Discoidal choppers	2	Curved-bit adzes	2
Straight-bit axes	3	Pick	1
Curved-bit axes	6	Pebble scrapers	2
Rectangular axe	1	Discoidal scraper	1
Stemmed axes	4	End and side scrapers	2
Waisted axe	1	Pebble hammerstone	1

CHIPPED-AND-POLISHED TOOLS

Curved-bit axe	1	Chisels	4
Curved-bit adzes	3		

CHIPPED-PECKED-AND-POLISHED TOOLS

Curved-bit axes	2	Broad axe	1

POLISHED TOOLS

Axes	6	Straight-bit chisels	2
Broad axes	2	Curved-bit chisels	4
Flat adzes	2	Gouge	1

HSIA-MA-T'AN SITE. At the first rapids above Hsia-ma-t'an, Nelson walked up the Yangtse for about one mile to a tributary stream and found 46 stone implements along the way:

CHIPPED TOOLS

Pebble axes (unfinished celts)	7	Chisel	1
Curved-bit axes	8	Double-edged knives (unfinished	
Rectangular axes	2	celts)	3
Stemmed axe (celt)	1	Pebble hammerstones	3

CHIPPED-AND-POLISHED TOOLS

Straight-bit axes	2	Polishing stone	1
Curved-bit axes	4		

CHIPPED-PECKED-AND-POLISHED TOOLS

Curved-bit axes	2	Broad axes	2

POLISHED TOOLS

Curved-bit axes	8	Broad axes	2

TAI-HSI SITE. This is situated in a big valley coming into the Wushan gorge from the right at the village of Tai-hsi. Nelson walked up this valley for two miles and found 38 stone implements on the surface. They were:

CHIPPED TOOLS

Pebble axes	3	Stemmed axe	1
Discoidal choppers	2	Curved-bit adze	1
Straight-bit axes	2	Chisel	1
Curved-bit axes	7	Discoidal scraper	1
Broad axe	1	Pebble hammerstones	3
Rectangular axes	2	Ordinary flakes	4

CHIPPED-AND-POLISHED TOOLS

Curved-bit axe	1	Chisel	1

CHIPPED-PECKED-AND-POLISHED TOOLS

Curved-bit axes	4	Adze	1

POLISHED TOOLS

Axe	1	Narrow-bit chisel	1
Broad axe	1		

At the entrance of the valley at Tai-hsi, Nelson discovered a neolithic deposit exposed in the face of an escarpment and in one place cut through by a gully. The sectional exposures of the deposit are shown both along the strike and the back of the hill as a result of the cutting of the gully. The deposit ranges in thickness from 1 to 2 ft. on the left (south) to about 18 ft. on the right (north). Some ruins of an old Han dynasty fort are scattered nearby on the surface of the valley with debris of historic potteries. A cultivated field is situated in front of the neolithic deposit and it has also yielded prehistoric artifacts.

Although Nelson did not excavate the site, yet he made a careful investigation of the deposit, noting the cultural objects which had been exposed by the gully according to their depths in the deposit. Worked stones were found at least 14 ft. down. They are mostly chipped implements which Nelson calls unfinished celts or blanks. Pottery of several types was seen from the surface to the bottom. Fish bones are very plentiful at all levels, but only a few animal bones were noticed. One human arm bone was found about 12 ft. down. The cultural debris also contains streaks of ashes but only in spots. Clay, or hill wash, constitutes the matrix of the debris. Only at the right end a sterile layer of nearly 6 ft. thick overlies the culture debris (**17,** 75). Four stone implements were recovered from the deposit *in situ* together with a large number of potsherds and animal bones. I venture to list the specimens in Table 2, giving the depths at which they were said to have been found (**19,** no. 315–32). Nelson thinks that this is a promising site for excavation.

TABLE 2. Artifacts from the Tai-hsi Cultural Deposit

| Depth | Old Han Fort | Cultivated Field | Culture | | Debris |
			Stone Implements	Pottery	Animal Bones
Surface	Impressed grey ware Glazed hard ware	—	—	—	—
1 ft.	—	Polished celt Stone ring Masked tile Bronze pin (?)		Plain fine brown ware	Fish bones
2 ft.	—	—	—	Plain coarse brown ware	
4 ft.	—	—	1 Curved-bit axe chipped-pecked-polished	Cord-marked coarse red ware Cord-marked fine grey ware	Fish bones
6 ft.	—	—	1 Curved-bit axe chipped-pecked-polished (scraper)	Plain coarse red ware	
8 ft.	—	—	2 Curved-bit axes chipped	Plain coarse red ware	Fish bones
9 ft.	—	—	—	Plain fine red ware	Fish bones
10 ft.	—	—	—	—	Fish bones
12 ft.	—	—	—	—	Human bones
14 ft.	—	—	Chipped axes	—	—

6. K'UEI-CHOU 夔 州 (**17, 18, 19**)

In the district of K'uei-chou, two prehistoric sites were investigated by Nelson. One was found in front of the city of K'uei-chou and the other is near the village of Kao-wei-tzŭ 高 桅 子 above the city.

34

K'UEI-CHOU SITE. This is situated on the foreshore in front of the city of K'uei-chou. Five worked stones were found here: a chipped discoidal scraper; a chipped pebble knife; two chipped-and-polished curved-bit axes; and two chipped-pecked-and-polished axes of the curved-bit type. Another chipped discoidal scraper was found on a beach on the left bank of the Yangtse five miles above the city.

KAO-WEI-TZŬ SITE. This is situated on the left bank of the Yangtse near Kao-wei-tzŭ village. Nine stone implements and nine potsherds are recorded. The stone artifacts are:

CHIPPED TOOLS

Curved-bit axes	2	Discoidal scraper	1
Straight-bit adze	1		

POLISHED TOOLS

Curved-bit axes	2	Curved-bit chisel	1
Broad axe	1	Polishing stone	1

The potsherds consist of four types:

Plain coarse red ware	Stamped coarse red ware
Cord-marked coarse red ware	Cord-marked coarse grey ware

7. YÜN-YANG 雲陽 (17, 18, 19)

In the district of Yün-yang, six prehistoric sites were discovered by Nelson. They are located at Ku-lin-t'o 古林沱, San-pa-hsi 傘把溪, Ma-fên-t'o 馬糞沱, Hsin-lung-t'an 與隆灘, Chi-liang-t'o, and Hsiao-chiang 小江.

KU-LIN-T'O SITE. This is situated on the right bank of the Yangtse. Nelson did not find any prehistoric indications, but his assistant, Mr Yen, picked up eight stone tools near the village. They are: a chipped pebble axe, a chipped curved-bit axe, a chipped discoidal chopper, a chipped discoidal scraper; three chipped-and-polished curved-bit axes; and a polished narrow-butted axe.

SAN-PA-HSI SITE. This is situated on the left bank of the Yangtse near the village at the entrance of the small stream, San-pa-hsi. 15 stone artifacts were discovered here:

CHIPPED TOOLS

Discoidal choppers	3	Short axes	2
Broad axe	1	Discoidal scrapers	2
Rectangular axe	1		

CHIPPED-AND-POLISHED TOOLS

Straight-bit axe	1	Ordinary flakes	3
Curved-bit axe	1	Polishing stone	1

MA-FÊN-T'O SITE. This is on the left bank of the Yangtse. A chipped-and-polished curved-bit axe and an adze of the same type are reported from this locality.

HSIN-LUNG-T'AN SITE. On the right bank of the Yangtse at the Hsin-lung rapids, two chipped discoidal scrapers, a polished axe and a polishing stone were found.

CHI-LIANG-T'O SITE. This is situated near the entrance of the Chi-liang stream which flows into the Yangtse. Six stone artifacts were found on the left bank of the river and 30 on the right bank. About a mile above the entrance on the left bank of the stream another 24 stone implements were discovered. These tools may be classified as follows:

CHIPPED TOOLS

Pebble axes	13	Curved-bit adze	1
Discoidal choppers	2	Chisel	1
Curved-bit axes	6	Pick	1
Broad axes	2	Discoidal scrapers	5
Rectangular axes	4	Single-edged knives	4
Stemmed axes	6	Double-edged knives	2
Waisted axe (double notched flake)	1	Pebble hammerstone	1

CHIPPED-AND-POLISHED TOOLS

Straight-bit axe	1	Chisels	2
Curved-bit axes	4	Polishing stone (celt)	1
Stemmed axe	1		

CHIPPED-PECKED-AND-POLISHED TOOL

Broad axe	1

POLISHED TOOL

Curved-bit chisel	1

A large number of notched pebbles, which were manufactured with the help of metal tools, were collected in this locality. Nelson has told the author that he was informed that these artifacts are still in use by the fishermen along the gorges as net-sinkers. Therefore, he suggests separating these modern artifacts from the prehistoric material.

HSIAO-CHIANG SITE. Prehistoric remains are reported from two localities near the village of Hsiao-chiang. One is situated in a field on the left bank of the Yangtse about two miles above the village. Three types of pottery were found in the field: the cord-marked coarse red ware, the plain coarse grey ware and the cord-marked coarse brown ware. They were found scattered in the field together with other kinds of modern potsherds.

The second locality is on the left bank of the Yangtse about five miles above the village. Here Nelson found a polished axe and a polished adze of the curved-bit type.

8. WAN-HSIEN 萬 縣 (16, 17, 18, 19)

In the district of Wan-hsien, Nelson discovered four prehistoric sites. They were located at Pa-yang-hsia 巴 陽 峽, Chang-tso-t'an, Wan-hsien and Pai-shui-hsi 白 水 溪.

PA-YANG-HSIA SITE. This is located on the right bank of the Yangtse near the Pa-yang gorge. Four stone implements were recovered from this locality: two chipped pebble axes, one chipped chisel, one chipped single-edged knife and one polishing stone adapted from a pebble.

CHANG-TSO-T'AN SITE. Several localities where prehistoric remains were found have been observed on both banks of the Chang-tso rapids. Three stone tools were collected on the right bank below the rapids, five on the left bank at the same point of the river, four on the right bank two miles above the rapids and another four also on the right bank about four miles above the rapids. These implements may be classified as follows:

CHIPPED TOOLS

Pebble axe	I	Curved-bit adze	I
Discoidal chopper	I	Chisel	I
Curved-bit axes	4	Discoidal scraper	I
Stemmed axe	I	Flake knife	I

CHIPPED-AND-POLISHED TOOLS

Straight-bit axe	I	Curved-bit adzes	4

WAN-HSIEN SITE. Prehistoric remains have been reported from two different localities at Wan-hsien. One is situated on the right bank of the Yangtse five miles below the city. One chipped perforator was found here and Nelson describes it as an oval bi-faced flaked core. The other site is on the left bank, just opposite the oil tanks below the city. Six stone implements, consisting of one discoidal chopper, one chipped chisel, one chipped single-edged knife, one pebble hammerstone, one chipped-and-polished curved-bit axe and one polished axe, were found on the foreshore.

PAI-SHUI-HSI SITE. Nelson found one chipped curved-bit axe on the right bank of the Yangtse about half a mile below the village of Pai-shui-hsi. He also notes about 30 axes given to the Peking Museum and considers it a promising site for excavation.

9. CHUNGKING 重慶 (9, 26)

In the district of Chungking one polished axe and two polished chisels were purchased by Baber (9, 129–30). According to the information he obtained, these implements were found in association with stone coffins near the city. The localities at which they were unearthed were not given.

Graham (26, 48) mentions five 'paleoliths' found by Edgar between I-ch'ang and Chungking and 'a large number of neoliths and paleoliths' found between Chungking and Chia-ting, but no definite localities are mentioned. 'A well-made neolithic axe', which was a polished axe or celt, is said to have been found 'at Chungking'.

10. LU-CHOU 瀘州 (10)

Edgar (10, 86) reports a polished adze of the curved-bit type from a locality near the city of Old Lu-chou. It is some distance from the Yangtse and about 30 ft. above the high water mark. The adze was found lying beneath some worn sandstone and Edgar concludes that it was unearthed in the adjacent fields.

11. NA-HSI 納溪 (10)

Edgar (10, 86) describes a chipped-and-polished pebble which looks like a single-edged knife. It was found about seven miles below Na-hsi in a sandstone cleft which had probably been exposed by erosion. The tool was splintered from a piece of water-worn debris.

12. SUIFU 叙府—I-PIN 宜賓 (10, 13, 26, 28)

Edgar (10, 86) reports two prehistoric sites in the district of Suifu. One is situated about 15 miles below the city of Suifu, and he found a flattish pointed stone implement which may be called a chipped pick, near the flood-water level. The other site is about 30 miles upstream from the city. Edgar has not given the number of stone implements found in the site; all he describes is a side scraper. Dye (**13**, 66–71) describes five other artifacts which Edgar collected from this site.

Graham (**26**, 48; 51) refers to a third site, also discovered by Edgar after a flood near Suifu. It was a camp site and had been exposed by the freshet. Seven stone tools were picked up from this deposit. Dye (**13**, 69) also describes a polished chisel found by Thomas Cook near the city.

The stone implements of Suifu may be classified as follows:

CHIPPED TOOLS

Stemmed axes (hoes)	3	Double-edged knife	1
Picks (Mousterian)	4	Flaked knives (Mousterian knives)	S
End scraper (thumb scraper)	1	Waisted pebble (grooved	
Side scrapers (Mousterian scrapers)	S	hammerstones)	2

CHIPPED-AND-POLISHED TOOLS

Curved-bit axe (neolithic axe)	1	Flaked knives	2
Picks (Mousterian)	2	Blade	1

POLISHED TOOLS

Point-butted axe	1	Cores (limestone tools of	
Narrow-bit chisel	1	undetermined shapes)	M

13. KUNG-HSIEN 珙縣 (**27, 28**)

The district of Kung-hsien lies along the upper An-ning-ho 安甯河, a tributary of the Yangtse, which flows into the great river at Chiang-an-hsien 江安縣. No prehistoric sites have been investigated in this district, but Graham (**27**, 90–1) purchased at Kung-hsien over two hundred neolithic implements, which were said to have been found near the borders of Szechwan, Kweichow and Yünnan provinces. Most of these artifacts were made of hard igneous rock, but some were of soft limestone. Graham has not published all the stone tools in his collection, but according to the album he prepared for the Peabody Museum at Harvard (**28**), they may be classified as follows:

CHIPPED TOOLS

Pebble axes	4	Coulter-type knives	S
Rectangular axes	2	Sickle-type knives	S
Picks	5	Hammerstones	S
Points	3	Cores (limestone tools of	
Side scrapers	S	undetermined shapes)	M

POLISHED TOOLS

Axes	M	Curved-bit adzes	2
Broad axes	S	Narrow-bit chisel	1
Narrow-butted axes	S	One-shouldered punch	1
Point-butted axes	S		

14. YUAN-MOU 元謀 (20, 21, 22, 23)

Lung-kai is a market town on the right bank of the Yangtse, at the most southern curve of the great river in northern Yüan-mou hsien, Yünnan. The site is situated on the top of a hill some distance back from the Yangtse on the left bank of the tributary stream Tso-ning-ho 苴甯河. It is a habitation site and Nelson brought back 178 stone implements and a small collection of potsherds which were found associated with them as well as modern debris. The artifacts from Lung-kai may be classified as below:

Stone implements

CHIPPED TOOLS

Pebble axes	6	Perforator	1
Curved-bit axes	15	Discoidal scraper	1
Rectangular axes	2	End scraper and flakes	41
Stemmed axes	4	Flaked knives	32
Curved-bit adzes	3	Pebble hammerstones	5
Picks	3	Waisted pebbles	2

CHIPPED-AND-POLISHED TOOLS

Curved-bit axes	16	Curved-bit adzes	5
Straight-bit axe	1	Chisels	11
Celt fragments	20	Rubbing stone	1
Straight-bit adzes	3		

POLISHED TOOLS

Vertical-grooved axe	1	Perforated knives	3
Narrow-bit chisel	1	Polishing stone	1

Pottery

Cord-marked coarse grey ware	11	Incised fine grey ware	4
Plain coarse brown ware	5		

THE T'O VALLEY

There is only one site reported from the T'o river valley. It was first discovered by the owner of the land in 1931 and an excavation was carried out by D. C. Graham in 1934.

15. HAN-CHOU 漢州—KUANG-HAN 廣漢 (29, 30, 31)

The site is situated at T'ai-p'ing-ch'ang, a village about six miles to the north-west of the city of Han-chou. It was found on the top of a hill which rises 40 to 50 ft. above the surrounding plain. A short distance to the east of the spot on which the excavation was conducted, some ruins of a Han city were found (**29**, 116–17).

The excavation was preliminary in nature. Three trenches each 40 ft. long and 5 ft. wide and several test holes were dug with successful results. The primary object of Graham's excavation was to investigate the actual condition of the pit, in which the owner of the land unearthed a large number of sacrificial implements of jade and sandstone, including discs, chisels, axes, spear blades, knives, etc. The excavation disclosed not only more ceremonial implements in the pit, but also ornaments of jade such as beads and flakes. Graham (**29**, 118–19) suggests that the pit was a grave.

Besides the so-called burial, Graham also found an undisturbed cultural stratum a little way under the surface of the site and he concludes (**29**, 118) that the level was the refuse heap of an ancient pottery kiln. The stone and jade implements unearthed in this level are similar in shape and in material to those found in the pit. A group of potsherds was recovered from the cultural level and they fall into two classes, a coarse, cord-marked red ware and a fine grey ware.

The discovery of a large number of beautifully made jade sacrificial implements at this site suggests that the culture here represented is of a later date than other prehistoric cultures known in this region. Therefore, the T'ai-p'ing-ch'ang culture will be discussed independently in a separate article (*see* p. xiv).

THE MIN VALLEY

There are eight districts along the Min river where stone implements have been found. The artifacts were mostly found at random and few sites could be definitely located.

16. CHIA-TING 嘉定 (10, 26)

According to Graham (26, 48), Edgar found a large number of neoliths and paleoliths' between Chungking and Chiating, mostly above the high-water mark along the Yangtse and the Min. Only in one case (10, 86) has Edgar tried to indicate the exact spot of his discovery. This is a chipped-and-polished axe which he found on the right bank of the Fu-wên river 符 文 水, 15 miles above the city of Chia-ting. It was lying just below the flood mark and was covered with hardened clay which suggests its having been once embedded in the red sandstone formation so common in the province. A chipped pick from the Edgar collection is described as an 'Asturian-like pick or fist-axe' by Graham (26, 51; 54) who also reports a 'crude fist-axe' with secondary chipping. The latter implement was found between Chia-ting and Yachou and was covered with old patination.

17. O-MEI 峨 嵋 (13, 27)

About 25 specimens of stone tools were found by Barter, Freeman, Foster and others at Mt O-mei, near a summer resort, Hsin-k'ai-ssu 新 開 寺, which is a little less than 5000 ft. above sea level. At the foot of the sacred mountain, two stone implements were found near Hsiao-t'ien-chu 小 天 竺 (27, 91). According to Dye (13, 69), the O-mei specimens, as far as workmanship and material are concerned, might have come from the same camp as those found in Suifu. They may be classified as follows:

CHIPPED TOOLS

Flaked knives	6 (?)

CHIPPED-AND-POLISHED TOOLS

Curved-bit axes	S	Flaked knives	6 (?)
Pebble knives	S		

18. CHENGTU 成 都 (10, 13, 26)

In the district of Chengtu, Edgar found a pebble hammerstone at the lower end of the plain. Being an isolated discovery, he could not decide whether it was a a piece of road metal or a crude human implement (10, 86).

Dye (13, 71) picked up a stone implement on the campus of West China

Union University outside the city. This may be called a chipped-and-polished pebble knife.

Graham (**26,** 51) also found a few sandstone axes near Chengtu.

19. P'ÊNG-HSIEN 彭縣 (**13**)

In the district of P'êng-hsien, Mrs W. J. Mortimore obtained a pottery horse-head from a well at a depth of 12 ft. under the surface. This is in a deposit of pebbles and silt, and Dye (**5,** 72) maintains that it would require at least 2000 years to aggrade 12 ft. At the same level near the pottery was a stone artifact, but Dye (**13,** 75) has failed to describe it. (After handling the pottery I am inclined to believe that it is a Liu-li-ch'ang ware.)

20. KUAN-HSIEN 灌縣 (**10, 13, 26**)

In the district of Kuan-hsien, in a limestone cave about 80 miles upstream from the city, Edgar (**10,** 86–7) found a stone implement, which may be taken to be a pebble axe. In the same cave he also discovered a rubbing stone ('implement sharpener') and a 'prehistoric curio'. Dye (**13,** 69–71) describes two chipped waisted picks and a chipped curved-bit axe from the Kuan-hsien plain collected by Edgar. However, the exact location of these finds is unknown.

Graham (**26,** 51) reports some fine 'palaeoliths and neoliths' from the districts of Kuan-hsien, Wên-ch'uan, Wei-chou and Li-fan. They were found on the banks of the Min river and one of its tributaries where the altitude is between 2500 and 4000 ft. above sea-level. Of the chipped tools, there are axes, picks, hammers and scrapers. Polished axes and chisels are all very well shaped. He concludes that there are fewer 'neoliths' than 'palaeoliths', i.e. that chipped tools are more dominant in this region than polished ones.

21. WÊN-CH'UAN 汶川 (**26**)

In the district of Wên-ch'uan, stone implements have been found on the banks of the Min river. The chipped stones consist of axes, picks, hammers and scrapers and the polished tools are axes and chisels. The polished tools are rarer than the chipped tools (**26,** 51).

22. WEI-CHOU 威州 (**10, 13, 26**)

In the district of Wei-chou, Edgar (**10,** 87) found a point-butted celt on a bank of the Min river a few miles from the city. It was in water-worn debris of clay, sand and stones. The deposits are probably of glacial origin. He also found a crude polished grooved axe in a rock shelter hundreds of feet above the river. In an ancient Chinese settlement site, he discovered a polished broad axe, a 'clumsy prehistoric weapon' and a 'prehistoric hammer', slightly grooved near the poll end.

A very interesting find was made at Wei-chou. A piece of painted pottery was found associated with some stone artifacts in a thick wall which was built around A.D. 680. The earth that contained these prehistoric objects might have been taken from ancient debris nearby. Among the stone artifacts found in the same wall, Dye (**13**, 66) describes a discoidal chopper.

Graham (**26**, 52) illustrates the outline of a chipped-and-polished (?) axe (of 'typical megalithic type'), which was rectangular in shape.

23. LI-FAN 理番 (**13**, **26**)

In the district of Li-fan, Dye (**13**, 67) describes a chipped curved-bit axe and a neatly polished narrow-bit chisel. Graham (**26**, 51) mentions chipped axes, picks, hammers and scrapers that were found here. Some polished axes and chisels were also discovered, but the polished tools are less numerous than the chipped tools.

THE TA-TU VALLEY

There are four districts in the Ta-tu valley where stone implements have been found. These are mostly scattered surface finds and few actual sites have been located.

24. K'ANG-TING—TATSIENLU 打箭鑪 (**12**, **13**, **25**, **26**)

The city of K'ang-ting, better known to the western reader as Tatsienlu, is the provincial capital of Hsikang. The district of K'ang-ting, which is governed from the city of the same name, covers a very wide area extending over parts of both the Ta-tu valley and the Ya-lung valley. Seven prehistoric sites in this region have been investigated by Edgar. Five of the sites are located in the Ya-lung valley and will be dealt with in the following section. Only the remaining two are located in the Ta-tu valley and will be considered here. One of these two sites is situated near a town called Chê-to 折多 and the other is ten miles north of the provincial capital on the caravan route.

CHÊ-TO SITE. This is situated about ten miles south-west of K'ang-ting city on the main road to Ya-chiang 雅江. Artifacts were found on a terrace, which Edgar maintains to be formed of debris from an ancient glacier. These artifacts are mostly small and of crude workmanship, and are much weather-worn. Some large crude stone implements which were also very much worn were found in the gutters nearby. Edgar attributes them to the same original owner as the implements from the terrace (**12**, 56–8). Edgar has not included details of any of these implements in his report.

From this site Graham (**26**, 51) mentions four chipped implements: one short axe, two picks (flat-top point) and one end (thumb) scraper. A well-fossilized bone punch is also reported from this site. These implements were found in a glacial deposit, it is stated.

K'ANG-TING SITE. This is situated on the northern caravan route about ten miles from the city. Stone artifacts were found on what looked like a moraine. They are mostly much weather-worn axes, scrapers and knives. Edgar (**12**, 57–9) did not find anything of interest below the site.

Dye (**13**, 71) describes a chipped pick from K'ang-ting (?) as a 'savage little implement'. Bowles (**25**, 125) records two chipped pebble scrapers as having been found here by Edgar.

25. TAN-PA 丹 巴 (**12**)

The city of Tan-pa is situated on the Ta-chin river 大 金 河, a tributary of the Ta-tu. A camp site was found in a canyon about 7000 ft. above sea-level. The chipped stone implements that were found by Edgar (**12**, 57; 59) are mostly of friable mica schist and are heavy crude tools. Edgar maintains that the topography of the neighbourhood provided a suitable environment for prehistoric men, but he fails to describe the implements.

26. MAO-KUNG 懋 功 (**26**)

The city of Mao-kung is about 35 miles east of Tan-pà. In this district, Edgar found over 60 chipped stone tools (**26**, 51) in 'dry and protected spots'. Some of them are made of soft slate and are very much water-worn. Graham mentions four types of implements: axes, picks, scrapers and hammerstones, but he has not given the exact number of tools of each type.

27. FU-PIEN 撫 邊 (**12, 26**)

The city of Fu-pien is some 30 miles north of Mao-kung. Edgar (**12**, 57; 59) found here a prehistoric site in the loess deposit along the Hsiao-chin river 小 金 河, another tributary of the Ta-tu. He maintains that this site would be the best centre for an investigation of this basin. But most of the implements he found were from wayside debris. Graham (26, 51) describes a chipped short axe of igneous rock with very old patination and another of sandstone with finger-hold depressions.

THE YA-LUNG VALLEY

In reporting on the prehistoric sites in the Ta-tu valley, I have purposely omitted mention of the investigation made by Bowles in 1930–1. The archaeological material he obtained in the Ta-tu and the Ya-lung valleys was treated collectively (25), and it is almost impossible to disentangle it and assign it to separate sites. Bowles (25, 122; 126) visited 15 prehistoric sites in the loess deposit. One of these was found near K'ang-ting, another to the north of Fu-pien, and the rest are also situated in Tao-fu and Lu-ho 鑪霍. He also investigated four rock shelters, two lying to the south-west of K'ang-ting and two to the west of Tan-pa. Scattered finds are reported from 15 localities, two to the west of Fu-pien, seven to the south-west of K'ang-ting, and six on the caravan route from K'ang-ting to Tao-fu. I shall give Bowles's cultural division of the two valleys in the following paragraphs before going into the various sites in the Ya-lung valley.

Bowles (25, 121–41) classifies the artifacts found in western Szechwan and eastern Hsikang under two general categories. One consists of the objects associated with deposits of loess or in the vicinity of loess. The other includes those bearing no proximal relationship to loess, found scattered at random along the caravan routes, along valley bottoms and more especially at points of juncture of rivers, streams or roads. Bowles has tabulated the principal differences in the materials and technique between these two groups as follows (25, 123):

1. Specimens of the first group are inclined to be smaller and show finer secondary work than the second.

2. The majority of the first group show definite attempts to produce points and gouge-like cutting edges, whereas those of the second group are seldom pointed or sharpened.

3. Most of the first group are made of hard stone, whereas the other group are of softer stone.

4. Most of the first group appear to be household utensils, whereas the other group appear to be associated with tilling, digging and other agricultural pursuits.

5. Only in the loess deposits were there other associated articles such as pottery, bone implements, charcoal, red ochre and human remains. These were found *in situ*.

Thus Bowles's collection of Szechwan-Hsikang archaeological material may be grouped under two headings:

ARTIFACTS FROM LOESS DEPOSITS

CHIPPED STONE TOOLS.   About 300 specimens:

Points	5 illustrated
Scrapers	4 illustrated
Combination of points and scrapers	1 illustrated
Pebble (large) scraper	1 illustrated
Perforators (borers?)	4 illustrated
Flakes in iron ore	3 illustrated
Pebble hammerstone	1 illustrated

POTTERY.   Mostly found in the loess deposit at about 4 to 7 ft. below the surface. The sherds fall into types:

Incised or appliqué coarse red ware	Plain fine grey or black ware

RED OCHRE.   A pot full of ochre was found at a depth of about 5 ft. in an undisturbed loess and another lump in redeposited loess at a depth of 7 ft. They were found associated with pottery and a hammerstone.

CHARCOAL.   Pieces of charcoal were found lying together, ranging from 5 to 8 ft. deep in loess deposits.

BONE IMPLEMENTS.   Two worked bones (of yak) were found embedded in the loess. One was embedded at a depth of 4 ft. and the other was obtained from an old gravel pit, at 6 or 8 ft. below the surface. They are points or borers.

OTHER REMAINS.   Some human and animal bones were also found at about the same level as the above artifacts in the loess. The human bones have no indication of any great age but the animal bones have been identified as those of dogs, yaks, sheep and rodents which exist in the vicinity to-day.

ARTIFACTS FROM NON-LOESS SITES

These sites fall into numerous categories such as rock shelters, caves, the junctions of rivers, valleys, roads, mountain paths, gravel pits, etc. The much-weathered stone implements which had probably never been reworked by polishing may be mere pebbles which were adapted for practical purposes. They may be classified as follows:

Axes (hoe type)	3	Sickle knives	3
Picks	6	Hammerstone	1 illustrated
Coulter knives	7	Pitted stones	3 illustrated

Let us now return to the site report for the Ya-lung valley, where prehistoric artifacts have been reported from four districts. Tao-fu and Lu-ho will be treated as one district.

28. K'ANG-TING 康定 (12, 26)

In the western part of the K'ang-ting district, which occupies the Ya-lung valley, Edgar has visited five sites. They are, from south to north, situated at Yü-lung-shih 玉龍石, A-tê 阿德, Cho-lung (Zhurihak'a) 捉龍 (?), Ying-kuan-chai 營官寨 and T'ai-ning 泰甯 respectively.

YÜ-LUNG-SHIH SITE. This is situated on the southern caravan route from K'ang-ting, at Ri Mo Chong, 14,400 (12, 57) or 14,500 (12, 58) ft. above sea-level. Edgar found some chipped stone implements showing 'intelligent purpose'. These artifacts were chiefly gathered on the river banks and in gutters and are of a type similar to those from Cho-lung which will be mentioned presently.

A-TÊ SITE. The exact location of this site is not recorded. Graham (26, 53) mentions a collection of stone tools from A-tê: four discoidal scrapers, several short axes, two small scrapers and a sickle knife. With the exception of the small scrapers which are made of quartz crystal and of flint respectively, the collection includes only black igneous rock.

CHO-LUNG SITE. This is situated on the southern caravan route from K'ang-ting. Edgar (12, 57; 58) found chipped stone artifacts at a col-like feature 14,850 ft. above sea-level. The culture was similar to that of the Chê-to terrace in the Ta-tu valley. Graham (26, 53) reports that the Cho-lung stone implements consist of 60 small and 10 large chipped tools. They may be classified as follows:

Axes ('fist-axes')	S	Perforators (graver punch)	S
Short axes	S	Side scrapers ('saw-toothed')	S
Points (spear points)	3	Sickle-typed knives	S

YING-KUAN-CHAI SITE. Ying-kuan-chai is a military fort, stationed at the junction of two plains, on the road from K'ang-ting to Li-t'ang 裏塘 about 36 miles from Chê-to. Edgar (12, 58) found nothing *in situ*. Ruins of architectural construction were abundantly found everywhere in the site and the chipped stone artifacts were all gathered from heaps of ruined stone and from walls of farmhouses. Graham (26, 48, Pl. 2) mentions two picks, one of which he calls an 'Acheulean' fist axe, some short axes and several pebble scrapers.

T'AI-NING SITE. T'ai-ning is a little town on the caravan route half-way between K'ang-ting and Tao-fu. Graham (26, 53) reports on two chipped axes, one of meteorite and the other of white quartz. The meteorite was un-earthed by a gold digger and was patinated. The exact locality of the find has not been given.

29. LI-HUA 理化—LI-TANG (26)

Li-hua, better known as Li-tang, is one of the largest trading centres along the K'ang-ting–Lhasa caravan route. Graham (26, 51) mentions a chipped stone scraper of igneous rock obtained at Li-hua, but fails to give the exact location of the find.

30. TAO-FU AND LU-HO (12, 24, 25, 26, 33)

The valley of Tao-fu, which extends north-westward into the district of Lu-ho, is the richest region in prehistoric sites among the districts we have reviewed. Here for a distance of about 15 miles, a large complex of terrace deposits of the alluvial fan type exist and all along the escarpment of this terrace, one group of important sites after another has been discovered by various investigators. Bowles and Edgar located 13 sites and Andersson found 17. Neither party followed the standardized system of romanization in spelling the names of the sites and I have no way, at present, of finding out the Chinese characters for some of them. Neither do I know how many sites in Bowles's list have been revisited by Andersson, who failed to give a complete list of the sites he studied (33, 73). Andersson, as a result of his investigation, maintains that all the 17 sites within the Rotsung-Cholöna terrace complex are located near the front terrace, the only exceptions being Zu-wo and Yung-chi which are high up on the more elevated reaches of the terrace fans and the Yibi site, which is located on the low land near the river.

Bowles (25, 127) finds that all his sites are located on the southern extremities of the deposits which occur chiefly along the eastern face of the valley. The 13 sites which he found (25, 126) are Tao-fu (Dawo, with two sites), Siniang-kou, Chiato, Ta-chai (Tachiai, with two sites), Bréi, Chachie, Hato, Garadrong, Zonga, and Güi (with two sites). Among them the Güi site, near Sharatang and the Chachie site, are of special importance. Güi has yielded the largest and richest find and Chachie, although a smaller site, has produced smaller and more refined implements (25, 128). The stone artifacts and pottery which Bowles discovered in the Tao-fu valley have already been mentioned in con-nexion with artifacts from the loess deposits above.

In view of the fact that we have Bowles's report on the Tao-fu valley, the miscellaneous accounts given by Edgar (**12**, 57; 59), Heim (**24**, 176) and Graham (**26**, 53) are of little importance. However, it may be interesting to note that of all the stone implements discovered by various investigators in the Tao-fu valley and in other sites of the Ya-lung valley mentioned above, no polished implements have yet been reported. Graham (**26**, 53) notes that they have not appeared, so far, in the 'China-Tibetan' border, which is 7000 ft. above sea-level. The geographical distribution of the stone implements reported is given in Table 3.

Andersson (**33**, 73) has given a brief account of the material which Ch'i Yen-pei excavated in the Tao-fu valley. His main interest was in the painted pottery, but the investigation was negative. He classified the pottery of this district into two groups, a red ware and a grey ware. These may mark two different cultures, he says, because the red ware consists mostly of small sherds while the grey is also represented by large fragments. Ch'i's excavations were undertaken principally in the grey pottery deposits, where stone artifacts were found in association with them. These tools are 'elegantly cut in slate and possess shapes hitherto entirely unknown'.

CHAPTER III

STONE IMPLEMENTS

AMONG the prehistoric artifacts discovered by various investigators in Szechwan, stone implements comprise the major part. Most of these stone tools are surface finds and, as there is hardly any stratigraphy for reference, it follows that this material has to be studied from the typological point of view.

The typology which I have used for the stone artifacts of Szechwan is based primarily on the technique by which they were manufactured. The artifacts are classified in four groups: (A) chipped implements; (B) chipped-and-polished implements; (C) chipped-pecked-and-polished implements; and (D) polished implements. Each of these four groups is subdivided into various types according to the function and the shape of the artifact.

In the following pages, I first describe the chief characteristics of each group, which is subsequently divided into types with a detailed description of the implement and its distribution in Szechwan. Then I try to trace its distribution in other parts of eastern Asia. In every case, I cite the closest parallels possible, giving the reference to the plate or figure in question. It is true that in the case of a few generalized types, such as scrapers, knives and flakes, which are often without regular shapes, comparisons with other implements elsewhere cannot always be exact and may not have great value, but the majority of the implements are specialized tools, which can be clearly identified when they occur in any area and their appearance elsewhere in eastern Asia throws much light on the relationships of the lithic industries of this marginal area.

For comparison, I have used material from the following regions (see Map 3):

Siberia: the Yenisei valley, the Baikal region, the Amur valley and Kamchatka.

Japan: the Kurile Islands, Hokkaidō, Tōhoku, Kantō, Kansai, Shikoku, Kyūshū, Ryūkyu and Korea.

Manchuria: Kirin, Heilungkiang, Fêngtien and Jehol.

Mongolia and Sinkiang.

North China: Chahar, Suiyüan, Ninghsia, Kansu, Shensi, Shansi, Hopei, Shantung and Honan.

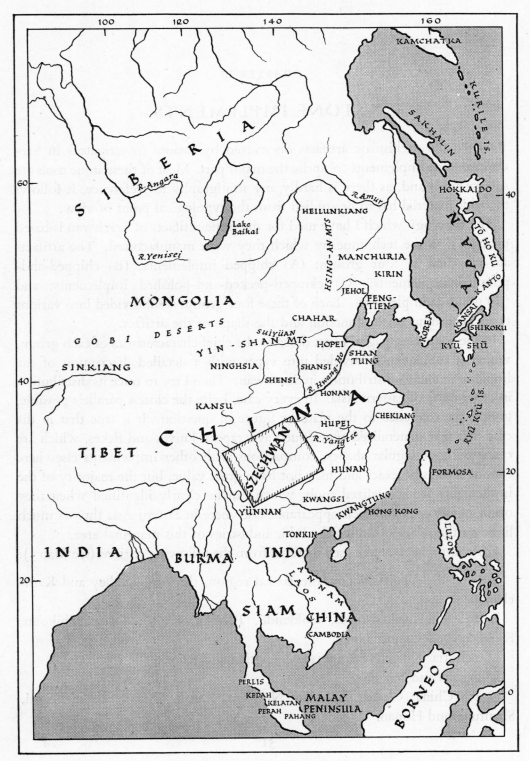

MAP 3. Szechwan and eastern Asia.

South China: Chekiang, Yünnan, Kwangsi, Kwangtung and Formosa.
Indo-China: Tonkin, Annam, Laos, Cambodia and Siam.
Malaya: Pahang, Perak, Kelantan, Kedah and Perlis.

In every case I also indicate, whenever possible, the type of site, level or stratum in which the comparative artifacts have been found. In most cases the authors of the reports referred to assign the deposits to the palaeolithic period or neolithic period, but here and there new terms have also been used. The Japanese archaeologists divide the neolithic age of Japan into two periods, the Jomon and the Yayoi, according to the two types of pottery characteristic of these periods. In Hongkong, Father Finn (256, Part 9, 127) employs the word 'epimiolith' to describe 'objects which must be regarded as much older than Neolithic'. In Indo-China, Mansuy and Colani adopt the terms 'Hoabinhien' and 'Bacsonien' for two long parallel series of implements, the older of which they describe in each case as palaeoliths and the younger of which they consider to be protoneoliths.

The assignment of prehistoric remains to the palaeolithic or the neolithic period is often very arbitrary and the dating differs with every region. The palaeolithic period in northern China and Siberia is generally regarded as Pleistocene in date, while remains of the Hoabinhien and Bacsonien cultures in Indo-China have not been found definitely associated with Pleistocene fauna or formations. The Malayan palaeoliths are said to resemble the Hoabinhien on one hand and to be akin to the Sumatra types on the other, but there is not enough geological and palaeontological evidence to justify assigning them a Pleistocene date. The microlithic culture of Siberia, Mongolia and Sinkiang may date back to the very beginning of post-Pleistocene times and hence belong to the mesolithic period, but in North China and Manchuria many microliths survived into Aeneolithic times. The neolithic period in Honan without much question ended a little before the rise of the Shang culture, or around 1500 B.C., but in Kamchatka it may have continued as late as A.D. 1000. However, I use the words in their cultural sense, as reported by the authors, without prejudice to the case. As to the time element involved, the terms used represent the chronological sequence in the areas in question and to that extent they have some value.

GROUP A: CHIPPED STONE IMPLEMENTS

The chipped stone industry of Szechwan is based primarily on the technique of pebble-flaking. I have used the word 'pebble' regardless of the size. Most of the Szechwan artifacts retain some of the pebble surface, so in the following description I shall use 'outer surface' to indicate the one that has retained more of the original pebble surface. The 'inner surface' has generally received more chipping, though it may retain the surface of the bulb of percussion.

There are a number of stone tools from Szechwan which may be recognized as merely pebbles or stones of desirable shape. Some axes, picks, scrapers, knives and hammers belong to this type and in several cases, especially with the limestone implements, it is difficult to distinguish them from ordinary pebbles. Some other tools such as the pebble axe, the pebble scraper, the single- and the double-edged knives and the waisted pebble are pebbles of suitable shape chipped into the desired cutting edge. These generally show no secondary chipping. The majority of the chipped stone tools are quite elaborately worked and the shape of the implements varies according to their function. In most cases, a flake is first knocked off from a pebble and secondary trimming or flaking is applied to render the flake into the desired form. The use of ordinary flakes is not unknown, but they are very limited in number. Only a few flint blades have been found in the region.

The materials of these river pebbles are chiefly quartzite, quartz, sandstone and limestone. Slate, flint, granite, mica schist, diorite, falsite, and other igneous rocks are also used. Bowles (**25,** 123) maintains that the artifacts associated with loess deposits are mostly made of hard stones, while those found disassociated from these deposits are generally of soft stones. This generalization may be true for the artifacts of the western part of the region, but on the foreshore of the river banks, especially along the Yangtse, quartzite and sandstone implements are by far the most numerous.

The chipped stone implements may be classified into the following sub-groups:

AXES

An axe, as here defined, is a relatively large and heavy implement, with a cutting edge consisting of a double bevel on one or seldom both ends of the tool. It is used for hewing or chopping and in some cases for digging. The chipped stone axes of Szechwan may be divided into nine types:

1. PEBBLE AXE (Pl. 1. 1): made of a selected oblong pebble with flaking at the bit end and at one side of the tool. The poll end and the other side retain the original pebble surface and the cross-section is oval. Some show more flaking on both sides, on both ends and on both surfaces than this specimen, leaving little pebble surface.

With the exception of one specimen from Kwan-hsien, in the Min valley, all the pebble axes were found in the Yangtse valley.

The pebble axe is a common type of stone tool found in eastern Asia. It has a very wide distribution, stretching from the Malay peninsula to Siberia, where implements of this type have been found in an early neolithic level at Monastyr, in the Yenisei valley (77, Fig. 6E). In Japan, pebble axes have been found associated not only with the Jomon (at Saitama, Kantō, 172, Fig. 9; Ubayama, Chiba, 125, Pl. 17. 5; Ninomiya, Tōkyō, 164, Fig. 64; Nio, Ehime, 166, Fig. 3 A), but also with the Yayoi pottery (at Todoroki, Higo, 108, Pl. 41.6; Iyo, Shikoku, 123, Fig. 1; Takada, Kyūshū, 121, Fig. 5 A). In Manchuria, specimens have been discovered with neolithic remains at Ninguta, Kirin (196, Fig. 3. 4) and also with microlithic tools at Linsi (201, Fig. 70) and East Onyuto (212, Pl. 34. 84–5), Jehol. In north China, pebble choppers of various shapes used by *Sinanthropus* (229, Fig. 9. 34) and the Upper Cave man (247, Pl. 1. 7), at Choukoutien, may be considered as the early types of the pebble axe, and in south China they have been excavated from the Kwangsi caves at Wu-ming-hsien (260, Fig. 11) which are probably mesolithic in date. This implement is quite at home in Indo-China, where it has been unearthed in association with the Hoabinhien (at Lang Kay, Tonkin, 290, Fig. 23–6; Yen-lac, Annam, 291, Pl. 42. 1, 3, 7, 9) and also with neolithic tools (at Bac Son, Tonkin, 282, Pl. 6. 1, 2; Bau Tro, Annam, 281, Pl. 2. 11). In Siam, it has been found in Tam Pra (298, Fig. 6. 1) and has been considered neolithic. Most of the reports on prehistoric remains of the Malay peninsula consider the pebble axe as palaeolithic (313, Pl. 41. 4–6; 324, Pl. 9. 2, 3, 6), but it has been found associated with pottery (as at Gua Debu, Kedah, 324, Pl. 5. 4) and with other neolithic tools (as at Gua Bintong, Perlis, 328, Fig. 5. 2).

2. DISCOIDAL CHOPPER (or SCRAPER) (Pl. 1. 2): made of a thick flattish pebble, flaked into a disc with a sharp edge, at a moderate angle, all around. One surface is more flaked than the other. It may have been used as a chopping tool. Some have a steeper angle at the edge than this specimen. Some are oval in shape. The edge is generally battered, and some specimens are so much worn

that the edge is more or less rounded. I am inclined to think that this implement was used not only for chopping but also for stone pecking. The much-worn edge of the tool suggests an active striking on a hard surface and the most battered chopper tends to resemble a hammerstone, which usually is discoidal or spherical in shape.

It must be pointed out, too, that the discoidal chopper occurs only in the Yangtse gorges, where the chipped-pecked-and-polished tools have been found.

So far, no discoidal chopper has been found in Siberia and Japan. In Jehol, it has been reported from Hung-shan-hou I, Ch'ih-fêng (**206,** Fig. 50), and at Sung-chia-ying-tzŭ, Ch'ao-yang (**195,** Pl. 2. 16). In these localities, the specimens were found associated with microlithic implements and other neolithic artifacts. The Ch'ih-fêng chopper is slightly square in outline. The discoidal choppers, which were unearthed in the *Sinanthropus* deposit (**229,** Fig. 7) and in the Upper Cave (**334,** Fig. 4B), at Choukoutien, seem to have been chipped from cores rather than pebbles. A 'palaeolithic' implement, which was made of a discoidal pebble, has been reported from Hongkong (**259,** Fig. 1), but the cutting edge of the tool, unlike most of the Szechwan implements, was worked only half-way around the disc. In Indo-China, the discoidal chopper has been discovered in the Hoabinhien (at Xom Kham, **286,** Pl. 4. 8) and in the Bacsonien sites (at Keo Phay, **279,** Pl. 5. 1). In the Malay peninsula, this type of implement was found mostly in the lower cultural levels, such as those of the sites at Gua Madu, Kelantan (**434,** Pl. 2), Gua Debu and Gua Kelawar, Kedah (**324,** Pl. 5, 6, 9). The specimens from these sites and those from Perak were generally reported as 'palaeoliths'.

3. CURVED-BIT AXE (Pl. 1. 3): made of a river pebble, flaked all over, with a roughly oval outline and an oval cross-section. Generally, a curved-bit axe has two straight sides, which are usually parallel to each other. The bit end and the poll end are mostly round in outline. Some have a straight poll end. There are a few cases in which this implement has been made of a pebble flake. In such cases, the flake is trimmed at both sides and the tool is usually thin and flat. This may have been used as a hoe, for digging rather than chopping, which is a job for heavier implements.

The curved-bit axe is one of the chief implements in this region. It has been found in large quantities in almost every district. In fact the straight-bit axe, the broad axe and the rectangular axe may all be taken as variations of this type.

The curved-bit axe is one of the most common stone implements of eastern Asia. In Siberia, it has been found in the early neolithic level of Označennaja (**77,** Fig. 6 A) in the Yenisei valley. It has also been found in the Kurile Islands (**79,** Pl. 13. 10), where the implement seems to have been retouched. In Japan, the curved-bit axe has been excavated in every region, for example: at Shiri-beshi, Hokkaidō (**159,** Fig. 86); Kamegaoka, Tōhoku (**119,** Fig. 4. 7); Asa-shimura, Kantō (**140,** Fig. 10); Todoroki, Kansai (**108,** Pl. 41. 2); Kita, Shikoku (**127,** Fig. 6. 1–6); Fukuoka, Kyūshū (**148,** Fig. 1. 4–5); Tôsandô, Korea (**126,** Fig. 36). The specimens from Japan were found associated not only with the Jomon or Yayoi pottery, but also with bronze artifacts as in the site of Fukuoka. A large specimen from the Kamiyo site, Tōhoku (**167,** Fig. 5) was grooved, probably through use. Some axes from Yamatogawa, Kawashi (**174,** Fig. 1. 2, 8–10) are lozenge-shaped in cross section and they were found associated with the Yayoi pottery. Some specimens have been found at the site of Seikori, Korea (**141,** Fig. 14–15) and they were associated with the 'Kammkeramik'. In Manchuria, curved-bit axes have been found in the neolithic sites of Ninguta, Kirin (**192,** Fig. 4. 1) and Shih-pei-ling, Ch'ang-ch'un (**198,** Fig. 7. 8, 10), and in Jehol, at Ta-miao (**202,** Fig. 13. 3), Ch'ih-fêng (**206,** Fig. 50), East Onyuto (**212,** Pl. 34, 71), and Linsi (**189,** Pl. 36. 2–5). Some of the Ch'ih-fêng specimens are small in size. This might have been due to the influence of the microlithic culture that dominated the Mongol–Manchurian plateau in neolithic times. In northern China, the curved-bit axe has been found in the neolithic sites of Ta-lai-tien, Honan (**242,** Fig. 6) and of An-ting, Kansu (**189,** Pl. 39. 4). This type of implement has also been found at Atogolan (**258,** Fig. 4 C), a neolithic site in Formosa. In Indo-China, axes of this type have been found in the prehistoric sites of the Hoabinhien (at Yen Luong and Tchong Doi, Tonkin, **289,** Pls. 13, 14), the lower neolithic (at Keo Phay; **279,** Pl. 1. 1–2), the neolithic (at Dong Thuôc, **279,** Pl. 11. 6), and the upper neolithic (at Ba Xa, **284,** Pl. 14) stages. Some of the specimens from Lang Kay Tonkin, have been described as *coups de poing* (**290,** Fig. 28). Some *coups de poing* of this type have also been reported from Cham Tong, in Siam (**298,** Fig. 3. 7). In the Malay Peninsula, some implements of this type have been recognized as similar to the 'Sumatra type' (**313,** Pls. 40, 43, 44) and considered palaeolithic, and in a level below the neolithic deposit at Ulu, Kelantan (**333,** Pl. 50. 14), some more have been reported as of the 'Hoabinhien' type. But most of the curved-bit axes found in this peninsula were associated either with pottery (as at Gua Debu, Kedah, **314**, Pl. 5. 1–2) or with other neolithic remains (at Gua Bintong, Perlis, **328**, Fig. 5. 1).

4. STRAIGHT-BIT AXE (Pl. 1. 4): made from an oblong pebble, flaked all over, with an almost straight bit end, a rounded poll end and nearly parallel sides and an oval cross-section. Some are less regularly chipped than the specimen illustrated.

The straight-bit axe was found in only two districts in the Yangtse gorges— five from Wu-shan and one from Wan-hsien. It may be a local variation of the curved-bit axe.

But outside Szechwan, axes of this type have been reported from a neolithic site in Kamchatka (**84**, Pl. 1. 6), from the Yayoi site of Izumi, Kyūshū (**109**, Pl. 5. 18) and from the neolithic site of Tôsandô, Korea (**126**, Pl. 3. 2). In Indo-China, this implement has been unearthed in a Hoabinhien site at Lang Vo, Tonkin (**286**, Pl. 11. 14) and in a neolithic site at Da But, Annam (**297**, Pl. 7. 5).

5. BROAD AXE (Pl. 1. 5): made of a flake of a river pebble, with flaking on the split surface producing a curved sharp cutting edge at the bit end. The poll end, and the two sides, are roughly straight, with the latter almost parallel to each other. On the other surface, the pebble surface is retained. This type is called broad-axe because the width of the tool in comparison with the length is much greater than in the case of the ordinary curved-bit axe.

The broad axe was only found in the districts of Kuei-chou, Wu-shan and Yün-yang, along the Yangtse.

This type of stone tool has been reported from the Jomon-Yayoi site at Tado, Kantō, in Japan (**138**, Fig. 7). It has also been found at Linsi, in Jehol (**189**, Pl. 40. 4). South of Szechwan, this implement has been unearthed in the Hoabinhien site of Sao Dong (**286**, Pl. 2. 1) and the Bacsonien site of Bac Son (**275**, Fig. 9), in Tonkin, and also in the Hoabinhien level at Kelantan in the Malay peninsula (**334**, Pl. 1. 5).

6. RECTANGULAR AXE (Pl. 1. 6): adapted from a rectangular block of stone, with a rectangular outline and cross-section. The bit end is roughly chipped into a sharp edge, which is somewhat curved. Generally, a rectangular axe is made of a pebble or a pebble flake. In both cases, the material is chipped and retouched into an artifact with rectangular outline, though not necessarily with a rectangular cross-section.

This type of implement is chiefly found in the Yangtse valley.

In Japan, specimens of this type have been found only in the Kantō region and almost always in association with the Jomon pottery (at Hiratoyama, **130,** Fig. 6; Asashimura, **140,** Fig. 2. 2; and Gau Hida, **145,** Fig. 2). In northern China, the squared chopper used by *Sinanthropus* (**229,** Fig. 2) may be regarded as a primitive type of this tool. In Indo-China, this implement has been reported from the Hoabinhien level at Sao Dong (**286,** Pl. 7. 3) and from the Bacsonien site of Bac Son (**282,** Pl. 10. 4). Some specimens of this type, labelled as palaeoliths, have been reported from Gua Debu, Kedah, in the Malay Peninsula (**324,** Pl. 6. 4), but those from Ulu, Kelantan (**333,** Pl. 49. 12, 51. 16) have been found associated with neolithic artifacts.

7. SHORT AXE (Pl. 1. 7): made of a thick flattish pebble, with a straight flat top or poll end and a circular cutting edge which is flaked from both sides. Both surfaces of the tool retain the smooth pebble surface. The straight flat top is sometimes adapted from the edge of a pebble, but generally it is flaked at a very steep angle. The implement is not meant for hafting.

The short axe was found abundantly in the Ya-lung valley at K'ang-ting. It is also reported from I-tu and Yün-yang along the Yangtse, and Wu-pien.

It has generally been accepted that the short axe is one of the typical stone artifacts of Indo-China and probably originated there. But it is interesting to find that this type of stone tool has a wide distribution outside of Indo-China and Szechwan. In Siberia, it has been reported from the early neolithic level of Jessaulovo, in the Yenisei valley (**77,** Fig. 8 p); in Japan, from the Jomon-Yayoi site at Yoshii, Kantō (**156,** Fig. 12. 9); in Jehol, at Kao-chia-ying-tzŭ (**189,** Pl. 16. 28); and in Suiyüan, from the upper palaeolithic level of Shui-tung-kou. An implement used by *Sinanthropus* (**229,** Fig. 31) may be classified under this type. In southern China, the short axe has been reported not only from the Kwangsi caves (**260,** Fig. 8) but also from Lamma Island (**256,** Part 9, Pl. 11). In Tonkin, it is a typical artifact of the Hoabinhien stages (at Lang Kay, **290,** Fig. 1–15; Yen Luong, **289,** Pl. 13. 7–8; Tchong Doi, **289,** Pl. 14. 7; Lang Neo, **286,** Pl. 7. 6; and Sao Dong, **286,** Pl. 2. 11, 19), but it has also been found in Bacsonien sites (Keo Phay, **279,** Pl. 7. 2). In the Malay peninsula, the short axe has been reported as a Hoabinhien type (Kelantan, **334,** Pl. 1. 2, 3) or as a palaeolith (Gua Debu, **324,** Pl. 6. 5, 6).

8. STEMMED AXE (or hoe) (Pl. 1. 8): may also be called 'shouldered axe'. It is made of a flake of river pebble, trimmed at the poll end into a stem, which is meant for hafting. The poll end is usually straight while the bit end is convex

and is chipped into a sharp edge. The outer surface retains the original pebble surface. The implement is generally flat and may have been used as a hoe.

The stemmed axe occurs quite frequently in the Yangtse valley, but as yet it is unknown in other districts.

Outside Szechwan, the stemmed axe has been found in the Kurile Islands (**79**, Pl. 13. 13). In Japan, most discoveries of the implement were made in Tōhoku (at Kamegaoka, **119**, Fig. 4. 8) and in Kantō (at Hiratoyama, **130**, Fig. 6; Kurume-mura, **175**, Fig. 18) where the stone tools were found associated with Jomon pottery. Some specimens from the Fujiyama site in Shizuoka (**116**, Fig. 1 B, C) have long stems, those from the Nagano site (**112**, Pl. 11) vary in size and shape and one of the two artifacts from Ishikawa (**168**, Fig. 3. 7) has two grooves. In Manchuria, the stemmed axe has been reported from the neolithic sites of Ninguta, Kirin (**196**, Fig. 4. 1) and of Tieh-ling, Fêngtien (**198**, Fig. 3. 1); in Jehol, from Ta-miao (**202**, Figs. 4, 6. 1), Linsi (**201**, Fig. 98) and Ch'ih-fêng (**206**, Fig. 50; **189**, Pls. 41, 42); in Honan, from the late neolithic site at Yangshao (**233**, Fig. 1 A); and in Formosa, at Atogolan (**258**, Fig. 4 B). In Indo-China, the stemmed axe has been found in the Hoabinhien level at Sao Dong (**286**, Pl. 3. 8), but it has also been found in the neolithic workshop at Ban Mon, Son La (**289**, Pl. 3. 1) where some bronze artifacts were unearthed. Stone artifacts of this type have been reported from the Malay peninsula as palaeoliths (at Gua Debu, **324**, Pl. 5. 3, 5), but in the Gua Kelawar site, Kedah (**324**, Pl. 9. 4), and in the Guak Kepah site, Province Wellesley (**326**, Pl. 32. 3, 10, 12), it has been found associated with pottery and neolithic tools.

9. WAISTED AXE (Pl. 1. 9): made from a pebble flake, with retouch at both ends and notched at the waist from both sides. The chipping is done on the inner surface while the other retains the pebble surface. The implement may have been hafted and used as a hoe for digging. The cutting edge produced artificially at both ends distinguishes the implement from a waisted pebble, which may be used as a net sinker or a hammer.

The waisted axe was found only in the Yangtse gorges, at Wu-shan and Yün-yang. Two specimens have been reported so far.

The waisted axe enjoyed the greatest popularity in Japan, where it has been found in practically every neolithic site. In Hokkaidō (as at Ishikari, **136**, Fig. 4. 1), in Tōhoku (as at Kamegaoka, **119**, Fig. 4. 9) and in Kantō (as at Okori, **99**, Pl. 17. 1), it has almost always been found associated with Jomon pottery, while in Kansai (as at Kōmura, **104**, Pl. 19. 8) and in Kyūshū (as at

Ibusuki, **102**, Pl. 30. 1, 2), the associated pottery has been mostly Yayoi. In Siberia, the waisted axe has been found at Ladeiki, in the Yenisei valley (**73**, Pl. 4. 11); in Manchuria, at Fu-shun, Fêngtien (**181**, 215), and in Jehol (**189**, Pl. 42. 2, 5–7); in Formosa, at Kōto-sho (**245**, Fig. 2. 1); in Indo-China, at Bac Son (**282**, Pl. 18. 7) and in the Malay peninsula at the neolithic sites of Ulu, Kelantan (**333**, Pl. 51. 15) and Guak Kepah (**326**, Pls. 31, 32). The Ulu specimen is necked rather than waisted.

ADZES

An adze is also a relatively large and heavy implement, with a cutting edge consisting of a single bevel on the bit end of the tool. It was undoubtedly used for hewing or chopping and perhaps was never used for hoeing. The chipped stone adzes of Szechwan consist of two types:

10. CURVED-BIT ADZE (Pl. 2. 1): may also be called a pebble adze. It is made of an oblong pebble, with a few flakes removed at the bit end to form the convex cutting edge, which is usually very much worn. The rest of the tool retains the pebble surface and looks like a polished tool. The poll end is round and the sides are roughly parallel to each other. The cross-section is oval. Some axes of this type are more elaborately chipped than the illustrated specimen, but they all have a single bevel at the bit end of the tool.

The curved-bit adze was found along the Yangtse but none has yet been reported from other districts.

In Kamchatka, curved-bit adzes have been found at Kavran (**79**, Pl. 9. 12, 19) and around Lake Kuril (**79**, Pl. 7. 18–29). Artifacts from the latter site are described as scrapers. In Japan, adzes of this type have been found in the Jomon sites of Okadaira (**100**, Pl. 10. 9, 14) and Hiratoyama (**130**, Fig. 6), Kantō, and in the Jomon-Yayoi sites at Tado, Kanagawa (**138**, Fig. 7) and at Kita, Ehime (**127**, Fig. 6, 10, 16). The implement has also been found in the Hoabinhien levels in Trieng Xen, Tonkin (**286**, Pl. 5. 19) and in Perak (**313**, Pl. 41. 2).

11. STRAIGHT-BIT ADZE (Pl. 2. 2): made of a thick flattish pebble with flaking on both sides and at the bit end. The poll end retains the pebble surface, as does the outer surface also, while flakes are mostly removed from the inner surface. The cutting edge is fairly straight and has a single bevel. Some implements of this type have been adapted from a pebble flake, but in most cases they are relatively large and heavy.

The straight-bit adze has been found so far at Kuei-chou, Wu-shan, Yün-yang and K'uei-chou, along the Yangtse.

In Siberia, straight-bit adzes have been found in an early neolithic site along the Angara river (**77**, Fig. 8 C, G), in the Yenisei valley and from the Chita site (**72**, Pl. 2. s6) on the upper Amur. The Chita specimen is small and flat.

CHISELS

A chisel is a relatively small implement with a cutting edge either of a single bevel or of a double bevel, on one or both ends of the tool. Owing to the size of the implement, it cannot have been used for hewing or chopping but it may have been used either as a gouge or as a scraper.

12. CHISEL (Pl. 2. 3): made of a pebble flake, trimmed into a roughly oblong outline, with fairly straight and almost parallel sides and arched ends, which are both very sharp, suggesting that it may have been used as a scraper. The flaking is done on the inner surface, while the outer retains the original pebble surface. Some chisels are adapted from a small flattish pebble. Most of them have a battered poll end.

The chisel was exclusively found in the Yangtse gorges. No specimen of this type has yet been reported from other districts.

Outside Szechwan, the chipped chisel has been found in the late neolithic site of Lake Kuril, Kamchatka (**78**, Pl. 11. 14); at the neolithic site of Tao-miao, Jehol (**202**, Fig. 13. 1); and in the Hoabinhien level of Trieng Xen, Tonkin (**286**, Pl. 5. 13).

PICKS

A pick is a relatively large and heavy implement with a point at the bit end. It was probably used exclusively for digging. Chipped stone picks have been found in large numbers in Szechwan and they may be classified into seven types:

13. SUB-TRIANGULAR PICK (Pl. 2. 4): made of a large pebble flake with a pointed bit end and an arched poll end. The sides are roughly straight forming an acute angle at the point. Unlike most of the axes and the adzes of this region, flakes are removed from both surfaces, though the outer one still retains a large portion of the pebble surface. In some cases, the poll end is trimmed by flaking and a triangular pick is thus produced.

This type of pick has been found at I-tu below the Yangtse gorges.

Outside Szechwan, sub-triangular picks have been found in the Hoabinhien site at Lang Kay, Tonkin (**290,** Fig. 27) and in the neolithic site at Gua Kerbau, Perak (**340,** Pl. 44. 1).

14. STRAIGHT-BUTTED PICK (Pl. 2. 5): made of a pebble block with a pointed bit end, which is chipped into shape. The sides are roughly straight and parallel to each other and the poll end is straight and almost at right-angles to the sides. Most of the surface of the tool retains the pebble surface.

This type of pick was discovered in the Ya–lung valley, and no parallel has yet been found in other regions of eastern Asia.

15. STEMMED OR SHOULDERED PICK (Pl. 2. 6): made of a large pebble, elaborately chipped into a pointed implement with a stem probably for hafting. A very small portion of the natural pebble surface is retained.

The stemmed pick was found in the Hsikang region.

In the Malay peninsula, some stone artifacts from the neolithic site of Nyong, Pahang (**320,** Pl. 14. 2, 4) may be classified as belonging to this type.

16. WAISTED PICK (Pl. 2. 7): made of a large pebble flaked into a pointed implement with symmetrical notches near the poll end of the implement. The notches may have been made for the purpose of hafting. The implement is symmetrical and is slightly rounded from top to bottom. A slight rubbing has been found at the bit end which may have been due to use.

This specimen was found at Kwan-hsien in the Min valley.

The waisted pick has been found at Ch'i-kou-chin-tzŭ, Hami, Sinkiang (**190,** Fig. 12) and at the Nyong site, Pahang (**320,** Pl. 14. 6). The Hami artifact is considered neolithic in date.

17. POINT-BUTTED PICK (Pl. 2. 8): made of a large pebble, chipped into a pointed implement with a pointed poll end. The outline of the implement is roughly diamond-shaped with one corner projected into a point, which forms the bit end of the implement.

A few specimens of this type of pick were found in the Ya-lung valley, and no parallel has yet been found in eastern Asia.

18. ELONGATED PICK (Pl. 3. 1): made probably of a large long pebble, chipped elaborately into a long pointed implement. It may have been hafted for digging as a slight depression can be observed at the middle section of the implement. The cross-section is probably round.

Two elongated picks were found in the Ya-lung valley.

In Siberia, the elongated pick has been reported from the early neolithic level of Čadobec on the Yenisei (**77**, Fig. 8 Y). In Japan, artifacts of this type from Hiratoyama (**130**, Fig. 6) and Nagano, Kantō (**112**, Pl. 11. 1) have been found associated with Jomon pottery, while those from Kōmura, Kansai (**103**, Fig. 5; **104**, Pl. 19. 6) were associated with Yayoi pottery. In Indo-China, the pick has been unearthed in the Hoabinhien levels at Xom Kham (**286**, Pl. 4. 2), in the lower neolithic level at Keo Phay (**279**, Pl. 5. 2) and in the neolithic level of Lai Ta, Bac Son (**283**, Pl. 4. 5). Artifacts of this type have also been found in the neolithic sites of Gua Madu (**334**, Pl. 3. 3) and Gua Pulai (**324**, Pl. 14. 3), in the Malay peninsula.

19. LEAF-SHAPED PICK (Pl. 3. 2): made of a large flat piece of stone, chipped into a leaf-shaped implement with a point at the bit end. Some implements of this type have a more pointed bit end than is shown in the illustration.

Most examples of this type of implement were found in Hsikang.

A 'crude cleaver' from Peresselentscheskij Point on the Yenisei (**73**, 37; Fig. 7. 1) may be classified under this type. The Kōmura artifact (**103**, Fig. 4. 3–4) seems to belong also to this type, but it was discovered among Yayoi pottery. In Manchuria, this implement has been found in the neolithic site of Shih-pei-ling, near Ch'ang-ch'un (**198**, Fig. 7. 1) and in Hung-shan-hou I, Jehol (**206**, Fig. 48). The latter specimens are pointed at both ends. In Tonkin, the leaf-shaped pick has been found in the Hoabinhien site of Lang Kay (**290**, Fig. 29) and Sao Dong (**286**, Pl. 3. 4), in the lower neolithic level of Keo Phay (**279**, Pl. 2. 1, 3, 4) and in the neolithic site of Bac Son (**282**, Pl. 1). A specimen has been reported from Perak (**313**, Pl. 43. 3) and is described as palaeolithic.

POINTS

A point is usually a smaller implement than the chopping and digging tools described above. It is a piercing tool with a sharp point for the purpose. It is generally small and this renders it suitable for a projectile point. Hence, I include the so-called spear-head in this group.

20. FLAKE POINT (Pl. 3. 3): made of a large flake which may have been removed from a core with a prepared striking platform. The materials used for the lithic industry of Szechwan are chiefly quartzite and sandstone, which, in the process of flaking, are harder to control than flint. Therefore the flake points do not usually assume any definite shape. A few examples of this type of implement have been reported from Wu-shan and Kung-hsien along the Yangtse.

The flake point has been found among the palaeolithic remains of Zabochka (**89**, Fig. 11. 1, 3) in the Yenisei valley and at Verkholenskaia Gora, near Irkutsk (**75**, Pl. 4. 1). Specimens from the latter are made of pebble flakes with retouch. A few points from the site of Kōmura, in Kansai, may be classified under this type, but they were found associated with Yayoi pottery (**104**, Pl. 18. 15; 19. 5). In Manchuria a flake of this type has been found at the Ku-hsiang-tun site, Harbin (**199**, Fig. 11D), which has been called palaeolithic in date, on not too good evidence. In Jehol, this implement has been found associated with the microlithic tools and other neolithic artifacts at Linsi (**189**, Pl. 10. 1; **201**, Fig. 58) and at Ch'êng-tê (**195**, Pl. 26. 26). The flake point is a common artifact in the palaeolithic sites of northern China. It has been found in the *Sinanthropus* deposit (**229**, Fig. 28–30) and in the palaeolithic site of Shui-tung-kou, Suiyüan (**30**, Pl. 23. 25). The Suiyüan specimens are of various shapes and are products of a flake industry, with retouching. South of the Yangtse, the flake point has been reported from Lamma Island (**256**, Part 9, K–O) and the Kwangsi caves (**260**, Fig. 2). The Lamma island point is considered palaeolithic and called 'epimiolith'. In Indo-China, this implement has been excavated from the Hoabinhien site of Sao Dong (**286**, Pl. 3. 21), and the neolithic site of Da But (**297**, Pl. 8. 3); in Siam, at Tam Kradam (**298**, Fig. 8. 5–6); in the Malay peninsula, in a cave in Perak (**313**, Pl. 41. 1). The specimen from the cave is described as a 'Mousterian' type.

21. SPEAR-HEAD (Pl. 3. 4): made of an ordinary flake of stone, chipped into a pointed-and-stemmed artifact. Graham (**26**, 6) gives an outline of the implement and states (**26**, 53) that three specimens were found at K'ang-ting, in the Ya-lung valley.

A pointed-and-stemmed implement has been found in the palaeolithic level at Aphontova Gora (**68**, Fig. 3), in the Yenisei valley. Some spear-heads of pressure flaking technique have been found in Kamchatka (**84**, Pl. 1. 4; **85**, Pl. 6. 1), and other implements like them in the Kurile islands. The latter at least are probably metal age in date (**90**, Pl. 3. 5–6). In Japan, spear-heads of this type have been found at the Yayoi site of Yamato-gawa (**174**, Fig. 44. 4). The specimen which bears the closest resemblance to the Szechwan type has been found in the Hoabinhien site at Som Jo, Tonkin (**286**, Pl. 10, 11). In Siam, it has been unearthed in the neolithic site of Tam Kradam (**298**, Pl. 8. 3).

PERFORATORS

A perforator is a piercing instrument, not necessarily small, with a point for piercing or gouging. It is a rare type in the Szechwan industry. Four implements are described below to represent the possible types of this group of implements.

22. BI-FACIAL PERFORATOR (Pl. 3. 5): made of a pebble elaborately chipped in the bi-face technique, that is, flaked on both sides, with a specially prepared point. The implement resembles a *coup de poing* and retains a small portion of the pebble surface at the poll end. The cross-section is oval. This is an isolated specimen, showing the perfection of quartzite flaking achieved by the prehistoric people along the Yangtse.

A perforator of this shape has been found in the palaeolithic site of Zabochka on the Yenisei river (**89**, Fig. 10. 7), but it is uni-facial. In Japan, the bi-facial perforator has been discovered in the Yayoi site of Kōmura (**103**, Pl. 7. 8, 28; **96**, Pl. 24. 7); in Suiyüan, at Shui-tung-kou (**220**, Pl. 29. 6); in Tonkin, at Bac Son (**282**, Pl. 21. 17) and in the Malay peninsula, at Gunong Pondok, Perak (**313**, Pl. 44. 1).

23. FLAKE PERFORATOR (Pl. 3. 6): made of an ordinary flake with a sharp point, which is rendered more perfect by a 'burin stroke' at the tip of the point. Therefore, the implement may also be called a graver.

This specimen was found at Lung-kai, on the Yangtse.

In the Baikal region, flake perforators have been unearthed from the upper palaeolithic level of Mal'ta (**88**, Fig. 22. 5, 7, 8). In Japan, the perforator has been found at Kōmura (**103**, Pl. 7. 9) and at Idzumi, Kyūshū (**109**, Pl. 5. 20), associated with Yayoi pottery. A few specimens of this type have also been discovered at Shui-tung-kou, Suiyüan (**220**, Pl. 27. 1–2) and at the Hoabinhien sites of Sao Dong and Lang Neo, in Tonkin (**286**, Pl. 3. 18; 9. 23).

24. RETOUCHED PERFORATOR (Pl. 3. 7–8): made of an ordinary flake of stone without any definite shape, with secondary chipping at the point. Most of these retouched perforators were found in the Tao-fu valley.

In the Yenisei valley, the retouched perforator has been found in the palaeolithic site of Aphontova Gora (**73**, 43. Fig. 9c); in Kantō, in the Jomon-Yayoi site of Yoshii (**156**, Fig. 12. 14); in Kansai, at Kōmura (**104**, Pl. 24. 11) associated with Yayoi pottery; in Manchuria, at Ku-hsiang-tun (**199**, Fig. 14); in Jehol, at Linsi (**201**, Fig. 62); in Suiyüan, at Shui-tung-kou (**220**, Pl. 27. 16); in Indo-

China, in the Hoabinhien stratum of Sao Dong (**286**, Pl. 3. 27) and in the neolithic level of Bau Tro, Annam (**281**, Pl. 3. 10); and in Siam, at the neolithic site of Tam Kradam (**298**, Fig. 8. 1).

SCRAPERS

A scraper is a tool shaped to suit the user's grasp, with a scraping edge at one or both ends, or at one or both sides, or with a combination of several edges at any of the above locations. The size of the scraper varies a great deal. Some may be as large as a small axe while others may be very small. They can be divided into eight types:

25. PEBBLE SCRAPER (Pl. 4. 1): made of a small pebble, flaked into a scraper with a sharp convex scraping edge. Chipping is applied on one face of the pebble and worked almost all the way round, leaving about one-third of the pebble untouched for grasping. The outline of this specimen is roughly discoidal but generally scrapers of this type do not have a definite shape. Any pebble of suitable form may be flaked into a scraper, usually leaving a portion untouched for grasping.

Another variation of the pebble scraper is illustrated in Pl. 4. 2. The implement is also made of a pebble, but it is chipped into suitable shape, with secondary flaking at the sharp scraping edge.

The pebble scraper has been found in I-tu, Kuei-chou and Wu-shan in the Yangtse valley. In the Min valley it occurs only at Chengtu. In the Ta-tu and the Ya-lung valleys, the implement occurs rather frequently in K'ang-ting and in Mao-kung and one specimen was reported from the Tao-fu valley.

The pebble scraper is a common stone tool in the Yenisei valley. It has been found in the palaeolithic deposits of Peresselentscheskij Point (**73**, 39, Fig. 7. 4), Aphontova Gora (**73**, 41, Fig. 8. 3), Batani (**73**, 50, Fig. 15. 4), Zabochka (**89**, Fig. 8. 1) and Kepernyi-log (**89**, Fig. 17. 7). It has also been found in the palaeolithic site of Zarubino, in the Baikal region (**83**, Pl. 1. 3–6) and in the neolithic site of Chita on the upper Amur (**72**, Pl. 2. 55). A pebble scraper has been reported from the Yayoi site at Kayama, Kantō (**152**, Fig. 4). In Jehol, it has been found at Linsi (**201**, Fig. 53, 68, 69; **189**, Pl. 7. 10), associated with microlithic artifacts; in Mongolia, at P'ang-chiang (**200**, Fig. 1. 13); in Suiyüan, at Shui-tung-kou and Sjara-osso-gol (**220**, Pl. 29. 10; 30. 8, 15); in Shensi, at Fa-sao-ho-wan (**222**, Pl. 8. 4) and in Hopei, in Locality 1 (**229**, Fig. 17) and 13 (**235**, Fig. 4) at Choukoutien. Some of the Linsi and Choukoutien specimens were retouched at the cutting edge. The pebble scraper has also been excavated from the Hoabinhien sites of Lang Kay (**290**, Fig. 19–22), Tchong Doi (**289**, Pl. 14. 3) and Sao Dong, and from the Bacsonien deposits of Keo Phay (**279**, Pl. 6. 4) in Tonkin. In the Malay peninsula it has been found at Gua Debu, Kedah (**324**, Pl. 7. 1) and at Gua Bintong, Perlis (**328**, Fig. 5. 4–6).

26. CORE SCRAPER (Pl. 4. 3): made of a stone core, with artificial chipping at the sharp scraping end. The inner surface is somewhat flat while the outer one is roughly convex. The chipping is done on the inner surface. Another variation of this type of implement is distinguished by the fact that the chipping for the scraping edge is done on both surfaces. The specimen illustrated (Pl. 4. 4) is a rather heavy tool and it might be taken for a chopper.

The core scraper is not a common artifact in Szechwan. One was found in I-ch'ang and several in the Ya-lung valley at K'ang-ting and Li-hwa.

The core scraper has been found in the palaeolithic levels of Zarubino and Zabaikalia, Trans-Baikal (**83**, Pl. 2. 1, 3. 7); in the so-called palaeolithic site of Ku-hsiang-tun, near Harbin (**199**, Fig. 12. 13); among the microlithic tools of Linsi, Jehol (**201**, Fig. 53); and P'ang-chiang, Mongolia (**200**, Fig. 1. 4); in the palaeolithic site of Shui-tung-kou, Suiyüan (**219**, Fig. 3; **212**, Pl. 22, 29); in the neolithic site of Bac Son (**284**, Pl. 20. 16) and in the Hoabinhien deposits of Sao Dong, in Tonkin (**286**, Pl. 2. 13). The Shui-tung-kou specimens represent artifacts of various shapes.

27. RECTANGULAR SCRAPER (Pl. 4. 5): made of a pebble flake, chipped from all sides and from both surfaces into a rectangular shape with four scraping edges. The tool is somewhat thin and flat, with a roughly convex outer surface. Another smaller specimen reported from K'ang-ting (**28**, Pl. 33. 5) seems to have a low pyramidal outer surface. The third specimen was found in I-ch'ang.

Outside Szechwan, the rectangular scraper has been found in the palaeolithic site of Peresselentscheskij Point (**89**, Fig. 27. 3) and in the neolithic site of Čadobec (**77**, Fig. 8v), in the Yenisei valley. The palaeolithic artifacts are mostly small with slight retouching. The rectangular scrapers of Ulan Kada, Trans-Baikal (**70**, Pl. 10. 88), are made by the pressure-flaking technique and are not comparable to the Szechwan type. In Japan, rectangular scrapers have been found at the Yayoi sites of Kōmura (**104**, Pl. 24. 4) and Tsutajima (**142**, Fig. 7. 4). In Jehol, it has been discovered at Linsi (**201**, Fig. 59–61), Ch'ih-fêng (**189**, Pl. 16. 25) and Chien-ping (**189**, Pl. 12. 3); in Chahar, at Nan-hao-chien (**189**, Pl. 39. 6); in Suiyüan, at Shui-tung-kou and Sjara-osso-gol (**220**, Pl. 30. 11); and in Hopei, at Locality 1 of Choukoutien (**229**, Fig. 25). Some quadrangular stone tools from the Hoabinhien sites of Lang Kay (**290**, Fig. 18), Keo Phay (**283**, Pl. 3. 4) and Sao Dong (**286**, Pl. 1. 15), in Tonkin, may be classified under this type. Stone tools of this shape have also been found in the neolithic site of Tam Pra (**298**, Fig. 4), Siam, and at Gua Debu (**324**, Pl. 7. 4, 5), Kedah.

28. DISCOIDAL SCRAPER (Pl. 4. 6): made of a thin flake of a pebble, trimmed and chipped into a discoidal shape, with scraping edge all around. The chipping was done from the inner surface, leaving the outer surface entirely with the original pebble surface. A discoidal scraper is distinguished from a discoidal chopper by its size. The chopper is the larger and heavier implement of the two.

Another variation of the discoidal scraper is an implement (Pl. 4. 7) made of a small flat pebble, chipped into the discoidal shape by removing flakes from both surfaces, instead of one. The original pebble surface is retained on both surfaces and the scraping edge consists of a double bevel.

The discoidal scraper is a common tool in the Yangtse valley. One specimen was found in the Min valley at Wei-chou and four at K'ang-ting, in Hsikang.

The discoidal scraper is also a common tool in the prehistoric sites of eastern Asia. In Siberia, specimens have been found in the palaeolithic sites of Peresselentscheskij Point (**89**, Fig. 25. 2, 7) and Mal'ta (**88**, Fig. 24, 25). A specimen has been found in the Yayoi site at Iyo, Shikoku (**123**, Fig. 2). The Ang-ang-hsi specimen of Tsitsihar, Heilungkiang (**191**, Fig. 15. 1) is flat and thin. The discoidal scraper has also been found at Ta-miao (**202**, Fig. 15. 4), Linsi (**201**, Fig. 28) and at Ch'ih-fêng (**212**, Pl. 33. 68) in Jehol. Most of these Jehol specimens were associated with the microliths and tools of neolithic type. In Suiyüan, scrapers of this type have been discovered at the palaeolithic sites of Shui-tung-kou and Sjara-osso-gol (**219**, Fig. 3; **220**, Pl. 21, 29, 30); in Kansu, at the Ch'i-Chia or 'early Yangshao' site of Lo-han-t'ang (**232**, Fig. 114); in Honan, at the neolithic site of Yangshao |(**233**, Fig. 1 B, C) and at Anyang (AMNH 2929); in Kwangsi, at Wu-ming (**260**, Fig. 5); and near Hongkong, on Lamma Island, where they were associated with bronze implements (**254**, Pl. 5. 5, 7). The discoidal scraper is very much at home in Indo-China and the Malay peninsula. There it has been reported from the Hoabinhien sites of Hoa Binh (**286**, Pl. 1. 21) and Tchong Doi (**289**, Pl. 14. 5); from the Bacsonien sites of Keo Phay (**279**, Pl. 6. 2), Giouc Giao (**282**, Pl. 4. 3), Bac Son (**282**, Pl. 13. 11) and Dong Lay (**284**, Pl. 12. 5), in Tonkin; from the neolithic rock-shelter, the protoneolithic remains and the 'palaeolithic' site at Gunong Pondok (**309**, Pl. 26. 1–2; **314**, Pl. 72; **313**, Pl. 42. 3); from the neolithic sites along the Tembeling river, Pahang (**311**, Pl. 52. 9); from the 'palaeolithic' cave of Perak (**313**, Pl. 41. 3); and from the Hoabinhien and neolithic deposits of Kelantan (**333**, Pl. 50. 14; **334**, Pl. 1. 4; 3. 2). Some of the Kelantan specimens are small and have a point. A discoidal scraper has also been found at Tam Pra, in Siam (**298**, Fig. 5).

29. END SCRAPER (Pl. 4. 8): made of a flake of stone chipped at one end into a scraping edge. The chipping was done from both surfaces. Generally the implement is small and does not have a definite outline. Some are chipped or retouched at the scraping edge from one surface only.

The end scraper was found along the Yangtse at I-tu, Wu-shan, Suifu, and Lung-kai, and at K'ang-ting and in the Tao-fu valley.

Most of the end scrapers found along the Yenisei and in the Baikal region are retouched. They were found in the palaeolithic levels at Zabochka, Kamen-nyi-log, Kepernyi-log, Peresselentscheskij Point (**89**, Fig. 8, 15, 17, 27) and Zarubino (**83**, Pl. 2. 8). In Japan, this implement has been found in Shizuoka (**147**, Fig. 9. 3) and at Kōmura (**104**, Pl. 24), associated with Jomon and Yayoi pottery respectively. It has also been discovered at Ku-hsiang-tun, near Harbin (**199**, Fig. 11 c); Linsi, in Jehol (**201**, Fig. 64) and Shui-tung-kou, in Suiyüan (**219**, Fig. 3; **220**, Pl. 24, 25). In Indo-China, the end scraper has been unearthed in the Hoabinhien site of Sao Dong (**286**, Pl. 3. 25) and in the neolithic deposits of Bau Tro (**281**, Pl. 3. 11), and in the Malay peninsula, at Ulu, Kelantan (**333**, Pl. 49. 12), Gua Debu (**324**, Pl. 7. 6–14) and Gua Bintong (**328**, Fig. 4. 25).

30. SIDE SCRAPER (Pl. 4. 9): made of a stone flake, chipped at one side to produce a scraping edge. The chipping was done from one surface only. Some specimens were chipped from both surfaces. Generally, this implement does not have a definite shape.

Side scrapers were found along the Yangtse at I-ch'ang, Wu-shan, Suifu, and Kung-hsien and in the Tao-fu valley.

Palaeolithic side scrapers of various shapes have been found numerously in Siberia. They are mostly retouched, and have been reported from Batani (**73**, 50, Fig. 15. 3), Aphontova Gora (**68**, Fig. 1–2), Zabochka (**89**, Fig. 11. 9, 11), Teleznyi-log, Kepernyi-log and Peresselentscheskij Point (**89**, Fig. 14,

17, 25) along the Yenisei river and from Zarubino (**83**, Pl. 1. 11), Verkholen-skaia Gora (**75**, Pl. 8–10, 12) and Mal'ta (**88**, Fig. 12. 4, 5) in the Baikal region. In Japan, this implement has been found in the neolithic sites of Shizuoka (**147**, Fig. 9. 4, 6, 8), Kōmura (**103**, Pl. 7. 3–7), Kagawa (**146**, Fig. 5. 9–10) and Ehime (**166**, Fig. 3 c). It has also been found at Ku-hsiang-tun near Harbin (**199**, Fig. 11 A); Linsi, in Jehol (**201**, Fig. 27, 29, 47–50); P'ang-chiang, in Mongolia (**200**, Fig. 1. 1); Shui-tung-kou and Sjara-osso-gol, in Suiyüan (**220**, Pl. 26, 30) and in the mesolithic caves of Kwangsi (**260**, Fig. 12). In Tonkin, this implement has been unearthed from the Hoabinhien site of Sao Dong (**286**, Pl. 3. 22), from the lower neolithic site of Giouc Giao (**282**, Pl. 4. 1) and from the neolithic site of Bac Son (**282**, Pl. 9. 9). A specimen from Tam Kradam, Siam (**298**, Fig. 9) has a point in addition to its cutting edge. In the Malay peninsula, the side scraper has been found at Gunong Pondok (**309**, Pl. 26. 3–5), Gua Debu (**324**, Pl. 7. 21, 22), Gua Bintong (**328**, Fig. 4. 24) and in Kelantan (**334**, Pl. 3. 1).

31. CONCAVE SCRAPER (Pl. 4. 10): made of a flake which was chipped at one side into a concave scraping edge. The retouching was done from one surface.

The other type (Pl. 4. 11) was made of a pointed pebble with a concave scraping edge on one side of the implement. The chipping of the scraping edge was probably done from both surfaces. It is a heavier tool than the one described above.

Concave scrapers were found in the Ya-lung valley, especially in the sites at Tao-fu.

Outside Szechwan, the concave scraper has been reported from Ladeiki (**73**, Pl. 4. 10) in the Yenisei valley; from Linsi, Jehol (**201**, Fig. 51); Shui-tung-kou, Suiyüan (**220**, Pl. 23, 10); Choukoutien, Hopei (in Locality 1, **229**, Fig. 21, 22; Upper Cave, **234**, Fig. 2); Yangshao, Honan (**233**, Fig. 1 H) and Lang Neo, Tonkin (**286**, Pl. 7. 9).

32. COMBINED BORER AND SCRAPER (Pl. 5. 1): made of a flattish flake of stone, roughly quadrangular in outline, with one angle projecting to a point. The sides were retouched to form straight scraping edges while the projection was chipped into a point for boring. This specimen was found at Chachie-Bréi, in the Tao-fu valley.

The 'complex scrapers' of *Sinanthropus* (**229**, Fig. 35; **236**, Fig. 8) may be classified under this type, which has also been found at Linsi, Jehol (**201**, Fig. 46).

In Indo-China, complex implements of this type have been discovered in the Hoabinhien site of Sao Dong (**286**, Pl. 1. 12) and in the neolithic sites of Bac Son (**282**, Pl. 11. 7) and Bau Tro (**281**, Pl. 3. 16). It has also been reported from Tam Kradam in Siam (**298**, Fig. 9).

KNIVES

A knife is an implement with one or two sharp cutting edges. The size and the shape vary greatly according not only to the material of which the implement is made, but also to the way in which it was used. In some cases, it may be distinguished from a scraper only by having a straight cutting edge, which does not serve well in scraping. Curved edges, both convex and concave, are not uncommon. There are five types of chipped stone knives represented in the Szechwan material:

33. SINGLE-EDGED KNIFE (Pl. 5. 2): made of a flattish pebble, chipped at both ends and on one side. At one side it was retouched from both surfaces into a sharp cutting edge, which is slightly curved. The other side was left untouched. Both surfaces retain a large portion of the original pebble surface. Some specimens were retouched from one surface for the cutting edge, while the ends of others were left untouched as well as one side. This implement might have been held in the hand for cutting as well as scraping.

The single-edged knife was found along the Yangtse, at Wu-shan, Kuei-chou, Yün-yang, Wan-hsien and Na-hsi and in the Ya-lung valley, at K'ang-ting.

Outside Szechwan, the single-edged knife has been found in the palaeolithic horizons of Aphontova Gora (**81**, Pl. 1. 5; 2. 1), Zabochka (**89**, Fig. 8. 5) and Peresselentscheskij Point (**89**, Fig. 25. 5) along the Yenisei river. The cutting edge of the implement was retouched. In Japan, a knife of this type has been found at Ishikawa, Kantō (**168**, Fig. 3), associated with Jomon pottery. Besides the cutting edge, the implement has also a point for piercing. Another specimen of the single-edged knife has been unearthed in the neolithic site of Tôsandô, in Korea (**126**, Pl. 3. 8). In Tonkin, this implement has been excavated in the Hoabinhien sites of Sao Dong (**286**, Pl. 2. 18) and Tchong Doi (**289**, Pl. 14. 2) and in the Bacsonien deposits of Keo Phay (**279**, Pl. 4. 3) and Giouc Giao (**282**, Pl. 4. 2).

34. DOUBLE-EDGED KNIFE (Pl. 5. 3): made of a flattish pebble with two chipped cutting edges at the sides. The edges were flaked from both surfaces, which retain most of the pebble surface. Both ends of the implement are arched, retaining the original outline of the pebble. Some implements acquired

their cutting edges by being chipped only from one surface. In most cases, a pebble of the desired shape was used in the manufacture.

The double-edged knife was found in Wu-shan and Suifu, along the Yangtse river.

Double-edged knives have been reported from the Jomon site of Ishikari, in Hokkaidō (**150**, Fig. 4. 18). A specimen of this type has been found in the Tôsandô site of Korea (**126**, Pl. 3. 9) and as it is semi-lunar in shape, it may possibly be the prototype of the polished semi-lunar knife. The double-edged knife has also been found in the neolithic site of Da But, Annam (**297**, Pl. 3. 10).

35. FLAKE KNIFE (Pl. 5. 4): made of a flake of a pebble, trimmed at one side and at one end into an oval outline. The trimmed side and end are thicker than the other side and end, which were slightly retouched to produce a sharp cutting edge. The implement is small and might have been held between the fingers for cutting. It could have been used as a scraper also. The outer surface retains most of the pebble surface. Other implements of this type do not have a regular shape, but they are generally thin and flat.

The flake knife was found along the Yangtse at Wan-hsien and Suifu, and in the Min valley at O-mei.

The palaeolithic flake knife of Zabochka (**89**, Fig. 10. 1) may perhaps be classified under this type.

36. COULTER-TYPE KNIFE (Pl. 5. 5): made of a large flake of a pebble, chipped into the shape of a coulter, with a concave cutting edge. Chipping was done on both surfaces leaving slight traces of the original pebble surface. Other implements of this type are mostly made of limestone and are very much weather-worn so that it is hard to distinguish the much-rubbed surface from that of the original pebble. The implement is generally quite flat and was probably hafted.

The coulter-type knife was found in Kung-hsien on the Yangtse and in the Tao-fu valley.

Outside Szechwan, the coulter-type knife has been found so far only in the Hoabinhien site of Lang Neo (**286**, Pl. 9. 17) in Tonkin.

37. SICKLE-TYPE KNIFE (Pl. 5. 6): adapted from a sickle-shaped pebble with slight retouching on the inner side. The rest of the pebble was left untouched, except the shorter end, which was slightly battered. Other implements of this type are mostly made of soft stone and are very much worn. No evidence of hafting was observed by Bowles (**25**, 141).

Several sickle-type knives were found in Kung-hsien; many at K'ang-ting; and three in the Tao-fu valley.

The sickle-type knife has been found in the palaeolithic level of Aphontova Gora (**81**, Pl. 2. 3); in the lake-shore deposit of Hu-chou, Chekiang (**262**, Fig. 4) and in the Hoabinhien level of Keo Phay, Tonkin (**283**, Pl. 2. 4).

HAMMERSTONES

A hammerstone is a relatively large and heavy tool, usually made of hard stone. The shape varies a great deal, ranging from spherical to elongated. It bears no cutting edge. It may be held in the hand or hafted for pounding. The pitted stone and the waisted pebble are included in this group of pounding tools.

38. PEBBLE HAMMER (Pl. 5. 7): made of an elongated pebble with round cross section. Both ends show traces of pounding. Pebbles of any shape may be used for the purpose.

The pebble hammer was found along the Yangtse at I-tu, Wu-shan, Yün-yang, Wan-hsien and Lung-kai and in the Tao-fu valley.

The use of pebbles as hammers is natural and hence the use of such implements is widespread and parallels do not have great significance. Hammerstones of this sort have been found in the neolithic site of Chita, on the upper Amur (**72**, Pl. 2). One specimen from this site is grooved. In Kamchatka, this tool is common in the neolithic sites (**82**, Pl. 1. 12; **85**, Pl. 10B) and in Japan it has mostly been found associated with Jomon ware, as at Tochigi (**143**, Fig. 11. 13), Ubayama (**125**, Fig. 17. 13, 14), Ninomiya (**164**, Fig. 7), Ekoda (**175**, Fig. 3) in Kantō and at Nio (**166**, Fig. 3B) in Shikoku. This implement has also been found at Djalai-nor, near Manchuri, Heilungkiang (**208**, Fig. 2); at Yangshao, Honan (**233**, Fig. 1E); on Lamma Island, near Hongkong (**254**, Pl. 4. 1, 4); and in the Kwangsi caves (**260**, Pl. 2. 1). In Tonkin it has been excavated in the Hoabinhien site of Trieng Xen (**286**, Pl. 5. 10) and in the neolithic deposits of Pho Binh Gia; and in the Malay peninsula, in the rock shelter of Gunong Pondok (**309**, Pl. 25), among the protoneolithic remains of Kelantan (**334**, Pl. 5. 2) and in a neolithic site in Perak (**313**, Pl. 47).

39. HAMMERSTONE (Pl. 5. 8): made of a spherical stone, which may originally have been a pebble. Traces of pounding cover practically the entire surface of the stone. The shape of other hammerstones varies a great deal. Some are roughly spherical, some oval, some discoidal (Pl. 5. 9) and some are very

irregular. It seems to me that most of these hammerstones are probably much-worn discoidal choppers.

Hammerstones of this type were found in large numbers at I-tu below the gorges and at Mao-kung in the Ta-tu valley. Several specimens were found at Kwan-hsien, Wên-ch'uan, Wei-chou, and Li-fan in the Min valley, and in the Tao-fu valley.

The spherical or discoidal hammerstone has more commonly been found in Japan and Manchuria. In Japan, the spherical hammerstone seems to have been used more in the south and associated more often with the Yayoi pottery, as stones of this shape have been found in the sites of Idzumi, Kyūshū (**109**, Pl. 6), Tsutajima, Shikoku (**142**, Fig. 7. 1), Todoroki (**108**, Pl. 42. 10–12) and Kōmura, Kansai (**104**, Pl. 18. 14). Some discoidal hammerstones have been found at Tochigi, Kantō (**143**, Fig. 11. 11, 12) and at Korekawa, Tōhoku (**119**, Fig. 6. 4), associated with Jomon pottery. This distribution may be purely accidental. In Manchuria, spherical and discoidal hammerstones have been found side by side at Shih-pei-ling, Kirin (**198**, Fig. 7, 10) and at Hung-shan-hou, Jehol (**206**, Fig. 49). They have also been discovered at Kao-li-chai, in Pi-tzŭ-wo, Fêngtien (**182**, Pl. 38. 13, 14) and at Ch'êng-tzŭ-yai I and II, Shantung (**237**, Pl. 37. 26). Stones of this type from the neolithic deposit of Nyong, Pahang (**320**, Pl. 15. 6–7) are described as 'potting stones'.

40. PITTED STONE (Pl. 6. 1): made of an irregular piece of stone with a pit on one side. Other specimens were pitted on both sides. In others considerable pits were formed. In no case, however, is the boring or pitting completed through the centre. The implement may have been used as a boring anvil, a tent peg pounder or an agricultural tool.

Pitted stones were observed by the scores in the fields of Hsikang, but only three were collected as specimens.

Pitted stones have been frequently found in the Jomon and the Yayoi sites in Japan, for example, in Kantō, at Tado (**138**, Fig. 7) and Nagano (**112**, Pl. 15); in Kansai, at Tsukumo (**107**, Pl. 23); in Shikoku, at Kita (**127**, Fig. 8. 1–3); and in Kyūshū, at Ibusuki (**110**, Pl. 30. 3–6). It has also been found in the neolithic site of Shih-pei-ling, Kirin (**198**, Fig. 8. 9); in the Hoabinhien site of Lang Vo, Tonkin (**286**, Pl. 11. 16) and in the *Sinanthropus* level at Choukoutien (**229**, Fig. 36). The *Sinanthropus* implement is named 'pitted boulder'. But on Lamma Island (**254**, Pl. 4. 2) and in the prehistoric workshop of Ban Mon, Tonkin (**289**, Pl. 2. 15) the pitted stone has been found associated with bronze.

41. WAISTED PEBBLE (Pl. 6. 2): made of a cylindrical pebble with a groove chipped near the upper end, probably for hafting, as it is very much worn. The lower end may be very much battered. The specimen illustrated was found in Wei-chou.

Other types of the waisted pebble are made of flat oval-shaped pebbles with a notch on each side. The notches were chipped from both surfaces. The specimen illustrated in Pl. 6. 3 bears some traces of pounding at each end and these suggest that the stone may have been used as a hammer. The other specimen (Pl. 6. 4) with two small notches at the sides was probably a net sinker. It was made in the same technique as the former one.

The flat waisted pebble was found at Suifu and at Lung-kai, on the Yangtse.

The waisted pebble is another common stone artifact of eastern Asia. Besides the type we have described from Szechwan, there are several other varieties. On the west coast of Kamchatka (85, Pl. 7B) the pebble was notched at the ends and not at both sides; at Kavran and Lake Kuril on the peninsula (78, Pl. 10, 11) some pebbles were notched at both sides and ends and were grooved through use; and at Vladivostok (80, Fig. 10–12), the pebble was not notched, but grooved both horizontally and vertically. A pebble from Ishikari, Hok-kaidō (136, Fig. 4. 7) was notched on the ends; another from Yokohama (120, Fig. 7. 1) was grooved all around at the waist; another specimen from Tsukumo, Kansai (107, Pl. 23) was notched on the ends and grooved vertically. Another pebble from Cho Ganh, Tonkin (289, Pl. 6. 1) was neither notched nor grooved, but scratched around the waist, and in the Malay peninsula among the protoneolithic tools of Gunong Pondok (314, Pl. 71), a pebble was notched and grooved horizontally and vertically and was also pitted. In any case waisted pebbles seem to be very numerous throughout the whole of eastern Asia. They have been found, for example, at Ōmori, Kantō (99, Pl. 17. 2); Seikori, Korea (142, Fig. 12; 15. 8); Ang-ang-hsi, Manchuria (192, Fig. 12. 2); Hung-shan-hou, Jehol (206, Fig. 27. 16, 17); Aksu, Sinkiang (190, Fig. 15); Wu-ming-hsien, Kwangsi (260, Pl. 2A); Lamma Island, Hongkong (254, Pl. 4. 5); Shinjo, Formosa (257, Fig. 5A) and Tam Nang Anh, Haut-Laos (303, Fig. 36).

MISCELLANEOUS IMPLEMENTS

Among the chipped stone tools of Szechwan are a number of artifacts which cannot be assigned to any of the types described above. They have no definite shape of their own. Most of them are ordinary flakes or fractured pebbles, which bear so few traces of rechipping that it is doubtful whether they were artifacts at all. Others are limestone pebbles, which may have been artifacts, but which are now so weather-worn that they are hardly distinguishable from ordinary river pebbles, so I choose to neglect them altogether.

GROUP B:
CHIPPED-AND-POLISHED STONE IMPLEMENTS

The chipped-and-polished stone tools of Szechwan are simply chipped tools with some polishing at the edge. By grouping them together into one class, I do not mean to suggest that they belong to a different industry altogether. In fact the same technique of manufacturing chipped implements was employed, plus the art of polishing. The pebble flaking which formed the basis of the chipping industry and dominated the whole production was also prominent in the present group of stone tools. The same material, that is, river pebble, was used not only in its entirety, as in the case of some axes, adzes, knives and rubbing stones, but also in the flake form, trimmed into the desired shape. The only difference lies in the fact that the retouching of the edge in the chipped stone tool was replaced by polishing, which produced a more regular sharp edge than did the chipping.

It is interesting to note that this new technique of polishing was not applied to every type of chipped tool. Among the forty-one types of chipped implements, only eight types have been treated with the polishing technique. They are the curved-bit axe, the straight-bit axe, the stemmed axe, the curved-bit adze, the straight-bit adze, the triangular pick, the pebble knife and the flake knife of the coulter type. The points and the scrapers were not polished.

Among the chipped-and-polished stone implements of Szechwan, four new types may be observed, viz. the chisel, which is rectangular in shape; the pointed pick, which may be a combination of the elongated and the leaf-shaped types; the blade; and the polished pebble. The typical specimens of this class of stone tools will be described below:

I. CURVED-BIT AXE (Pl. 6. 5): made of a large elongated pebble, chipped into an oval outline with arched ends and roughly parallel sides. Chipping was done only on the inner surface while the other retains the original pebble surface, which is rather convex. The bit end was ground from the inner surface. The cross section of the implement is oval. Other specimens of this type of tool are made of pebble flakes, chipped into shape and polished at the bit end. Generally they are all oval in cross section. Some implements have a straight poll end and they are usually thin and flat.

The curved-bit axe was found mostly in the Yangtse valley. With the exception of Pa-tung, K'uei-chou, Chungking, Lu-chou, Na-hsi and Kung-hsien, the implement was reported from every district. A few were also found at Chia-ting and Omei in the Min valley, but no specimen was collected in the Ta-tu and Ya-lung valleys.

The comparison of the chipped-and-polished axes of Szechwan with those found in other regions of eastern Asia presents a difficult technical problem. The stone tools of Group B, as I have pointed out, were polished only at the bit end, while most of the implements of other regions which had been grouped under this category were probably polished not only at the cutting edge, but also over the surfaces. The descriptions of these tools generally do not emphasize the difference between these two techniques or stages. So in this preliminary study, it is almost impossible to stick strictly to my own definition of Group B. Some unfinished implements of Group D may have slipped into the comparison for this type and for the other types of this group that follow.

Curved-bit axes of Group B have been found in the early neolithic level of Maklakovo (77, Fig. 8 B) and in the frozen gravel (69, Pl. K. 1, 2) in the Yenisei valley. In Kamchatka they have been reported from the prehistoric sites on the west coast (85, Pl. 6. 12), at Tarja (79, Pl. 16. 5) around Lake Kuril (78, Pl. 11. 12) and in the Kurile Islands (90, Pl. 3. 3). Some of these sites are probably metal age in date. In Japan axes of this type have been found associated with Jomon pottery (for example, at Shiribeshi, Hokkaidō, 159, Fig. 88) and with Yayoi pottery (at Todoroki, Kansai, 108, Pl. 41. 1, 3). They have also been discovered in the neolithic sites of Tôsandô (126, Pl. 3. 4) and Seikori (141, Fig. 13), in Korea; and of Ninguta (196, Fig. 3. 1), Shih-pei-ling (198, Fig. 10. 3) and Linsi (189, Pl. 35, 36), in Manchuria. The specimen of this type from the Lop Desert, Sinkiang (211, Pl. 5. 18) is a fragment of an axe. The Bacsonien axes of Indo-China are exactly parallels of the Szechwan type. They were found in large quantities at Tchong Doi (289, Pl. 14. 13), Keo Phay (279, Pl. 6, 7), Pho Binh Gia (279, Pl. 8–10), Bac Son (282, Pl. 8, 9) and Na Chè (282, Pl. 4, 5). In the upper neolithic sites of Ban Mon, Tonkin (289, Pl. 1. 5), of Luang Prahang, Haut-Laos (273, Pl. 1) and of Somrong Sen, Cambodia (276, Pl. 2. 5), axes of this type were still present. In the Malay peninsula, implements of this sort have been discovered among the proto-neoliths of Kelantan (**334**, Pl. 4, 5) and Perak (**313**, Pl. 45), in the neolithic sites of Gua Debu (**324**, Pl. 5) and Gua Bintong (**328**, Fig. 4. 2, 23), in the workshop of Tanjong Malim (**308**, Pl. 24. 1–5) and in the rock shelter of Gunong Pondok (**309**, Pl. 26. 8).

2. STRAIGHT-BIT AXE (Pl. 6. 6): made of a thin flake of stone, probably split from a pebble, chipped on both surfaces, trimmed at both sides and the poll end and polished at the bit end. The cutting edge is roughly straight. The poll end is curved and the sides are roughly parallel to each other. The implement is flat in cross section. Other implements of this type are made of a pebble or a pebble flake, chipped and polished with ordinary technique. Some retain more pebble surface than others and some are more polished at the bit end. The cross section of the tools is either oval, or longitudinal or flat.

There are more straight-bit axes of this type than there are of the type which shows no polishing. This may be due to the fact that polishing produces a straight bit more easily than chipping.

Chipped-and-polished straight-bit axes were mostly found in the Yangtse valley, at I-tu, Pa-tung, Wu-shan, K'uei-chou, Yün-yang, Wan-hsien and Lung-kai. Only one specimen was reported from Wei-chou, on the Min river.

In the Yenisei valley, axes of this type have been found in the early neolithic level of Maklakovo (**77**, Fig. 8 A). In Kamchatka, this implement has been found in prehistoric sites around Lake Kuril (**85**, Pl. 10 B) and also in the Kurile Islands (**78**, Pl. 9. 4). The Kurile specimen has a pointed poll end. Specimens of this implement have also been discovered in the Jomon site of Ibaraki (**154**, Fig. 5. 8), Kantō; in the Kammkeramik site of Seikori (**141**, Fig. 16. 1–3), northern Korea; in the late neolithic site of Hung-shan-hou, Jehol (**206**, Fig. 46. 7); in a prehistoric site in the Lop Desert, Sinkiang (**211**, Pl. 5. 15); and in the neolithic site of T'eng-yüeh, Yünnan (**248**, Pl. 3. 14). In Indo-China, this implement is also typical of the Bacsonien industry and specimens have been found at Bac Son (**283**, Pl. 6. 1, 8), at Lang Cuom and Lang Rang (**284**, Pl. 2, 9). In the Malay peninsula, straight-bit axes have been found in the neo-lithic workshop of Tanjong Malim (**308**, Pl. 24. 6) in the neolithic deposits of Kelantan (**334**, Pl. 6. 5) and among the protoneolithic remains of Gunong Pondok (**314**, Pl. 71).

3. STEMMED AXE (Pl. 6. 7): made of a pebble flake, trimmed into a stem with an arched poll end and polished at the bit end. Chipping was done on the

inner surface while the other preserves the original pebble surface. The bit end is arched and sometimes almost semicircular in outline. The implement is thin and flat. Other implements of this type possess a more developed stem with roughly parallel sides and a straight poll end. Generally they are made of pebble flakes and are thin and flat.

The stemmed axe of this type was found in I-tu, I-ch'ang and Yün-yang, along the Yangtse river.

Stemmed axes of Group B have been found on the west coast of Kamchatka (**85**, Pl. 6. 15), in the Kurile Islands (**162**, Fig. 5) and in Sakhalin (**162**, Fig. 6), but they all represent more advanced types of the tool, in shape as well as in polishing technique. Specimens of the stemmed axe from Japan and China almost always have polished surfaces and their shapes are of the more advanced types. Some stemmed axes of the Bacsonien technique from Tonkin (**289**, Pl. 2. 12), Annam (**281**, Pl. 2) and Kelantan (**334**, Pl. 3. 4) may be grouped with the Szechwan artifacts. It is interesting to note that the stemmed axe becomes extinct in the polished industry of Szechwan, while in Indo-China, the shouldered axe has been developed in the Somrong Sen culture into the most perfect form of this artifact (cf. **306**).

4. CURVED-BIT ADZE (Pl. 6. 8): made of an oblong pebble with a few flakes removed at the bit end which was polished after chipping. The implement is oval in outline and in cross section and has a round poll end. Other curved-bit adzes of this group are made of pebbles and pebble flakes and are generally more elaborately chipped than the above specimen. In most cases the outer surface is flat, the inner surface convex, and the polishing applied at the bit end on the inner surface has produced a sharp edge consisting of a single bevel.

This type of implement was found at I-tu, Kuei-chou, Pa-tung, Wu-shan, Yün-yang, Wan-hsien and Lung-kai along the Yangtse river.

Outside Szechwan, curved-bit adzes of this group have been found in the prehistoric deposit on Lake Kuril in Kamchatka (**78**, Pl. 11. 18–20); in the neolithic site of Ishikari, Hokkaidō (**136**, Fig. 4. 2, 3, 6); associated with Kammkeramik in Seikori, Korea (**141**, Fig. 16. 6); and at T'êng-yüeh in Yünnan (**248**, Pl. 2. 8). More implements of this type have been excavated in Indo-China: in the Bacsonien level of Bac Son (**282**, Pl. 6, 8) and Lang Cuom (**284**, Pl. 5. 5) and in the neolithic deposits of Ban Tro, Annam (**281**, Pl. 7. 2) and Somrong Sen, Cambodia (**276**, Pl. 1. 2). Among the protoneolithic remains of Kelantan (**334,** Pl. 4. 1) and Gua Bintong (**328,** Fig. 4. 9) some curved-bit adzes have also been found.

5. STRAIGHT-BIT ADZE (Pl. 6. 9): made of a pebble flake; chipped into the usual shape, trimmed on both sides and at the poll end; and polished at the bit, forming a single-bevelled cutting edge. The ends are roughly straight and the sides are almost parallel, but slightly nearer to each other at the poll end. Chipping was done on the inner surface and the other retains the pebble surface. In the production of a pebble flake, the flake was removed from the pebble with one stroke, which produced a bulb of percussion, typical with a quartzite pebble. The flake is usually flat and thin. The inner surface of the specimen illustrated was not thoroughly chipped so that a part of the original bulb of percussion can still be observed.

Other implements of this type are made of a flat pebble or a pebble flake, chipped, trimmed and polished in the same way as the above specimen. The outline is generally rectangular and the cross section ranges from flat to oval. The polishing occurs only at the bit end.

Implements of this type were found at I-tu, Kuei-chou and Lung-kai, in the Yangtse valley.

The straight-bit adze seems to be one of the chief artifacts in the Kamchatka region, but here the implement is probably an unfinished tool of Group D, as some specimens are thin and flat in cross section, which is typical of the wholly-polished adze. The straight-bit adze has been found in Hokkaidō in the neolithic deposit of Ishikari (**136,** Fig. 5. 4); in Korea, associated with Kammkeramik at Seikori (**141,** Fig. 16. 4); and in Indo-China, in the Bacsonien site of Lang Cuom (**284,** Pl. 1. 3) and in the neolithic level of Somrong Sen (**276,** Pl. 2. 6).

6. CHISEL (Pl. 7. 1): made of a flake, probably from a pebble, chipped and trimmed into a rectangular outline, with straight parallel sides and ends. The implement is slightly curved and the bit end was polished on the convex surface, producing a single-bevelled cutting edge. The poll end is battered, with one corner missing. Other chisels are adapted from small pebbles or flakes. The ends may be curved or straight, but the sides are usually parallel to each other. Some retain much of the pebble surface.

Chisels of this type were found in I-tu, Kuei-chou, Pa-tung, Wu-shan, Yün-yang and Lung-kai, along the Yangtse.

Some chisels discovered on the west coast of Kamchatka (**85,** Pl. 7A) and around Lake Kuril (**70,** Pl. 11. 20) appear to be of this type, but the Kuril specimen has a pointed poll end.

7. PICK (Pl. 7. 2): made of a large pebble, chipped into a triangular outline, with an irregular poll end and the sides converging toward the bit, which is almost a point. The outer surface probably retains the pebble surface, while the inner shows two flat surfaces inclined to each other at an obtuse angle. One of these inner surfaces was ground and this may not have been with the intention of sharpening the point. Another specimen (Pl. 7. 3) shows some careful grinding on both surfaces at the pointed bit end. This implement has an arched poll end. The cross section is probably oval, while the former implement has an irregular oval cross section.

Picks of this type were found only at Suifu on the Yangtse and at Kwan-hsien in the Min valley.

No parallel for this type has yet been found in other parts of eastern Asia.

8. PEBBLE KNIFE (Pl. 7. 4): made of a large pebble flake; chipped and polished on the inner surface while the other retains the pebble surface. The poll end is straight while the bit end is slightly curved and well polished. Judging from the sketch of the implement, the cutting edge may have extended up the right side, thus making the implement a knife rather than an axe. A slight polishing was done on the inner surface also.

Pebble knives of this type were found at O-mei and Chengtu, on the Min river.

In other parts of eastern Asia no parallels have yet been found.

9. FLAKE KNIFE (Pl. 7. 5): made of a pebble flake which is slightly of a coulter shape, with flaking and grinding on the inner edge. The two ends are both very much worn and the outer edge is dull and probably far thicker than the cutting edge.

This type of chipped-and-polished knife was found in Suifu and O-mei.

No parallel has yet been reported from other regions of eastern Asia.

10. BLADE (Pl. 7. 6): a broad stone blade, chipped and polished, with a beautiful edge. The outline is almost discoidal. Dye (**13,** 71) seems to think that it belongs to a different culture which is not that of the pebble flaking industry which dominated this region. The implement is probably thin and flat. Judging from the sketch of the small implement, polishing was done only on one surface.

Two blades of this type were reported in Szechwan, one from Suifu on the Yangtse and the other from Kwan-hsien in the Min valley.

In other parts of Eastern Asia no blade of this type has yet been reported.

11. POLISHED PEBBLE (Pl. 7. 7): I include seven polished pebbles in this class of stone tool, because while polishing is observable on the edges of the pebbles (perhaps with the purpose of producing a cutting edge), the work was not completed. Moreover, most of the pebbles thus polished do not present a suitable shape for chipping into any kind of implement. They may be simply rubbing stones. Some of these pebbles were flaked, but the flaking does not seem to be artificial. These pebbles should be distinguished from the polishing and rubbing stones, which will be described later among the polished tools, because the polished pebble is an artifact which was in process of being polished, while the others are tools which were used to polish other artifacts.

This type of polished pebble was found on the Yangtse at I-ch'ang, Wu-shan, Yün-yang, Wan-hsien and Lung-kai.

Some polished pebbles of this type have been reported from the excavation of the neolithic deposit at Bac Son (**282**, Pl. 14. 11–12), Tonkin.

GROUP C: CHIPPED-PECKED-AND-POLISHED STONE IMPLEMENTS

The chipped-pecked-and-polished stone implements of Szechwan are a product of three techniques—chipping, pecking and polishing—which were combined to produce the tools of this new industry. When I speak of a new industry, I mean that the nature of the product is completely different from that of the two groups of stone tools already described. In those two groups, it is clear that the industry is fundamentally based on pebble flaking, but with the introduction of pecking, no pebble surface could be observed on the tool. Therefore, we may conclude that the pebble flaking probably came to an end or became, at least, a technique of no importance in this new industry.

With pecking, the manufacturer could easily reduce a ragged chipped surface to an even or smooth one. In some cases, he might peck the stone into shape without any preliminary chipping. The unfinished implement (Pl. 8. 1) shows how much pecking can do in shaping a tool. The artist could hollow out or leave in relief any part of the stone surface as he pleased. The new industry witnesses a higher technical development than that of the former groups.

6-2

But pecking does not produce a sharp cutting edge, which can best be obtained by grinding. Hence, while the new manufacturer might drop the art of flaking in some cases, he never discarded the art of polishing. Every new product was finished with a polished cutting edge. Pecking alone cannot be used as the basis of an industry.

Pecking has another advantage over chipping. With the new technique, the manufacturer can have better control over the stone in producing the desired shape. This is especially advantageous in working on materials like quartzite and sandstone. Chipping is swifter and fits better with materials such as flint, obsidian or other glossy substances. By having the material under better control time was sacrificed, but the Szechwan manufacturer produced better or more well-defined shapes.

The implements of the chipped-pecked-and-polished class can be divided into three main types: the curved-bit axe, the broad axe and the chisel, all three of which are common types of the two groups already described. Only two other types are found, each represented by a single specimen. The curved-bit adze has a pointed butt and the large axe has a groove. These five types are described below:

1. CURVED-BIT AXE (Pl. 8. 2): pecked into the shape of an ordinary celt, with a curved-bit end consisting of a double-bevelled cutting edge, which was carefully polished. No trace of chipping is observable on both surfaces. The sides are straight and closer to each other at the poll end, which is very much battered. Generally, the poll end is round and the whole outline is oval. The cross section of the tool is also oval.

This type of implement was found only in the gorges; it was very common at Wu-shan and I-tu, but few were found at I-ch'ang, Kuei-chou, Pa-tung and K'uei-chou.

The curved-bit axe of Group C has been found in the neolithic deposits at Tarja in Kamchatka (**79**, Pl. 16. 4). In northern Japan, the implement is usually point-butted and is found associated with the Jomon pottery (**161**, Fig. 1–3), but in Kyūshū, the specimens from Idzumi (**109**, Pl. 5. 19) and Okitsumiya (**135**, Fig. 4. 2) were associated with the Yayoi ware. In Fêngtien, this implement has been found in the neolithic sites at Tieh-ling (**198**, Pl. 12) and Pi-tzŭ-wo (**182**, Pl. 19. 6); in Jehol, at East Onyuto (**212**, Pl. 34. 82), associated with microlithic implements; in Shensi, at Yu-fang-t'ou (**189**, Pl. 38. 12, 13); in Kansu, at An-ting (**189**, Pl. 39. 1–3); and in Formosa, at Taihoku (**255**, Pl. 1. 8).

84

2. BROAD AXE (Pl. 8. 3): relatively broader than the curved-bit axe. No trace of chipping appears on the tool. It has two parallel sides, an arched, well-polished cutting edge, of the double-bevel type, at the bit end and a straight or slightly slanting poll end. Both ends are badly battered. The cross section is flat and rectangular. Some specimens of this type have a round poll end and in such cases the cross section is usually oval.

This type of implement was found in I-tu, I-ch'ang, Wu-shan and Yün-yang along the Yangtse.

No parallel for this type has yet been found in other parts of eastern Asia.

3. GROOVED AXE (Pl. 8. 4): an exceptionally large and heavy implement, probably first chipped out of a big stone. The pecking did not remove all the traces of chipping. The implement is not only polished at the bit end but also grooved horizontally at the upper end of the tool, i.e. the groove is nearer to the poll end than to the bit end, which consisted of a curved cutting edge with double bevel. The implement is oval in outline and lenticular in cross section. This implement, the only specimen of this type, was found in I-ch'ang.

No axe of this type has yet been reported outside Szechwan.

4. CURVED-BIT ADZE (Pl. 8. 5): an unusual shape for an adze. The implement was chipped and the pecking did not cover all the ragged chipped surfaces. The poll end is pointed and the two sides are roughly straight. The bit end is arched with a sharp cutting edge consisting of a single bevel, polished on the outer surface. The implement is slightly grooved in the middle probably for hafting. It is oval in cross section, with the inner surface slightly flattened. This is the only specimen. It was found at Kuei-chou in the Yangtse gorges.

A curved-bit adze, which was unearthed at Okadaira, Kantō (**100,** Pl. 10. 11), in association with Jomon pottery, may be classified under this type, but no traces of polishing at the cutting edge can be seen in the illustration.

5. CHISEL (Pl. 8. 6): a small implement with the surface partly pecked and partly polished. It is roughly rectangular in outline and oval in cross section. The two sides are straight and parallel to each other. The bit end consists of a single bevelled cutting edge, which is highly polished. The poll end is straight and much battered. This solitary specimen was found at Wu-shan, in the gorges.

Chisels of this type have been found in neolithic deposits at Tieh-ling, Fêngtien (**198,** Pl. 12. 8–9) and at East Onyuto, Jehol (**212,** Pl. 34. 74). A fine specimen from Shensi (**214,** Pl. 2. 1) is dated by Laufer to the period of the Chou dynasty.

GROUP D: POLISHED STONE IMPLEMENTS

The polished stone implements of Szechwan are the product of a rather highly developed lithic industry. The basic technique of this industry is polishing. Among the stone tools, there are quite a number (Pl. 9. 2) which bear witness that the stone had been chipped into shape before polishing. However, the polishing of this class of implement must be distinguished from the same technique employed to produce the artifacts of the previous two groups. In these cases, polishing was used only in sharpening the cutting edge, that is, a polished surface could only be seen at the bit end of a tool. But in the polished stone tools of the group now being described, the technique was used not only to sharpen the edge, but also to smooth the whole surface of the implement, transforming it into a beautiful artifact.

While not a single specimen of this class of polished tools shows any signs of having been pecked before polishing, we notice that this industry still made the best use of the raw material, that is the river pebble. The pebble surface, which did not stand in conflict with the desired polished surface, was usually retained, and in the case of the gouge (Pl. 10. 5), it is simply a pebble with a hollow ground out. However, the manufacturer knew his art well and did not depend entirely on the pebble to furnish a smooth, pleasant surface. He could produce any types of surface, which might be at any angle to one another. This accounts for the new and well-finished shapes developed in the axes, the adzes and the chisels which I shall describe presently.

Four new features of minor importance may be observed in this polishing industry. First, the grooving technique is better developed in this group than in the others. The vertical grooves (Pl. 9. 6) and the right-angled shoulder (Pl. 10. 4) are both beautifully executed. Secondly, the art of perforation was introduced (Pl. 10. 7). Thirdly, six new type of implement appeared. They are the one-shouldered punch (Pl. 10. 4), the gouge (Pl. 10. 5), the spear-head (Pl. 10. 6), the semi-lunar knife (Pl. 10. 7), the ring (Pl. 10. 8) and the mealing stone (Pl. 10. 12). Finally, some new materials, especially jade (Pl. 9. 6), were added to the stone list.

It is interesting to note that some of these new features and the new type implements are even better developed in the lithic industry of Han-chou (see p. xiv).

The polished stone tools of Szechwan may be classified as follows:

1. AXE OR CELT (Pl. 9. 1): a highly polished implement with a double-bevelled cutting edge at the bit end. The two sides are straight and almost parallel to each other. Both ends are very much battered, and the cross section is rectangular. The axe is the most common polished implement with many variations. The outline is mostly oval, but in some cases the poll end is narrower than the bit. The cross section is generally oval, but rectangular shapes are also common, and a lenticular or a flat cross section is also known. The sides are usually straight and rounded, but flat sides are not uncommon. The poll end is sometimes straight and arched. It may be arched and rounded but never arched and flat. The bit end is more usually arched than straight.

The polished axe or celt was found not only along the Yangtse at I-tu, I-ch'ang, Kuei-chou, Wu-shan, K'uei-chou, Yün-yang, Wan-hsien and Kung-hsien, but also along the Min river at Chengtu, Kwan-hsien, Wên-ch'uan and Li-fan.

The polished axe or celt is the most common type of stone implement used in eastern Asia during the neolithic period. This implement, with its many sub-types, can be found in practically every report on the prehistoric culture of the Far East. Many specimens have been excavated in the early neolithic level at Čadobec in Siberia (77, Fig. 8K), in the late neolithic sites of Gorin (77, Fig. 10G) and Chita (72, Pl. 1) on the Amur river, and among the prehistoric remains of Kamchatka (78, Pl. 9. 3; 79, Pl. 13. 11; etc.) and the Kurile Islands (90, Pl. 3). In Japan, specimens of the celt have been unearthed with Jomon pottery (Ishikari, 150, Fig. 4), with Yayoi pottery (Kōmura, 106, Pl. 7) and with bronze artifacts (Senjô-gatani, 132, Figs. 6, 8, 9). This implement has also been found associated with microlithic tools in Manchuria (Ang-ang-hsi, 191, Figs. 12, 13), in Mongolia (Urga, 181, 206) and in Sinkiang (Lop Desert, 213, Pl. 5). In Jehol, it has been excavated in the Bronze Age graves at Ch'ih-fêng (206, Figs. 8, 23). In China proper, this implement has not only been discovered in numbers in the neolithic sites, but also in the Shang (Anyang, 223, Fig. 5. 3–4), Chou (I-chou, 225, Figs. 1–3) and even Han (Peking, 241, Fig. 4) sites. In Indo-China, specimens have been found in the neolithic workshop of Ban Mon (289, Pls. 1, 2) and in the neolithic sites of Bau Tro (281, Pl. 2), Luang Prabang (271, Fig. 94) and Somrong Sen (276, Pl. 1). A few specimens have also been reported from Chong (285, Pl. 9), in southern Siam. In the Malay peninsula, specimens of celt have been found commonly in Perak

(307, Pl. 1A), Pahang (311, Pl. 52), Kelantan (316, Pl. 2; 326, Pl. 6), Kedah (224, Pl. 6) and Perlis (328, Fig. 4. 1).

2. BROAD AXE (Pl. 9. 2): a polished celt with oval outline and oval cross section. It is quite broad in proportion to its length, with straight rounded sides, roughly parallel to each other. The ends are both arched. Polishing was probably not finished as traces of chipping are present. Another type of broad axe is the rectangular axe (Pl. 9. 3), which is one of the most finished tools of the collection. It is rectangular in outline and cross section. The tool consists of five evenly polished flat surfaces: poll end, two sides and two surfaces. The latter meet at the bit end in a very acute angle and the cutting edge is slightly curved. A third variation of the broad axe is the low-butted axe (Pl. 9. 4) with a roughly triangular outline and oval cross section. The cutting edge at the bit end is convex and the poll end is arched. Other specimens may have a roughly semicircular poll end extending down the side to join the cutting edge. Generally, this kind of celt is thicker at the poll end than at the bit end.

The polished broad axe was found on the Yangtse at I-tu, Wu-shan, K'uei-chou and Kung-hsien. In the Min valley, it was found only at Wei-chou.

Outside Szechwan, specimens of the rectangular axe have been found in Siberia at Čadobec on the Yenisei river (77, Fig. 8) and at Vladivostok (80, Fig. 9); in Japan at Ishikari, Hokkaidō (150, Fig. 4. 12) and at Yokohama (153, Fig. 5); in Manchuria, at Pi-tzŭ-wo (182, Pl. 21. 8); in Indo-China, at Ban Mon (289, Pl. 1. 6), at Pho Binh Gia (272, Fig. 6) and at Ba Xa (284, Pl. 14) in Tonkin, as well as at Luang Prahang (302, Pl. 1. 5) in Laos; and in the Malay peninsula at Baling, Kedah (324, Pl. 19. 4). Specimens of the other two kinds of broad axe have been reported from Hida in Japan (170, Fig. 2. 1); Yangshao in Honan (217, Pl. 6. 14); Shuo-kuang-hsien in Shantung (181, Fig. 6); T'êng-yüeh in Yünnan (248, Pl. 2–4); Hai-fêng in Kwangtung (264, Fig. 7); Lamma Island near Hongkong (254, Pl. 3); Pho Binh Gia (279, Pl. 9), Dong Thuôc (279, Pl. 14) and Bac Son (282, Pl. 8. 10) in Tonkin; Somrong Sen in Cambodia (276, Pl. 1. 6); Chong in Siam (285, Pl. 9. 2); and Baling in the Malay peninsula (324, Pl. 17. 5).

3. POINT-BUTTED AXE (Pl. 9. 5): a new type of polished axe, with a pointed poll end. The cutting edge at the bit end is slantingly curved. The two sides are both rounded with one straight and the other slightly curved. They join at the poll end in a point. The cross section is oval. Other specimens have one or two flat and straight sides.

The point-butted axe was found at Suifu and Kung-hsien on the Yangtse and at Wei-chou in the Min valley.

The point-butted axe is a fairly common tool of eastern Asia. A large number of implements of this type have been excavated in Japan, from Hokkaidō in the north to the Ryūkyū Islands in the south, but this does not mean that this new type was originated in Japan. In the neolithic site of Gorin on the Amur river, a specimen of this type (**77**, Fig. 10c), which was chipped on the surfaces and was partly polished, may be considered a prototype of this point-butted tool. Specimens of this kind of polished axe have also been gathered in the Kurile Islands (**85**, Pl. 10b). In Japan, this implement was found associated with Jomon pottery (Kamegaoka, **119**, Fig. 4, 6) with the Yayoi ware (Kita, **127**, Fig. 2, 7), and also with bronze artifacts (Okitsumiya, **135**, Fig. 4. 3) and in Ryūkyū, with the Iha pottery (Ogido, **105**, Pl. 3. 12; Omonawa, **129**, Fig. 1). This implement has also been reported from Ch'ao-yang in Jehol (**189**, Pl. 37. 10), T'êng-yüeh in Yünnan (**248**, Pl. 1. 1), Somrong Sen in Cambodia (**276**, Pl. 1. 4) and Kelantan in the Malay peninsula (**334**, Pl. 6. 1). The Kelantan specimen is angular and not round or oval in cross section.

4. VERTICAL-GROOVED AXE (Pl. 9. 6): one of the most handsome and well-finished tools of the collection. The outline is roughly rectangular. The poll end is straight and the sides are slightly curved. The cutting edge at the bit is slanting. Both surfaces are well polished with a longitudinal groove on each surface probably for hafting.

This solitary specimen, which is made of whitish jade, was found at Lung-kai on the Yangtse, in Yünnan.

Horizontal-grooved axes have been reported from Hokkaidō (**162**, Fig. 4), Shantung (**237**, Pl. 24. 11; **213**, Pl. 11) and Formosa (**255**, Pl. 1. 6), but no vertical-grooved specimen has yet come to light in these regions. The only specimen that can be compared to the Lung-kai axe is one found at Pho Binh Gia, Tonkin (**272**, Fig. 7): 'Hachette polie en phtanite, avec sillon longitudinal sur le bord droit.' But the Lung-kai specimen is grooved on both surfaces.

5. CURVED-BIT ADZE (Pl. 9. 7): a roughly rectangular implement with a curved cutting edge consisting of a single bevel. Both the poll end and the two sides are straight and almost at right-angles to each other. The outer surface is convex and the inner surface is flat, thus producing a semi-oval cross section. Other specimens are simply celts with a single-bevelled cutting edge.

The curved-bit adze was found in Yün-yang, Lu-chou and Kung-hsien, on the Yangtse river.

In other regions of eastern Asia, specimens of the curved-bit adze have been reported in the late neolithic site of Gorin, on the Amur river (**77**, Fig. 10 C); in the late neolithic deposit of Kavran, Kamchatka (**78**, Pl. 9. 1); in the Jomon sites of Hokkaidō (**150**, Fig. 4. 1), Tōhoku (**119**, Fig. 4. 23), and Kantō (**99**, Pl. 13. 5; **100**, Pl. 10. 13) and in the Yayoi site of Yokohama (**153**, Fig. 1), in Japan; at Tôsandô (**126**, Fig. 36) in Korea; in the neolithic sites of T'ieh-ling (**198**, Fig. 2. 6), Pi-tzŭ-wo (**182**, Figs. 6, 7) and Ho-tung (**195**, Pl. 18. 55), in Manchuria; at the Yangshao site of Honan (**217**, Pl. 6. 15); in both lower and upper levels at Ch'êng-tzŭ-yai in Shantung (**237**, Pl. 35, 39); in the bronze age site of Hai-fêng, Kwangtung (**264**, Fig. 7. 5–7) and on Lamma Island near Hongkong (**254**, Pl. 1–3). In Indo-China, specimens of this type have been excavated in the neolithic workshop of Ban Mon (**289**, Pl. 1. 4, 7) and the late neolithic or aeneolithic sites of Luang Prahang (**271**, Fig. 95) and Somrong Sen (**276**, Pl. 1. 1). This implement has also been discovered at Baling (**324**, Pl. 18. 1) and Gua Bintong (**328**, Fig. 4. 22) in the Malay peninsula.

6. STRAIGHT-BIT ADZE (Pl. 9. 8): a broad and short implement with a straight single-bevelled cutting edge. The poll end is roughly curved, the sides straight and the cross section flattish-oval.

The straight-bit adze was found in I-ch'ang and Wu-shan, along the Yangtse.

Outside Szechwan, the straight-bit adze has a fairly wide distribution in eastern Asia. Along the Pacific coast, this implement has been reported from Tarja (**79**, Pl. 16. 6) and Kavran (**78**, Pl. 9. 15) in Kamchatka; from the Kurile Islands (**85**, Pl. 10 B); from Hokkaidō (**150**, Fig. 4. 2), Tōhoku (**119**, Fig. 4. 24), Kantō (**99**, Pl. 17) and Kyūshū (**148**, Fig. 1) in Japan; from Kōto-sho (**253**, Fig. 1) in Formosa; and from Lamma Island near Hongkong (**255**, Pl. 1. 7). On the mainland, adzes of this type have been found in Korea (**126**, Fig. 36; **160**, Fig. 4, 11), Fêngtien (**198**, Figs. 2–4; **182**, Fig. 6), Shantung (**213**, Pl. 10), Suiyüan (**241**, Fig. 32. 3), Honan (**217**, Pl. 4. 1), Chekiang (**261**, Fig. 1. 2; **262**, Fig. 5), Yünnan (**248**, Pl. 3. 13) and Kwangtung (**264**, Fig. 8). In the south, specimens of this type have also been excavated in Tonkin (**274**, Pl. 3. 6–9; **279**, Pl. 11. 3, 4), Cambodia (**276**, Pl. 1. 5), and Baling, Malay peninsula (**324**, Pl. 18. 4–6). Some of these stone axes have been found associated with bronze.

7. FLAT ADZE (Pl. 9. 9): a finely ground flat implement of even thickness, straight poll end, straight sides and straight bit. The poll end is narrower than the bit, which consists of a single-bevelled cutting edge. The implement has a thin and flat cross section and is incomplete.

The flat adze was found in I-ch'ang and Wu-shan, in the gorges.

Stone adzes of this type have been reported from the following sites: Yokohama, Japan (153, Fig. 2); Kôgendô, Korea (160, Fig. 7); T'ieh-ling (198, Fig. 4. 2) and Tan-t'o-tzŭ (182, Fig. 6. 8, 9) in Fêngtien; Lang Son (274, Pl. 3. 4, 5) in Tonkin; and Kelantan (334, Pl. 6. 9) in the Malay peninsula. In Kôgendô, the specimen was found associated with bronze.

8. CURVED-BIT CHISEL (Pl. 10. 1): a small polished implement with roughly rectangular outline and cross section. The poll end and the sides are straight while the bit end consists of a curved single-bevelled cutting edge. Other specimens are not as regularly shaped as this. Some have an arched poll end and others have curved sides.

The curved-bit chisel was found in the Yangtse valley at I-tu, I-ch'ang, Wu-shan, K'uei-chou, Yün-yang and Chungking. In the Min valley, it was found at Kwan-hsien, Wên-ch'uan and Li-fan.

Specimens of the curved-bit chisel have been found in Kamchatka (78, Pl. 9. 18), in the Kurile Islands (90, Pl. 3. 4), in Japan (118, Fig. 10. 4; 153, Figs. 6, 8; 139, Fig. 2. 31; etc.), in Korea (160, Fig. 4), in Fêngtien (193, Fig. 2. 5; 182, Fig. 7. 19), in Honan (223, Fig. 5. 5), in Shensi (214, Pl. 2. 2), in Yünnan (248, Pl. 4. 23), in Formosa (253, Fig. 3; 247, Pl. 1. 2, 5), in Tonkin (284, Pl. 14. 4, 8), in Laos (271, Fig. 87; 273, Pl. 2. 4), in Cambodia (276, Pl. 1. 7), in Pahang (320, Pl. 13. 6, 7) and in Kedah (324, Pl. 19. 7). Some of these specimens have been discovered in association with bronze tools.

9. STRAIGHT-BIT CHISEL (Pl. 10. 2): a small implement with the outline of a common celt and oval cross section. The poll end is arched, the sides straight and the bit end roughly straight, with a cutting edge consisting of a single bevel.

The implement was found in I-tu, I-ch'ang, Kuei-chou and Wu-shan along the Yangtse river.

Specimens of the straight-bit chisel have been found in Kamchatka (85, Pl. 6. 17), in the Kurile Islands (85, Pl. 10B; 79, Pl. 12. 6), in Tôhoku (118, Fig. 10. 1), in Kantô (155, Fig. 17. 2; etc.), in Kansai (174, Fig. 24B), in Kyūshū 148, Fig. 1), in Fêngtien (198, Fig. 4. 4; 193, Fig. 2. 7), in Chahar (221, Fig. 33), in Suiyüan (**241**, Fig. 32. 5, 6), in Shensi (**213**, Pl. 2. 3), in Honan (**223**, Fig. 5. 5; etc.), in Shantung (**237**, Pl. 36. 3, 4), in Formosa (**253**, Fig. 2. 2; etc.), on Lamma Island (**256**, Part 3. Fig. 1. 1), in Tonkin (**284**, Pl. 13), in Cambodia (**276**, Pl. 2. 1), in Pahang (**320**, Pl. 13. 4) and in Kedah (**324**, Pl. 19. 8). Some of these chisels have been found associated with bronze.

10. NARROW-BIT CHISEL (Pl. 10. 3): a small tool with a narrow cutting edge consisting of a double bevel. The implement is neatly polished with surfaces and sides at right-angles to each other. The cross-section is rectangular. This particular implement is broken. Other implements are not as well polished as this.

This type of implement was found in the Yangtse valley at I-tu, Wu-shan, Suifu, Kung-hsien and Lung-kai. It was also discovered at Li-fan in the Min valley.

The only parallel for the narrow-bit chisel, outside this region, has been found in the late neolithic level of Dong Thuôc (**279**, Pl. 11. 5) in Tonkin.

11. PUNCH (Pl. 10. 4): a polished pointed implement with the poll end grooved into a shoulder, probably for hafting. One of the sides is convex and the other concave, and they join in a point at the bit end. The point was probably used for boring.

This solitary implement was found in Kung-hsien, in the Yangtse valley, and no similar implement has yet been found in any other region of eastern Asia.

12. GOUGE (Pl. 10. 5): A cylindrical pebble with a highly polished hollow ground out at the bit end, producing a gouge-like cutting edge. The poll end is rounded and the sides roughly parallel. There is practically no distinction between the polished surface and the original pebble surface. The cross section is oval.

This neatly adapted implement was found in Wu-shan, on the Yangtse.

'A chisel of quartz schist' from the Cape of Nalacheva, Kamchatka (**78**, Fig. 18), almost exactly resembles the Szechwan gouge. In Japan, this type of implement has been found in Hokkaidō (**159**, Fig. 87), in Kantō (**100**, Pl. 10. 12; **117**, Fig. 8. 5) and in Kyūshū (**148**, Fig. 1). The last specimen seems to have been associated with bronze. Another implement of this type has been excavated from the Somrong Sen site (**276**, Pl. 3. 1) in Cambodia.

13. SPEAR-HEAD (Pl. 10. 6): a fragment of a nicely ground spear point. It is flattish in cross section with a sharp edge on both sides, which meet in a point. There is a vertical ridge on both surfaces at the end of the weapon, which suggests an imitation of a bronze implement.

This weapon was found in I-tu, below the gorges.

Most of the spear-heads of this type we know from other parts of eastern Asia belong to the bronze age. They have been found in Kyūshū (**148**, Fig. 5), in Korea (**160**, Fig. 2), in Fêngtien (**193**, Fig. 3), on Lamma Island (**254**, Pl. 7. 7, 9), in Tonkin (**274**, Pl. 4. 4–6) and in Pahang (**321**, Pl. 20).

14. PERFORATED KNIFE (Pl. 10. 7): a fragment of a small semi-lunar knife, with a perforation near the dull side. The other side consists of a sharp, roughly straight cutting edge. The end is curved. The cross section is flat, but it is thicker on the dull side than on the blade.

This implement was found at Lung-kai, on the most southern bend of the Yangtse.

The perforated knife of this type has a limited distribution in eastern Asia. From what we know at present, it has been found in Kantō (**112**, Pl. 40; **131**, Fig. 22), Kansai (**103**, Fig. 2; **104**, Pl. 18. 1–3; **174**, Figs. 21–4), Shikoku (**127**, Fig. 4. 17, 18; **146**, Fig. 8. 13), Kyūshū (**115**, Fig. 7; **148**, Fig. 3), Korea (**160**, Figs. 3, 4, 11), Kirin (**198**, Fig. 8. 11–12), Fêngtien (**182**, Fig. 5. 1–17; etc.), Jehol (**206**, Figs. 23, 50), Chahar (**221**, Fig. 33), Suiyüan (**241**, Fig. 32. 1–2), Kansu (**232**, Fig. 113), Shensi (**213**, Pl. 8. 2), Hopei (**241**, Figs. 4, 12; etc.), Shantung (**237**, Pl. 37. 2, 10), Honan (**217**, Pls. 1–2; **223**, Fig. 5. 1–2; etc.), Chekiang (**261**, Fig. 32; **262**, Fig. 2), Formosa (**255**, Pl. 2. 6; **268**, Fig. 3; etc.) and Lamma Island (**254**, Pl. 8). In Japan, this knife has been found in sites of the Jomon and Yayoi cultures, as well as associated with bronze artifacts, and it has several variations; in Manchuria, it has been found associated with microlithic implements and also with bronze artifacts; in northern China the use of this tool, with all its varieties, extended from the late neolithic period down to the time of the Han dynasty; and on the South China coast it has been reported from the neolithic as well as bronze age sites. The Kansu specimen is perforated and winged, with notches at the sides. The Formosa knife is winged but without notches at the sides. These two specimens may represent the most highly-developed type. We must bear in mind that only a few fragments have been found in Szechwan, including one from the Hanchou site, and this may indicate that the Szechwan area was marginal to the whole territory of this perforated knife culture complex.

15. RING (Pl. 10. 8): a fragment of a stone ring, well polished. It is flat, with the inner rim thicker than the outer edge. This isolated artifact was found at Wu-shan, in the gorges.

Outside Szechwan, stone rings of various shapes and sizes have been found in neolithic and bronze age sites in eastern Asia. Specimens are mostly fragmentary. In Siberia, they have been found on the Angara (**77,** Fig. 10) and the Amur rivers (**72,** Pl. 2. 510); in Japan, in Hokkaidō (**136,** Fig. 5, 19), in Tōhoku (**119,** Fig. 4. 30), in Kantō (**112,** Pl. 15. 2) and in Kansai (**174,** Fig. 24). They have also been found in Korea (**160,** Fig. 7), in Kirin (**198,** Fig. 8. 13), in Fêngtien (**193,** Fig. 2), in Jehol (**196,** Fig. 27), in Chahar (**200,** Fig. 3, 4), in Honan (**217,** Pl. 6; **233,** Fig. 3), on Lamma Island (**254,** Pl. 7, 8; **256,** Part 8), in Formosa (**258,** Fig. 5), in Tonkin (**279,** Pl. 10; **289,** Pl. 1), and in Cambodia (**276,** Pl. 4, 5). Some of the specimens from Hongkong and Tonkin are unfinished and illustrate the processes by which these ornaments were made. Some of the reported artifacts have been recovered from bronze age sites.

16. POLISHING STONE (Pl. 10.9): a highly burnished polishing stone, roughly spherical in shape, with one slightly flat surface. Other tools are almost discoidal. Another variety of the polishing stone is the rubbing pebble (Pl. 10. 10), which is a flat pebble, roughly discoidal, showing traces of rubbing on both surfaces. A third kind of the polishing stone is the whetstone (Pl. 10. 11), which was originally a pebble, which has been rubbed down on five sides. With the exception of the top surface, which retains the original pebble surface, the implement has become a rectangular cube. This type of implement was found at I-tu, I-ch'ang, Kuei-chou, K'uei-chou, Yün-yang and Lung-kai along the Yangtse.

Outside Szechwan, specimens of the polishing stone have been found in Japan (**119,** Fig. 4, 6), in Jehol (**206,** Fig. 49) and in Indo-China (**292,** Pl. 8. 4). Other specimens from Kamchatka (**78,** Pl. 11. 4–7), Japan (**134,** Fig. 7. 3; **143,** Fig. 12. 7), Shantung (**237,** Pl. 33. 1–2) and Lamma Island (**254,** Pl. 4. 3, 6) may be classified as whetstones. Some of the specimens mentioned above were found associated with bronze.

17. MEALING STONE (Pl. 10. 12): a fragment of a polished mealing stone, which is made of a flat piece of stone, with a ground out depression on the working surface. The fragment is too small to determine the shape of the tool, which may have been round or oval.

This grinding utensil was found in I-tu below the gorges.

Mealing stones of various sizes and shapes have been found in the neolithic and the bronze age sites of eastern Asia. In Japan, specimens have been reported from Kantō (**99,** Pl. 17. 9; etc.), Shikoku (**127,** Fig. 8) and Kyūshū (**109,** Pl. 6).

Others have been found in Korea (**126**, Pl. 3), in Kirin (**196**, Fig. 6), in Jehol (**201**, Figs. 73, 79, 80; etc.), in Shantung (**237**, Pl. 33), in Tonkin (**272**, Figs. 8–9); and in Perak (**307**, Pl. 1; **313**, Pl. 47).

SUMMARY

In the classification of the stone implements from Szechwan, I have divided the artifacts into four groups. The classification is based on the techniques of manufacture, which vary from simple to refined. I am inclined to think that these four industries may represent four stages of development in the prehistory

TABLE 3. Distribution of Lithic Industries in Szechwan

River Valley	District	Number of Sites	Groups of Stone Implements			
			A	B	C	D
Yangtse	1. I-tu	2	116	19	72	23
	2. I-ch'ang	8	60	6	9	8
	3. Kuei-chou	5	18	8	2	7
	4. Pa-tung	2	10	6	1	—
	5. Wu-shan	7	126	20	17	35
	6. K'uei-chou	2	7	2	2	5
	7. Yün-yang	6	64	17	1	5
	8. Wan-hsien	4	21	7	—	1
	9. Chungking	1+	—	—	—	4+
	10. Lu-chou	1	—	—	—	1
	11. Na-hsi	1	1	—	—	—
	12. Suifu	2	M	6	—	2
	13. Kung-hsien	1+	M	—	—	M
	14. Yüan-mou	1	M	57	—	6
Min	15. Chia-ting	1+	2	1	—	—
	16. O-mei	2+	6	M	—	—
	17. Chengtu	2+	1	1	—	S
	18. P'êng-hsien	1	—	—	—	—
	19. Kwan-hsien	2+	M	3	—	M
	20. Wên-ch'uan	1	M	—	—	M
	21. Wei-chou	1+	M	1	—	2
	22. Li-fan	1	M	—	—	M
Ta-tu	23. K'ang-ting	2	M	—	—	—
	24. Tan-pa	1	—	—	—	—
	25. Mao-kung	1	M	—	—	—
	26. Wu-pien	1	2	—	—	—
Ya-lung	27. K'ang-ting	5	M	—	—	—
	28. Li-hwa	1	S	—	—	—
	29. Tao-fu to Lu-ho	17+	M	—	—	—

TABLE 4. Distribution of Stone Objects and Pottery on the Yangtse

District	Site	Groups of Stone Implement				Pottery	Remarks
		A	B	C	D		
I-tu	Ku-lao-pei	★	★	★	★	★	
	Hsien-jên-ch'iao	★	.	.	★	★	
I-ch'ang	Site I	★	.	★	.	.	
	Site II	★	.	★	.	.	
	Site III	★	★	★	.	.	
	Site IV	★	★	★	.	.	
	Site V	.	.	.	★	★	
	Site VI	★	★	★	★ (4)	.	
	Huang-ling-miao	★	.	★	.	.	
	Ta-tung	.	.	.	★ (2)	.	
Kuei-chou	Miao-ho	★	★	.	.	.	
	Hsin-t'an	★ (2)	.	.	.	★	Pottery partly modern
	Hsiang-hsia	★	★	★	★	★	
	New Kuei-chou	★	★	★	★ (3)	.	
	Old Kuei-chou	★ (2)	.	.	.	.	
Pa-tung	Kuan-tu-k'ou	★	★	★	.	.	
	Huo-yen shih	★	★	.	.	.	
Wu-shan	L. Wushan gorge	★	★	★	★	★	
	Pei-shih	★	.	.	★ (1)	.	
	T'iao-shih	★	.	.	★ (2)	.	
	U. Wushan gorge	★	.	.	.	★	No association
	Wu-shan	★	★	★	★	★	
	Hsia-ma-t'an	★	★	★	★ (10)	.	In a stretch of about a mile
	Tai-hsi	★	★	★	★	★	
K'uei-chou	K'uei-chou	★	.	.	.	.	
	Kao-wei-tzŭ	★	.	.	★	★	
Yün-yang	Ku-lin-t'o	★	★	.	★ (1)	.	
	San-pa hsi	★	★	.	.	.	
	Ma-fen-t'o	.	★ (2)	.	.	.	
	Hsin-lung-t'an	★	.	.	★ (2)	.	
	Chi-liang-t'o	★	★	★	★ (1)	.	From several localities
	Hsiao-chiang	.	.	.	★	★	From two localities
Wan-hsien	Pa-yang-hsia	★	.	.	★ (1)	.	
	Chang-tso-t'an	★	★	.	.	.	
	Wan-hsien	★	★	.	★ (1)	.	From several localities
	Pai-shui-hsi	★	.	.	.	.	
Yüan-mou	Lung-kai	★	★	.	★	★	

★ Artifacts found at the site.

of Szechwan. The typology of the groups of stone tools, the distribution of these groups in the four river valleys of the region, the classification of the prehistoric sites along the Yangtse river, the association of the different types of stone tools with pottery and the comparison of these tools with examples from the lithic industries in other parts of eastern Asia, all contribute in one way or another to give support to this hypothesis.

Typologically, Group A, the chipped stone tools, is represented by forty-two types; Group B, the chipped-and-polished tools, by eleven; Group C, the chipped-pecked-and-polished tools, by five; and Group D, the polished implements, by seventeen. The richness of the stone types of Group A indicates that the industry must have had a long development and was comparatively dominant in this region. The other three industries were apparently secondary or late comers, if not actual imports, into this region.

TABLE 5. Types of Site on the Yangtse

Types of Site	Groups of Stone Tools found				Number of Sites
	A	B	C	D	
1	A	.	.	.	5
2	.	B	.	.	1
3	A	B	.	.	4
4	A	.	C	.	3
5	A	B	C	.	3
6	A	.	.	D	6
7	A	B	.	D	3
8	A	B	C	D	9
9	.	.	.	D	3

The distribution of the implements of these four groups in Szechwan is very interesting. According to Table 3, which shows the distribution of stone tools in the four river valleys, implements of Group A have been found in every valley; those of Groups B and D, in the Min and the Yangtse valleys; while the pecked tools were restricted to the Yangtse gorges alone. With these facts in view, it would not seem too far-fetched to assume that this region was probably inhabited first by a people who were masters of the pebble-chipping technique. Then, successive waves of outside influences, which are clearly represented by the products of the three other industries, came in, probably in later periods, but they never reached the mountainous areas in western Szechwan and Hsikang.

Along the Yangtse river, which has always been one of Szechwan's main routes of communication with the outside world, thirty-seven prehistoric sites have been investigated by Nelson. The result of his finds are tabulated briefly in Table 4, giving the association of these groups of stone tools in each locality. According to the association of the stone implements, the sites fall into nine types, as illustrated in Table 5, and it is interesting to find that these sites may also be classified into four stages, as follows:

Stage I: Sites yielding implements of Group A only:

Hsin-t'an	K'uei-chou
Old Kuei-chou	Pai-shui-hsi
Upper Wushan gorge	

Stage II: Sites yielding implements of Group B, or A and B:

Ma-fên-t'o	San-pa-hsi
Miao-ho	Chang-tso-t'an
Huo-yen-shih	

Stage III: Sites yielding implements of Groups A and C, or A, B and C:

I-ch'ang I	I-ch'ang III
I-ch'ang II	I-ch'ang IV
Huang-ling-miao	Kuan-tu-kou

Stage IV: Sites yielding implements of Groups A and D; A, B and D; A, B, C and D; or D only:

Hsien-jên-ch'iao	Hsiang-hsia
Pei-shih	New Kuei-chou
T'iao-shih	Lower Wushan gorge
Kao-wei-tzŭ	Wu-shan
Hsin-lung-t'an	Hsia-ma-t'an
Pa-yang-hsia	Tai-hsi
Ku-lin-t'o	Chi-liang-t'o
Wan-hsien	I-ch'ang V
Lung-kai	Ta-tung
Ku-lao-pei	Hsiao-chiang
I-ch'ang VI	

Table 4 also shows that the polished stone implements were found almost always associated with pottery. In each of the ten sites where the polished stone implements of Group D have been found in a larger number than merely three or four pieces, pottery has also been present. On the other hand, the chipped stone tools were found less often associated with pottery. Out of the five sites which have yielded only tools of Group A, three have been found free of pottery. The other two sites were represented only by two specimens each, which may quite possibly be of a later date.

It is interesting to note that at Tai-hsi, the only possible stratigraphic site we have at present, the chipped stone tools have been gathered from a depth of 14 ft. below the ground while pottery has been observed no deeper than 9 ft. (see Table 2).

I have gone into considerable detail in the comparison of the Szechwan stone objects with those of other regions in eastern Asia. The result of this comparative study has been tabulated in Table 6, which shows clearly the following facts:

(1) The stone implements of Szechwan are not the products of one or more independent lithic industries of its own. As a whole, they belong to one or more general culture-complexes of eastern Asia. Among the 75 types of stone objects found in Szechwan, only ten do not have any parallel in other parts of the Far East, and none of these ten types may be considered an essential and important artifact. Therefore, the stone artifacts of Szechwan, fundamentally a marginal area, must be studied in connexion with the cultural remains of a much larger region, eastern Asia.

(2) Among the 41 types of implements of Group A, 32 have been reported from other parts of eastern Asia as palaeoliths or, in Indo-China, as part of the Hoabinhien and Bacsonien cultures, the earliest stages of which are sometimes considered to be palaeolithic in date. Of the other nine types, three have some parallels from sites or levels of sites which have been classed as lower neolithic and four from upper neolithic horizons. It is thus a reasonable conclusion that the majority of this group of implements probably existed in this part of the world from palaeolithic down to the late neolithic period, when they gradually died out. Only five out of the 41 types have been found associated with bronze.

By drawing comparisons with the artifacts of palaeolithic sites in eastern Asia, I do not mean to suggest that actual specimens of chipped stone tools found in Szechwan are palaeolithic in date. Some of them may be, but most, if not all of them are probably late survivals of a technique which was first developed during the palaeolithic period. The real proof of a palaeolithic dating would have to be based on geological evidence and this is at present

TABLE 6. Types of Szechwan Stone Tools found in other parts of eastern Asia

Types of stone tools of Szechwan	Yenisei	TransBaikal	Amur	Kamchatka	Japan	Korea	Manchuria	Mongolia	Sinkiang	North China	South China	Indo-China (Siam)	Malay peninsula	Lower palaeolithic	Upper palaeolithic	Early neolithic	Late neolithic	Aeneolithic	Bronze age	Iron age
Group A																				
1. Pebble axe	★	.	.	.	★	.	★	.	.	★	★	★	★	.	×	×	×	.	.	.
2. Discoidal chopper	★	.	.	.	.	.	★	.	.	★	★	★	★	×	×	×	×	.	.	.
3. Curved-bit axe	★	.	.	★	★	★	★	.	.	★	★	★	★	.	×	×	×	×	.	.
4. Straight-bit axe	.	.	.	★	★	★	.	.	.	.	.	★	.	.	×	.	×	.	.	.
5. Broad axe	.	.	.	.	★	.	★	.	.	.	.	★	★	.	×	.	×	.	.	.
6. Rectangular axe	.	.	.	.	★	.	.	.	.	★	.	★	★	×	×	×	×	.	.	.
7. Short axe	★	.	.	.	★	.	.	.	.	★	★	★	★	×	×	×	×	.	.	.
8. Stemmed axe	.	.	.	★	★	.	★	.	.	★	★	★	★	.	×	×	×	×	.	.
9. Waisted axe	★	.	.	.	★	.	★	.	.	.	★	★	★	.	×	×	×	.	.	.
10. Curved-bit adze	.	.	.	★	★	.	.	.	.	.	★	★	.	.	×	×	×	.	.	.
11. Straight-bit adze	★	.	★	.	.	.	.	.	.	.	.	.	.	.	.	×	.	.	.	.
12. Chisel	.	.	.	★	.	.	★	.	.	.	.	★	.	.	×	.	×	.	.	.
13. Sub-triangular pick	.	.	.	.	.	.	.	.	.	★	★	.	.	.	×	.	×	.	.	.
14. Straight-butted pick	.	.	.	.	.	.	.	.	.	.	.	.	.	.	×	.	×	.	.	.
15. Stemmed pick	.	.	.	.	.	.	.	.	.	.	.	★	.	.	×	.	×	.	.	.
16. Waisted pick	.	.	.	.	.	.	.	.	★	.	.	.	.	.	×	.	×	.	.	.
17. Point-butted pick	.	.	.	.	.	.	.	.	.	.	.	.	.	.	×	.	×	.	.	.
18. Elongated pick	★	.	.	.	★	.	.	.	.	.	★	★	.	.	×	×	×	.	.	.
19. Leaf-shaped pick	★	.	.	.	★	.	★	.	.	.	★	★	.	.	×	×	×	.	.	.
20. Flake point	★	★	.	.	★	.	★	.	.	★	★	★	★	×	×	×	×	.	.	.
21. Spear head	★	.	.	★	★	.	.	.	.	.	.	★	.	.	×	×	×	.	.	.
22. Bi-facial perforator	★	.	.	.	★	.	.	.	.	★	.	★	★	.	×	×	×	.	.	.
23. Flake perforator	.	★	.	.	★	.	.	.	.	★	.	★	.	.	×	×	×	.	.	.
24. Retouched perforator	★	.	.	.	★	.	★	.	.	★	.	★	★	.	×	×	×	.	.	.
25. Pebble scraper	★	★	★	.	★	.	★	.	.	★	.	★	★	.	×	×	×	.	.	.
26. Core scraper	.	★	.	.	.	.	★	.	.	★	.	★	.	.	×	×	×	.	.	.
27. Rectangular scraper	★	.	.	.	★	.	★	.	.	★	.	★	★	×	×	×	×	.	.	.
28. Discoidal scraper	★	★	★	.	★	.	★	.	.	★	★	★	★	.	×	×	×	.	.	.
29. End scraper	★	★	.	.	★	.	★	.	.	★	.	★	★	.	×	×	×	.	.	.
30. Side scraper	★	★	.	.	★	.	★	.	.	★	★	★	★	.	×	×	×	.	.	.
31. Concave scraper	★	.	.	.	.	.	★	.	.	★	.	★	.	×	×	×	×	.	.	.
32. Borer and scraper	.	.	.	.	.	.	★	.	.	★	.	★	★	×	×	.	×	.	.	.
33. Single-edged knife	★	.	.	.	★	★	.	.	.	.	.	★	.	.	×	×	×	.	.	.
34. Double-edged knife	.	.	.	.	★	★	.	.	.	.	.	★	.	.	×	.	×	.	.	.
35. Flake knife	★	.	.	.	.	.	.	.	.	.	.	★	.	.	×	.	.	.	.	.
36. Coulter knife	.	.	.	.	.	.	.	.	.	.	.	★	.	.	×	.	×	.	.	.
37. Sickle knife	★	.	.	.	.	.	.	.	.	.	★	★	.	.	×	.	×	.	★	.
38. Pebble hammerstone	.	.	★	★	★	.	.	.	.	★	★	★	★	.	×	×	.	.	.	.
39. Hammerstone	.	.	.	.	★	.	★	.	.	★	.	.	★	.	.	.	×	×	×	.
40. Pitted stone	.	.	.	.	★	.	★	.	.	★	★	★	★	×	×	×	×	×	×	.
41. Waisted pebble	.	.	★	★	★	★	★	.	★	.	★	★	★	.	×	×	×	.	.	.

TABLE 6 (cont.)

Types of stone tools of Szechwan	Yenisei	TransBaikal	Amur	Kamchatka	Japan	Korea	Manchuria	Mongolia	Sinkiang	North China	South China	Indo–China (Siam)	Malay peninsula	Lower palaeolithic	Upper palaeolithic	Early neolithic	Late neolithic	Aeneolithic	Bronze age	Iron age
				Regions of Eastern Asia												Supposed dating in E. Asia				
Group B																				
1. Curved-bit axe	★	.	.	★	★	★	★	.	★	.	.	★	★	.	.	×	×	.	.	.
2. Straight-bit axe	★	.	.	★	★	★	★	.	★	.	★	★	★	.	.	×	×	.	.	.
3. Stemmed axe	.	.	.	★	.	.	.	.	.	.	.	★	★	.	.	×	×	.	.	.
4. Curved-bit adze	.	.	.	★	★	★	.	.	.	.	★	★	★	.	.	×	×	.	.	.
5. Straight-bit adze	.	.	.	★	★	★	.	.	.	.	.	★	.	.	.	×	×	.	.	.
6. Chisel	.	.	.	★	.	.	.	.	.	.	.	.	.	.	.	.	×	.	.	.
7. Pick	.	.	.	.	.	.	.	.	.	.	.	.	.	.	.	.	.	.	.	.
8. Pebble knife	.	.	.	.	.	.	.	.	.	.	.	.	.	.	.	.	.	.	.	.
9. Flake knife	.	.	.	.	.	.	.	.	.	.	.	.	.	.	.	.	.	.	.	.
10. Blade	.	.	.	.	.	.	.	.	.	.	.	.	.	.	.	.	.	.	.	.
11. Polished pebble	.	.	.	.	.	.	.	.	.	.	.	★	.	.	.	.	×	.	.	.
Group C																				
1. Curved-bit axe	.	.	.	★	★	.	★	.	.	★	★	.	.	.	.	.	×	.	.	.
2. Broad axe	.	.	.	.	.	.	.	.	.	.	.	.	.	.	.	.	.	.	.	.
3. Grooved axe	.	.	.	.	.	.	.	.	.	.	.	.	.	.	.	.	.	.	.	.
4. Curved-bit adze	.	.	.	★	.	.	.	.	.	.	.	.	.	.	.	.	.	×	×	.
5. Chisel	.	.	.	.	.	.	★	.	.	★	.	.	.	.	.	.	×	×	.	.
Group D																				
1. Celt	★	.	★	★	★	.	★	★	★	★	★	★	★	.	.	.	×	×	×	×
2. Broad axe	★	.	★	.	★	.	★	.	.	★	★	★	★	.	.	.	×	×	×	×
3. Point-butted axe	.	.	★	★	★	.	★	.	.	.	★	★	★	.	.	.	×	×	×	.
4. Vert.-grooved axe	.	.	.	.	.	.	.	.	.	.	.	★	.	.	.	.	×	×	.	.
5. Curved-bit adze	.	.	★	★	★	★	★	.	.	★	★	★	★	.	.	.	×	×	×	.
6. Straight-bit adze	.	.	.	★	★	★	★	.	.	★	★	★	★	.	.	.	×	×	×	.
7. Flat adze	.	.	.	.	★	★	★	.	.	.	.	★	★	.	.	.	×	×	×	.
8. Curved-bit chisel	.	.	.	★	★	★	★	.	.	★	★	★	★	.	.	.	×	×	×	.
9. Straight-bit chisel	.	.	.	★	★	.	★	.	.	★	★	★	★	.	.	.	×	×	×	.
10. Narrow-bit chisel	.	.	.	.	.	.	.	.	.	.	.	★	.	.	.	.	×	.	.	.
11. Punch	.	.	.	.	.	.	.	.	.	.	.	★	.	.	.	.	.	.	.	.
12. Gouge	.	.	.	★	★	.	.	.	.	.	.	★	.	.	.	.	×	.	×	.
13. Spear head	.	.	.	.	★	★	★	.	.	.	★	★	★	.	.	.	.	×	×	.
14. Perforated knife	.	.	.	.	★	★	★	.	.	★	★	.	.	.	.	.	×	×	×	×
15. Ring	★	.	★	.	★	★	★	.	.	★	★	★	.	.	.	.	×	×	×	.
16. Polishing stone	.	.	.	★	★	.	★	.	.	★	★	.	.	.	.	.	×	×	×	.
17. Mealing stone	.	.	.	.	★	★	★	.	.	★	.	★	★	.	.	.	×	×	×	.

lacking. Nelson's thorough investigation along the Yangtse river (**16,** 549) and Andersson's reconnaissance in the mountainous region of Hsikang (**32;** **33,** 68–9) both failed to disclose any traces of Pleistocene deposits in which artifacts were found. Therefore, until we have more specific facts to support it, we cannot assume the presence of palaeolithic man in Szechwan merely on the basis of the type of implements found there.

Being from a marginal area, and quite an inaccessible one, too, the chipped implements of Szechwan ought to be later in date than those found in North China or whatever the centre of culture may be. It seems safe for the present to assume that a part of these specimens are probably early neolithic in date, while others were much later.

(3) The typical artifacts of Group B show a continuation of some of the types of Group A tools. The majority of these two groups have been found lying side by side. Among the eleven types represented in Group B, four do not have any parallels in eastern Asia so far. They also happen to be implements of no particular importance. A comparison of Group B tools with similar implements elsewhere shows that the types belong to the early and the late neolithic periods in eastern Asia. None of them has yet been found associated with bronze.

(4) The industry of Group C seems to be based on a very special technique, which did not have a wide distribution in eastern Asia. Moreover, two out of the five types represented in Szechwan do not have any parallels at all in the entire region. It is interesting to note that the introduction of this technique in eastern Asia came at about the same time as that of the polished tools of Group D. The chipped-pecked-and-polished implements have mostly been found in late neolithic sites or levels, and in only one instance were they associated with bronze. Therefore, we may safely conclude that these pecked tools are later in date than the implements of Group B.

(5) Among the 17 types of polished stone implements (Group D) represented in Szechwan, only the one-shouldered punch stands without a duplicate in the entire region of eastern Asia. In this part of the world, polished tools seem to have been introduced or established in late or upper neolithic times. But unlike the implements of Group C, the polished implements seem to have maintained their popularity into the aeneolithic period and the bronze age. In three cases, they have been found in an iron age level, and they survived as late as the Han dynasty in North China.

In view of these five conclusions which we have drawn from our comparative study, it seems evident that the prehistory of Szechwan lies largely within the neolithic period of eastern Asia and comprises several stages of development. The stages are probably four, as represented by the four lithic industries, although the stages represented by the stone tools of Groups B and C are not as clear and distinct as are the first stage, represented by the chipped implements of Group A, and the last stage, characterized by the polished tools of Group D.

TABLE 7. Proposed Chronological Sequence for the Prehistory of Szechwan based on the Study of the Stone Artifacts

Stage	Valley			
	Ya-lung	Ta-tu	Min	Yangtse
IV				
III	Group A	Group A	Group A Group B Group D	Group A Group B Group C Group D
II				
I				

Although the evidence which has just been reviewed is not in all cases as conclusive as could be desired, the cumulative effect is fairly convincing. Accordingly, on the basis of the stone tools, I venture to propose a chronological sequence for the prehistory of Szechwan, as tabulated in Table 7. This table shows the development of the four lithic industries in the four river valleys of Szechwan.

CHAPTER IV

POTTERY

THE pottery specimens which will be described in this chapter form a small part of the archaeological material from Szechwan. They consist of potsherds only. These are very fragmentary; not a single whole vessel was found. They come from more than fourteen sites, viz. Ku-lao-pei, Hsien-jên-ch'iao, I-ch'ang site V, Hsin-t'an, Hsiang-hsia, lower Wushan gorge, upper Wushan gorge, Tai-hsi, Kao-wei-tzŭ, Hsiao-chiang, Lung-kai, P'êng-hsien, Wei-chou and the sites of the Tao-fu valley. The first eleven sites are in the Yangtse valley, the next two in the Min valley and the Tao-fu sites in the Ya-lung valley.

For the analytical study of this collection, I first of all classified the sherds into five groups, according to the colour of the ware: red, black, grey, brown and white. Each of these groups was then divided into two sub-groups, based on the fineness or the coarseness of the paste. The white pottery was represented by one sherd only, of fine texture, so there were only nine sub-groups. Each of these sub-groups was again divided into several types, according to the surface treatment or the decoration of the sherd. Thus, we had altogether 24 types of pottery.

From the analytical study of the 24 pottery types it was clear that, on the basis of the characteristics of the paste, this collection of potsherds could actually be grouped into six general classes. In each of these classes there may be slight variations and duplications with regard to colour, technique and other characteristics. I have called these classes A, B, C, D, E and F. The type or types of pottery that are included in each of them are listed below:

CLASS A

1. Plain coarse red ware.
2. Cord-marked coarse red ware.
3. Grooved coarse red ware.
4. Stamped coarse red ware.
5. Incised or appliqué coarse red ware.
6. Cord-marked coarse black ware.
7. Plain coarse grey ware.
8. Cord-marked or stamped coarse grey ware.
9. Plain coarse brown ware.
10. Cord-marked coarse brown ware.
11. Stamped coarse brown ware.

CLASS B

12. Plain or slipped fine grey ware.   15. Appliqué fine grey ware.
13. Cord-marked fine grey ware.   16. Plain or appliqué fine brown
14. Incised fine grey ware.   ware.

CLASS C

17. Plain or slipped fine red ware.   18. Painted fine red ware.

CLASS D

19. Plain fine black ware.

CLASS E

20. Stamped fine white ware.

CLASS F

21. Stamped fine black ware.   23. Stamped fine grey ware.
22. Comb-marked fine grey ware.   24. Incised fine brown ware.

CLASS A

1. PLAIN COARSE RED WARE (Pl. 11. 1). This type of pottery was found only in the Yangtse gorges, at the lower Wushan gorge, Tai-hsi and Kao-wei-tzŭ.

Colour. This ware is crimson or dark-red on the outer surface and brownish-red on the inner surface. It is unslipped. The surface is spotted with tiny white dots, due to the shell particles which are used in the paste.

Material. The paste is brown and rough, tempered with shell powder or silica particles, which show very clearly on the sherd surface. The amount of temper shown in the paste seems to indicate that the potter did not follow a definite proportion for the mixture, which is by no means carefully prepared. The ware is usually relatively soft but the hardness of the ware is greater when higher temperatures have been used in firing.

Thickness. The thickness of this ware is very variable; some medium, some thick. The illustrated specimen is 6–20 mm. thick.

Construction. It is obvious that no great pains were taken in the manufacture of this ware. The thickness is very variable, and the vessels were undoubtedly built by hand.

Surface treatment. The outer surface is smoothed, probably with the wet hand. In some cases, it appears to have been polished. The inner surface is always left untreated.

Shape. Several types of rim may be mentioned: a flaring rim, a horizontally everted rim and a flaring rim with a slight depression at the edge.

2. CORD-MARKED COARSE RED WARE (Pl. 11. 2–5). This type of pottery was found only in the Yangtse gorges, at Ku-lao-pei, I-ch'ang site V, lower Wushan gorge, Tai-hsi, Kao-wei-tzŭ and Hsiao-chiang.

Colour. This ware is generally dull red, but buff and yellowish-red are not uncommon. It is almost always unslipped. In one case only, a sherd from lower Wushan gorge, a red slip seems to have been used, but the traces are so slight that they are almost negligible.

Material. The paste of this ware is not at all well prepared. It is rough, coarse and unevenly mixed. The clay may be divided into two kinds: (1) brownish clay mixed with tiny particles of silica or sand (Pl. 11. 4, 5); (2) coarse greyish clay tempered with relatively big grains of sand, some of which are as large as 4 mm. in diameter. The former paste seems to be softer than the latter.

Thickness. The thickness of the sherds appears to be correlated with the quality of the paste. The specimen of the coarser paste, which is tempered with big grains of sand, is thicker than the specimen of the other material. The former is 7–18 mm. thick, while the latter is 4–8 mm.

Construction. This ware is undoubtedly handmade, but the technique seems to vary again with the paste. The coarser paste is very poorly prepared and the vessels with this kind of paste are crudely moulded. More care seems to have been employed in the making of the vessels with the finer paste.

Surface treatment. The surface treatment also varies with the paste. The surface of the vessels with coarser paste seems to have been left untouched, while the others are carefully smoothed with the wet hand, though not necessarily polished.

Decoration. The vessels of this ware are generally decorated with cord-marked designs, which may have covered the whole body except the rim and the neck. The cord-marks may also vary with the paste. The sherds of the coarser paste seem to carry coarser cord marks. The cord-marks of the less coarse sherds always seem to be arranged vertically, while those of the coarser sherds run vertically in some cases (Pl. 11. 3) and horizontally in others (Pl. 11. 2). Moreover, the latter vessels seem to have had an indented rim, made probably by nipping with the finger. In this way a scalloped effect is produced at the edge of the rim.

Shape. The vessels of the coarser paste seem to be larger than the others. The rims are either straight, or flaring, or straight but standing at an obtuse angle to the wall of the body (Pl. 11. 5).

3. GROOVED COARSE RED WARE (Pl. 11. 6). This type of pottery so far has been found only at Ku-lao-pei below the Yangtse gorges.

Colour. The colour is red and this is due to a sheet of red slip. The original surface of the vessels is slightly yellowish, which shows not only on the inner surface, but also on the outer surface under the slip.

Material. The paste of this ware is unique in the pottery of Szechwan. The clay is dark grey and soft, tempered with bits of vegetation, possibly grass. The texture is coarse and porous.

Thickness. The thickness of this specimen is 8·5 mm., so it ranks as one of the thick wares of the region.

Construction. The clay seems to have been carefully mixed with the vegetable matter and considerable care was taken in the building of the vessel. It is probably handmade, although, judging from the evenness of the grooves at the rim, the vessel might possibly be wheel-made. With only one sherd, it is very hard to be positive on this point.

Surface treatment. The surface of this ware seems to have been first smoothed with the wet hand and then slightly polished before the application of the slip. With the exception of traces lying in the grooves, all the slip has flaked off.

Decoration. The rim of the vessel, which is straight, is decorated with linear horizontal grooves, which run parallel to one another.

4. STAMPED COARSE RED WARE (Pl. 11. 7, 8). This type of pottery was found in the Yangtse gorges at the lower Wushan gorge and at Kao-wei-tzŭ.

Colour. This ware is generally red, but sherds of buff and grey sometimes occur. The range of colour is apparently due to variations in the firing.

Material. The colour of the paste ranges from black to buff and red and this is due to the degree of firing. The material is not very well prepared and may be divided into two kinds. One is clay mixed with big grains of sand, the same material as Type 2, paste 2, described above. The second kind is soft black clay mixed with sand and better prepared.

Thickness. The lower Wushan gorge specimen (Pl. 11. 7) is 7·5 mm. thick, representing pottery of medium thickness. The Kao-wei-tzŭ sherd (Pl. 11. 8) is 12 mm. thick, representing thick pottery. This ware is by no means uniform in thickness.

Construction. The vessels are crudely built and the firing is very uneven. The ware is evidently handmade.

Surface treatment. The surface of this ware is generally left untouched. A few sherds are roughly smoothed, probably with the wet hand.

Decoration. This ware is decorated with irregular stamped patterns. One specimen (Pl. 11. 7) shows stamping with depressions of various shapes and sizes, crowded together in a more or less horizontal fashion. The other sherd (Pl. 11. 8) shows some impressions of square, rectangular and triangular shapes scattered sparsely and unsystematically at the neck of a vessel. These impressions seem to have been made with the ends of wooden sticks.

Shape. The Kao-wei-tzŭ sherd comes from a vessel of unknown shape, with a straight rim, which is roughly indented, in the same fashion as the specimens shown in Pl. 11. 2, 3.

5. INCISED OR APPLIQUÉ COARSE RED WARE (Pl. 11. 9, 10). This type of pottery is common among the sites in the Tao-fu valley. It has been described by Bowles (25, 130–6).

Colour. The ware is generally light brick-red in colour, but it may range from ochre to black, according to the conditions of firing.

Material. The paste seems to be similar to that of the plain coarse red ware mentioned above, although in the present case the temper consists of particles of shale instead of powdered shell.

Thickness. The thickness of the sherds is medium and the thinnest of all measures 5 mm.

Construction. Handmade.

Surface treatment. The surface is smoothed by rubbing, but the process does not seem to have been carried very far and fingermarks are still visible on both sides.

Decoration. Decoration occurs probably on the shoulder of the vessel and is of two kinds: (1) an incised pattern (Pl. 11. 9), which is composed of a line running around the vessel horizontally, with diagonal short straight lines arranged parallel to one another; (2) appliqué work (Pl. 11. 10), consisting of a raised band, nipped probably with the finger to produce a scalloped pattern. Besides these designs, some irregular impressions appear on the inner surface.

Shape. The variety of form and thickness of the rim-sherds indicates the existence of several forms. One sherd shows that the vessel of which it was a part had a low ring of about 12 mm. in height for its base (**25, 133**).

6. CORD-MARKED COARSE BLACK WARE (Pl. 12. 1). This type of pottery is represented by one sherd only, found at Hsiang-hsia, in the Yangtse gorges.

Colour. The ware is black on the surface, the black colour extending for about 2 mm. into the body of the sherd. White spots of shell particles can be seen scattered on the surface.

Material. The paste is not very well prepared and is coarse and hard. The clay is brown in colour and mixed with grains of sand and particles of shell.

Thickness. The sherd is 11 mm. thick.

Construction. Handmade and crudely modelled.

Surface treatment. The surface is rough, probably left untouched, and is covered with unsystematic cord-marking.

7. PLAIN COARSE GREY WARE (Pl. 12. 2–5). This type of pottery was found in the Yangtse gorges, at Hsien-jên-ch'iao and Hsiao-chiang.

Colour. The ware is either grey or buff coloured. The sherds are generally much weather-worn and show a rough surface.

Material. The paste of this ware is coarse, as the clay is not very well prepared and the sand temper varies greatly in the size and shape of the grains.

Thickness. The thickness of the ware is 4·5–22 mm.

Construction. Handmade.

Surface treatment. The surface is smooth, probably produced with the wet hand, but not well polished.

Shape. The flat pointed legs (Pl. 12. 2, 3) and the rims (Pl. 12. 4, 5) suggest the existence of several shapes. The legs might belong to a *ting*-tripod, a very common type of vessel in North China.

8. CORD-MARKED OR STAMPED COARSE GREY WARE (Pl. 12. 6–8). This type of pottery was found in the Yangtse valley, at Kao-wei-tzŭ, Hsiao-chiang and Lung-kai. The ware is simply the plain coarse grey ware (Type 7), with the addition of stamped cord-marked designs. The string impressions are generally very carefully made, but irregular stamping is not unknown (as in Pl. 12. 8). The impressions were made by the beating process.

9. PLAIN COARSE BROWN WARE (Pl. 12. 9). This type of pottery was found in the Yangtse valley at Tai-hsi and Lung-kai.

Colour. The ware is generally brown and the colour varies from light brown, almost yellowish, to dark reddish brown.

Material. The paste is composed of a reddish-brown clay, tempered with white shell particles. It is exactly the same as that of the plain coarse red ware (Type 1) which, however, was probably more highly fired than this ware. The core is relatively soft, but some sherds are quite hard.

Thickness. The thickness of this ware ranges from 4–8 mm.

Construction. The sherds show that this ware was crudely built. There are no traces which might indicate the use of the wheel.

Surface treatment. The surface of this pottery is usually smoothed, probably with the wet hand, and in a very few cases it is polished.

10. CORD-MARKED COARSE BROWN WARE (Pls. 12. 10; 13. 1). This type of pottery was found in the Yangtse gorges, at Ku-lao-pei and Hsin-t'an.

Colour. The ware is brown, but the colour is usually tinged with grey. No dark brown sherd is present in this collection.

Material. The paste is made of dark grey clay, tempered with sand. It is hard and somewhat porous.

Thickness. The thickness of this ware is from 8–12 mm.

Construction. None of the sherds of this ware shows any evidence of the wheel technique. They are all handmade.

Surface treatment. The surface of this ware is left completely untouched after modelling and is rough and uneven.

Decoration. The cord-marks, which appear on the sherds, apparently were not produced with a beater but were probably made by a stamp after the vessels were constructed. There are two kinds: (1) rough rope-impressions made horizontally and arranged close together (Pl. 13. 1); (2) horizontal string impressions, which are arranged roughly parallel to one another.

11. STAMPED COARSE BROWN WARE (Pl. 13. 2). This type of pottery was found only in the Yangtse gorges, at Hsin-t'an. Except for the decoration, the ware is exactly similar to Type 9, the plain coarse brown ware, not only in colour and paste, but also in technique and surface treatment. The sherds are stamped, in no definite pattern, with impressions made by the ends of wooden sticks, which were square, rectangular or triangular in cross-section.

CLASS B

12. PLAIN OR SLIPPED FINE GREY WARE (Pl. 13. 3–7). This type of pottery was found in large quantity in the sites of the Tao-fu valley and at Hsien-jên-ch'iao below the Yangtse gorges.

Colour. The surface is generally grey in colour, which is of the light tone commonly known as silver grey. In the Tao-fu valley, some sherds are black outside and brown inside (**25,** 136). The grey ware from the Tao-fu valley, mentioned by Andersson (**33,** 73) may be of this type.

Material. There is almost no difference between the colour of the surface and that of the paste, which is soft, fine and even throughout (**25,** 136). No sand or other foreign substance can be discerned. Judging from the texture of the sherds, the clay was very well mixed.

Thickness. The thickness of the sherds varies greatly with their position in the vessel. A base piece may be 22 mm. thick, while the thinnest wall-sherd measures only 4·5 mm. On the whole, the thickness of this ware is medium. The handle piece (Pl. 13. 3) is about 20 mm. wide and 4 mm. thick.

Construction. This ware is generally moulded with the hands, but wheel-made sherds are also common.

Surface treatment. The surface of the pottery is usually smoothed and this was probably done on the wheel, as parallel striae can be found on the rim, the ring-foot, and the cylindrical stem of a vessel which was possibly a *tou*-cup. A large number of the sherds are white-slipped, the slip having been applied after the surface had been smoothed (Pl. 13. 6, 7).

Decoration. Very few of the sherds are decorated and the designs are nothing but horizontal parallel sunk or raised lines (Pl. 13. 4), the number of which does not exceed five in a group.

Shape. The sherds suggest a great variety in the shape of the vessels. The *tou* vessel, which is a bowl with a tall pedestal base, seems to be present. There are several kinds of rims and two kinds of bases. One base has knobbed legs which may have been three or four in number. The other is a ring-foot, similar to the low-rimmed base mentioned above. Bowles (**25,** 136) illustrates a modern vessel from Lato, which suggests the position of the handle piece on the original vessel. The upper end of the handle is attached to the neck, while the lower end is attached to the wall below the shoulder of the vessel.

13. CORD-MARKED FINE GREY WARE (Pl. 13. 8). This type of pottery was found at Tai-hsi in the gorges.

Colour and material. The colour and the material of this ware resemble exactly those of Type 12. The grey colour of the surface is light in tone and the paste is fine and soft.

Thickness. The specimen is 6 mm. thick.

Construction. Hand-modelled.

Decoration. The surface is covered with slanting and horizontal string paddle impressions, crossing one another.

14. INCISED FINE GREY WARE (Pl. 13. 9-11). This type of pottery was found in the Yangtse valley, at the upper Wushan gorge and at Lung-kai.

Colour. The surface is generally grey, the Wushan sherds being mostly of lighter tone, while specimens from Lung-kai are dark and slightly brownish. The difference in colour may have been caused by the different material used in these two places.

Material. The paste of the Wushan ware (Pl. 13. 11) is similar to the fine, soft grey material used in Type 12. Not only the material but also the method of making the surface treatment and the incised decoration are identical. The paste of the Lung-kai ware (Pl. 13. 9, 10) is different. It is dark grey, sometimes reddish-brown, slightly tempered with sand, highly fired, and hard.

Thickness. The thickness of the ware is medium. The Wushan sherds are about 5 mm. thick while the Lung-kai specimens range from 7-11 mm.

Construction. The Wushan ware is probably wheel-made, but the Lung-kai pottery is handmade.

Surface treatment. The surface of this ware is smoothed, probably with the wet hand. The Lung-kai sherds are not as evenly done as the Wushan fragments.

Decoration. The Wushan sherds are generally decorated with one or several horizontal incised lines near the rim or at the pedestal. The incision was evidently made by pressing a point on the pottery surface while the vessel was turning on the wheel. The incised patterns of the Lung-kai sherds are of two sorts: (1) slanting lines crossing one another, producing a series of lozenges; (2) slanting lines pointing toward one another in pairs, forming a herringbone pattern.

15. APPLIQUÉ FINE GREY WARE (Pl. 14. 1). This type of pottery was found at Hsien-jên-ch'iao, below the gorges. The colour, paste, thickness, technique and surface treatment are all similar to those of Type 12. The differ-

ence lies only in decoration. This ware is decorated with appliqué work, similar in technique to the decoration of some sherds of Type 5. There is a raised band of clay, nipped, probably with the fingers, producing a scalloped pattern.

16. PLAIN OR APPLIQUÉ FINE BROWN WARE (Pl. 14. 2–4). This type of pottery was found in the Yangtse valley, at the upper Wushan gorge, Tai-hsi and Hsien-jên-ch'iao.

Colour. The surface is generally brown, but sherds of greyish and reddish brown occur. There is no slip.

Material. The paste of this ware appears to be well prepared. It is fine and hard, slightly tempered with sand. The colour of the clay is grey or dark brown.

Thickness. The Wushan sherds are about 7 mm. thick and the rims and walls of the vessels do not seem to differ much in thickness. In the case of the Tai-hsi sherds, the base sherds are generally thicker than the walls. One base piece is 11 mm., while wall sherds may be as thin as 2·5 mm.

Construction. This ware is commonly handmade, but there are traces of striae on some sherds that suggest wheel technique.

Surface treatment. The surface of this ware is usually smooth, probably produced by the wet hand, but polished sherds (Pl. 14. 3) are not uncommon. The polishing was done possibly with a pebble.

Decoration. The Hsien-jên-ch'iao sherd (Pl. 14. 4) shows two series of scalloped 'pie-rims', nipped probably with the fingers, running parallel to each other, with incised slanting lines between them.

CLASS C

17. PLAIN OR SLIPPED FINE RED WARE (Pl. 14. 5–8, 11). This type of pottery was found in the gorges at Ku-lao-pei, Hsien-jên-ch'iao, Hsin-t'an and Tai-hsi.

Colour. This ware is either brick-red throughout, or red on both surfaces, with a grey core. Some sherds show patches of grey on the outer surface (Pl. 14. 6). The red colour is presumably produced by firing under oxidizing conditions and it varies from yellowish to blood red. The grey colour of the core is due to incomplete firing.

Material. The paste of this ware appears to be well prepared, as the clay is always fine and uniform. It may be divided into two kinds: (1) very fine clay (Pl. 14. 5, 6, 11) sometimes mixed with very fine sand. (2) Clay mixed with coarser sand (Pl. 14. 7). The colour of the paste varies from grey to brick-red. The firing was not uniform, as some sherds are soft (Pl. 14. 11) and others are hard (Pl. 14. 7).

Thickness. The thickness of the ware appears to vary with the paste. The sherds of very fine clay are always thinner than those of sand-tempered clay. The former are 3 to 6 mm. thick, while the latter are always more than 8 mm. thick.

Construction. The sherds are too fragmentary to show the method of making this ware. Judging from the even thickness of some of the sherds, a turn-table, if not a potter's wheel, may occasionally have been employed. Most of the sherds show evidences of hand modelling.

Surface treatment. The outer surface is always smooth and even, presenting an appearance much like that resulting from the wheel-technique. Some sherds are smoothed with the wet hand, some polished and some red-slipped and polished (Pl. 14. 8). The colour of the slip is either orange-red or crimson. In most cases, due to weathering, the thin layer of fine clay has flaked off considerably. It is better retained on the harder material.

Shape. As the sherds of this ware are in a very fragmentary state, no definite vessel shapes could be determined. However, the variety of form and thickness of the rim sherds indicates the existence of several forms of pots. One of them (Pl. 14. 11) may be the rim of a large jar, with one perforation, probably made for the attachment of a string for suspension.

18. PAINTED FINE RED WARE (Pl. 14. 9, 10). This type of pottery was found below the gorges, at Ku-lao-pei, and also at Wei-chou, in the Min valley.

Colour. This ware is terra-cotta or blood-red. The colour is very even, both on the outer and the inner surface, and this indicates that great care was taken in making and in firing.

Material. The paste of this ware appears to be similar to that of the plain ware described above (Type 17). It is very well prepared and the clay is fine and uniform, tempered with shell powder instead of sand. The colour of the paste is red and grey and the texture is hard.

Thickness. The thickness of the Ku-lao-pei specimen is 6·5 mm. It is a rim sherd, so the wall of the vessel may be thinner than this.

Construction. The manufacture of this ware was obviously more elaborate than that of the plain ware. Although the technique is the same, evidently hand-modelled, yet the preparation of the paste, the moulding of the vessel, the surface treatment and the firing all show the very great care taken in the process.

Surface treatment. The outer surface is slipped, very highly polished, smooth and even. It appears to have been smoothed first with wet hands, then rubbed with a polishing object, probably a pebble. The inner surface is not as highly polished as the outer, and finger marks are still evident.

Decoration. This ware is unique in that it is decorated with black painted curvilinear designs. Dye (**14,** 75) suggests that the black lines are from the brush work and 'are covered over with the circular sweep of the brush'. On the plate (Pl. 14. 10), the white part of the figure represents the terra-cotta surface. Both these sherds show what is often referred to as 'negative' paintings, i.e. the painting constitutes the background and the unpainted portions of the surface form the real design.

Shape. The Wei-chou sherd (Pl. 14. 10) is slightly convex and suggests a vessel or bowl or jar shape, which may be 25–30 cm. in diameter. The other sherd (Pl. 14. 9) is part of a horizontal everted rim.

Dye (**14,** 75) maintains that the Szechwan painted pottery suggests in colour and in pattern some of the pottery found by Andersson at Yangshao and Sha-kou-tun. While commenting on the Ku-lao-pei specimen, Nelson (**19**) points out that it is 'apparently typical of Yangshao ware'. We may safely conclude that these two specimens of painted ware from Szechwan belong to the group of painted pottery which flourished in North China during the later part of the neolithic period.

CLASS D

19. PLAIN FINE BLACK WARE (Pl. 15. 1). This type of pottery was found at Ku-lao-pei and Hsien-jên-ch'iao, below the gorges.

Colour. The ware is black in colour. On the surface, all black wares look alike, but if the paste is carefully examined, a difference in the colour of the paste may be observed. This fine black ware is black not only on the surface but also throughout the paste, unlike other black pottery of this region which has usually a red or grey core. Moreover, the sherds from Ku-lao-pei and Hsien-jên-ch'iao are thin and have a shiny surface.

Material. The paste is very well prepared, as the clay is very fine and carefully mixed. The clay seems to have been washed repeatedly and no temper of any kind is visible, even with a lower power microscope.

Thickness. The sherds of this ware are all very thin, measuring 2·5 to 4·5 mm. in thickness and the walls are very even.

Construction. Horizontal parallel striae are observable and these suggest that the wheel technique had reached a very high stage of development.

Surface treatment. The surface of this ware is very highly burnished, though only a few of the sherds still retain the original glossy surface, which is sometimes like black lacquer.

Decoration. In one specimen (Pl. 15. 1) a horizontal incised line appears on the surface.

CLASS E

20. STAMPED FINE WHITE WARE (Pl. 15. 2). A single sherd of white pottery was found at I-ch'ang Site V.

Colour. The ware is white both on the surface and underneath. The colour is milk white.

Material. The paste is well prepared; it may have been washed several times before the clay was used. The texture is fine and hard and there does not seem to be any foreign material. In fact the paste is pure china clay or kaolin, such as is used in making modern white stoneware and porcelain.

Thickness. The sherd is 6·5 mm. thick.

Construction. The evenness of the wall and the neatness of the horizontal groove over the stamped impression suggest wheel technique.

Surface treatment. The surface of the sherd seems to be well smoothed, if not polished, and stamped with a very fine chequer pattern, which is probably produced with a piece of textile pressed on the vessel, before the surface had dried.

Decoration. The chequer pattern is separated by a horizontal groove, which apparently was produced by pressing a round point on the chequered surface while the vessel was turning on a wheel.

CLASS F

21. STAMPED FINE BLACK WARE (Pl. 15. 3, 4). This type of pottery was found at the lower Wushan gorge.

Colour. The ware is generally black, but on the whole it is lighter than the plain black ware (Type 19). Dark grey is quite common.

Material. The paste is fine and was well prepared. The colour of the clay is grey. The texture is soft and no sand or any foreign material can be found.

Thickness. The thickness of the ware is 5–7 mm.

Construction. Horizontal parallel striae indicate that a wheel technique of a very high stage was used in the manufacture.

Surface treatment. The rim sherd (Pl. 15. 3) shows a very highly burnished surface, which may have been produced by the same technique as in Type 19. This specimen shows, however, considerable crackling on the smooth surface.

Decoration. The sherds are decorated with two kinds of stamped design. The first is a combination of rectangular impressions and vertical grooves (Pl. 15. 3). The impressions form a horizontal line a short distance below the neck of the vessel and the grooves are placed between the impressions and are parallel to one another. The second kind of stamped design is chequered (Pl. 15. 4).

22. COMB-MARKED FINE GREY WARE (Pl. 15. 5, 6). This type of pottery was found at Hsien-jên-ch'iao, below the gorges.

Colour. The surface is generally grey in colour, but terra-cotta is not uncommon and some sherds are buff-coloured. The difference in colour is presumably due to differences in the firing.

Material. The paste of this ware is grey and seems to be quite well prepared. It is tempered slightly with particles of silica and the texture is fine and soft.

Thickness. The thickness of the sherds is medium, ranging from 7 to 12 mm.

Construction. The sherds are in part wheel-made.

Surface treatment. Some sherds are left untouched, others are smoothed probably with the wet hand, but most of them have a polished surface.

Decoration. The sherds are decorated with comb-marks. There are also always horizontal incisions or bands where the comb-marks are obliterated. The decoration seems to cover the whole outer surface of the vessels except the neck and a part of the shoulder. The pattern suggests an imitation of basketry. The parallel comb-marks are arranged like wickerwork, in which the horizontal incised lines represent a visible horizontal warp while the depressed bands may represent a group of horizontal warps or other decoration.

Shape. The number of rims suggests that several forms existed.

23. STAMPED FINE GREY WARE (Pl. 15. 7–9). This type of pottery was found at Hsien-jên-ch'iao, below the gorges.

Colour and material. The colour and the material of this ware are the same as those of Type 22. It ranges from grey to terra-cotta in colour and the fine and soft paste is slightly tempered with silica particles. It is partly wheel-made.

Surface treatment and decoration. The only difference between this ware and Type 22 lies in the decoration. This stamped ware is ornamented with corrugated paddle impressions, which represent imitations of basketry. The technique of stamping does not vary from that of Type 21, but the designs are new. One sherd (Pl. 15. 7) presents a slanting chequer pattern with horizontal grooves running parallel to one another. The second specimen (Pl. 15. 8) seems to represent an imitation of wrapped twined weaving, in which the turns of the wrapping are oblique on the outside of the basket. The third specimen (Pl. 15. 9) represents an open chequer pattern, in which the chequers are arranged horizontally, with horizontal grooves representing the warp or group of warps.

A close examination of these specimens and the cord-marked wares indicates that the impressions were made with a beater, which might have been made of a thin rectangular strip of wood, bound round with string or carved with the desired pattern.

24. INCISED FINE BROWN WARE (Pl. 15. 10, 11). This type of pottery was found at Hsien-jên-ch'iao, below the gorges.

Colour. This ware is generally brown, but the colour shades from light grey to dark brown.

Material. The paste seems to be composed of the same material as that of the plain brown ware (Type 16). The colour of the clay varies from grey to brown to red. One sherd (Pl. 15. 11) actually is made of a paste which is grey in the middle and reddish brown on the surface. The clay is mixed slightly with sand and the texture is usually fine and hard.

Thickness. The thickness of these sherds is medium, ranging from 4 to 10 mm.

Construction. This ware seems to be carefully manufactured. The paste is well prepared and the construction was carefully done. The evenness of the walls and the striae on the surface suggest wheel-technique, though some vessels may be hand-modelled.

Surface treatment. The surface has been treated with care after the vessel was modelled. It seems first to have been smoothed with the wet hand then polished with a pebble. The ware is so well fired that the surface is somewhat glossy.

Decoration. This ware is decorated with incised ornament. The incisions are of two kinds: (1) slanting lines, produced by a point, crossing one another in series of lozenges (Pl. 15. 10); (2) short vertical slanting lines, indented with the finger nail, arranged in a series of horizontal bands, which may be an imitation of basketry (Pl. 15. 11).

OTHER POTTERY OBJECTS

Three spindle whorls were found at the Hsien-jên-ch'iao site. They are made of coarse brown paste tempered with sand, and the shape is that of a disc, with a perforation in the centre. The edge is slanting at a steep angle. Two of the specimens are broken fragments, the third (Pl. 15. 12) measures 41 × 13 mm., but the perforation is only partly drilled.

The disc-shaped spindle whorl in pottery was quite a popular object in the late neolithic times of China and Indo-China. Specimens have been found at Shih-pei-ling in Kirin (**198**, Fig. 6. 3), Sha-kou-tun in Fêngtien (**177**, Pl. 8. 20), Pi-tzŭ-wo at the tip of the Liaotung peninsula (**182**, Fig. 6. 23–6), Hung-shan-hou, Jehol (**206**, Fig. 27; 46), Yangshao and Ta-lai-tien in Honan (**217**, Pl. 6. 2; **242**, Pl. 9. 8–9), Lamma Island, near Hongkong (**256**, Part 9, Pl. 11), Shinjo in Formosa (**257**, Fig. 5) and Somrong Sen in Cambodia (**276**, Pl. 3. 15–16). Some of the Hung-shan-hou specimens and those of Lamma Island were found associated with bronze. Another specimen has been reported from a site at Hsuan-hwa in Hopei (**241**, Fig. 20. 3), which is supposed to be Han or Pre-Han in date.

SUMMARY

The ceramic art of prehistoric Szechwan may be summarized as follows:

COLOUR

In Szechwan we can find nearly all the colours of Chinese prehistoric wares, the main colours being red and grey. The plain fine black ware, Class D, may be taken as an intrusive element and the other types of black pottery are mainly variations of Class A. The brown variation of the grey wares in Classes A, B and F is probably produced by some chemical change that takes place when the pot is in the fire; therefore it is always a secondary colour. The white ware of Class E is clearly a late intrusion, so far found only at one site, in the Yangtse valley east of the gorges.

MATERIAL

The paste of Class C consists of fine clay carefully prepared, while the material of Class D is even finer. The paste of the black ware is of pure clay, while that of the red ware is sometimes tempered with fine sand. The coarse grey ware is made of material which is either naturally or artificially mixed with grains of sand, some of which are as big as a tiny pebble. The paste for Classes B and F is on the whole the same, a well-prepared clay mixed with fine sand, but the texture is different. Class B seems to be softer than F. The hardness of the latter ware is probably due to a higher temperature at firing. The paste of the white ware is very fine and no foreign material seems to be present.

THICKNESS

I have classified the thickness of the potsherds as thin, medium and thick: 4 mm. and less would be thin; 5–8 mm., medium; and over 8 mm. thick. With the exception of the fine black ware, which is mostly thin, and the coarse grey ware, which is almost always thick, the Szechwan potsherds are generally of medium thickness.

METHOD OF MANUFACTURE

The technique of making pottery in prehistoric Szechwan seems to be very simple indeed. Hand-modelling was the basic technique. At times a beater was also employed, as shown by some of the cord-marked sherds. The fragmentary condition of this collection makes it impossible to study the primitive methods of construction in a more detailed manner. The wheel-technique seems to have been introduced with the fine black ware and those sherds which were produced by this technique may be later in date than the handmade ware. The white ware and the hard grey ware are also wheelmade and may be considered the latest products of all the pottery classes.

SURFACE TREATMENT

I call a surface untouched when it is rough and uneven. I call it smooth when it is smooth and even, and this was effected probably with the wet hand. A polished surface is very smooth and was produced by rubbing with a pebble or a piece of bone, while a burnished surface is so highly polished that it becomes glossy. Technically, these four methods of surface treatment form a natural sequence of technical development: untouched, smoothed, polished and burnished. The sherds of coarse grey ware have only untouched or smoothed surfaces. The fine grey ware sherds of Class B are generally smoothed, but a few are polished. The red ware is polished; the black, burnished; and the hard grey ware either smoothed or burnished. The surface of the white ware seems to have been prepared for stamping, so an ordinary smooth surface would probably be good enough for the purpose.

The chronological sequence of the Szechwan pottery, which I have ventured to advance above, is based on the method of construction. It may be supported by reference to surface treatment. Classes A and B may be the earliest wares of the collection, and were still dominant when the other classes were introduced. Then probably came the red ware, with its technique of polishing. Polished grey sherds of Class B may be considered to be a combination of old and new techniques. These were followed by the fine black ware with its technique of burnishing. The later ware also shows this more developed method of surface treatment.

DECORATION

The majority of the Szechwan potsherds are either plain or cord-marked. Plain wares are common in the first four classes, A–D. Cord-marking, which may be taken as a type of stamping, was used only on the earlier wares, Class A and B, on which stamped, incised or appliqué patterns may also occasionally be found. Grooved and slipped decoration on these earlier wares are very rare and may have been a late development. The red ware is either slipped or painted, while the fine black ware is mostly plain and occasionally has incisions. The later pottery, Classes E and F, shows a general tendency to imitate basketry either by incision or by stamping.

The description of these six classes of pottery appears in Table 8.

TABLE 8. The Six Classes of Szechwan Pottery

Class	Type	Colour	Material	Thickness	Technique	Surface	Decoration
A	1–11	Grey Red Brown Black	Coarse	Thick	Handmade	Untouched Smoothed	Plain Cord-marked Grooved Incised Stamped Appliqué
B	12–16	Grey Brown Red	Fine	Medium	Handmade Wheel-made	Smoothed Polished	Plain Cord-marked Slipped Incised Appliqué
C	17–18	Red Grey	Fine	Medium	Hand-modelled	Polished	Plain Slipped Painted
D	19	Black	Fine	Thin	Wheel-made	Burnished	Plain Incised
E	20	White	Fine	Medium	Wheel-made	Smoothed	Stamped (Basketry)
F	21–24	Grey Brown	Fine (hard)	Medium	Wheel-made	Smoothed Burnished	Incised Stamped (Basketry)

TABLE 9. Distribution of the Six Classes of Pottery

Site	Class and Type of Pottery					
	A	B	C	D	E	F
Ku-lao-pei	2, 3, 10	—	17, 18	19	—	—
Hsien-jên-ch'iao	7	12, 15, 16	17	19	—	22, 23, 24
Site 5, I-ch'ang	2	—	—	—	20	—
Hsin-t'an	10, 11	—	17	—	—	—
Hsiang-hsia	6	—	—	—	—	—
Lower Wushan gorge	1, 2, 4	—	—	—	—	21
Upper Wushan gorge	—	14, 16	—	—	—	—
Tai-hsi	1, 2, 9	13, 16	17	—	—	—
Kao-wei-Tzŭ	1, 2, 4, 8	—	—	—	—	—
Hsiao-chiang	2, 7, 8	—	—	—	—	—
Lung-kai	8, 9	14	—	—	—	—
Wei-chou	—	—	18	—	—	—
Sites of Tao-fu	5	12	—	—	—	—

GEOGRAPHICAL DISTRIBUTION

The distribution of these six classes of pottery among the prehistoric sites of Szechwan is given in Table 9, which shows readily that the data are by no means complete. Only a few potsherds were discovered in the Min valley and, up to the present, none has been reported from the Ta-tu. These two valleys require a more thorough investigation. However, the geographical distribution of the various classes may be traced from these incomplete data and the conclusions to be derived therefrom deserve more than a passing notice.

Classes A and B both have a wide distribution to the east and south along the Yangtse and to the west in the Tao-fu valley. We may assume from this distribution that they may have dominated the other valleys as well. In fact they are the only classes which seem native to Szechwan. Class C was found only on the northern border in the upper Min valley at Wei-chou and on the eastern border in the Yangtse gorges. Class D appears only on the eastern border below the Yangtse gorges. Classes E and F were found also only in the eastern portion of the gorges (see Map 4).

In view of these facts, the distribution of the six classes cannot clearly support any proposed chronological sequence of the Szechwan pottery, such as I have just suggested on the basis of evolution in the method of construction and the surface treatment. Classes A and B, probably the earliest and possibly native wares, apparently dominated the entire region and were still the chief product of the prehistoric Szechwan potter even after the introduction of the other classes, as shown by their presence at many sites in association with sherds of those groups. Also it must be clearly stated that the native wares (Classes A and B) numerically form the major part of the collection. Class C is represented by a very moderate number of sherds, which must be considered as imports. Only a few sherds of Class D and one sherd of Class E were found and these were undoubtedly foreign wares. The number of sherds of Class F is higher than those of Class C, yet they are still very few in comparison with the large representation of Classes A and B.

The Szechwan pottery of Classes A and B may have survived in this region for a very long period of time. It would be very helpful if we could group these potsherds into sub-classes that might represent different stages of development. Unfortunately, the present material does not allow such a close study. The association of the pottery types in each site with other pottery types and

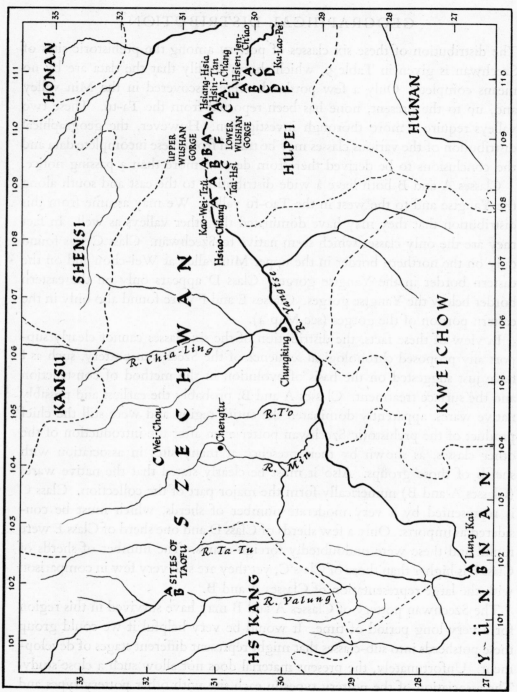

MAP 4. Distribution of the six classes of prehistoric pottery in Szechwan.

with the different groups of stone tools (Tables 4 and 9) does not throw much light on the problem. As for Class A, the sites of the Yangtse gorges have yielded all the eleven types, except Type 5, and three types have been found at Lung-kai, in Yünnan, and in the Tao-fu valley. But Lung-kai has produced Types 8 and 9, while Tao-fu only Type 5. The distribution of Class B is obscure also. Tao-fu in Hsikang produced Type 12; Lung-kai in Yünnan, Type 14; while the sites in the gorges contained Type 12, 15 and 16 in one, Types 14 and 16 in another and Types 13 and 16 in the third. Moreover, the wide range of colours, red, black, grey and brown, render it unlikely that they should be due solely to firing. The present classification of A and B pottery is based only on the coarseness and fineness of the paste. This is, of course, by no means conclusive. We need more material for a more detailed and satisfactory classification. For the present, however, the sixteen types may be regarded as one complex, intimately bound together as they are by common features of colour, construction, surface treatment and decoration.

The geographical distribution of the imported pottery classes, C, D, E and F, does not permit us to break them down definitely with respect to their relative chronological position. There is no way of telling which of the four classes was first introduced into this region. Technically, Classes E and F are probably younger than the other two classes, but three of the four types of Class F were found associated with those of Classes C and D at Hsien-jên-ch'iao. Table 9 and Map 4 indicate that Class C may have entered this region from the north as well as from the east, while Classes D, E and F all came in by the eastern route. But this does not necessarily mean that the red pottery appeared in Szechwan before the other three classes, in spite of the fact that similar pottery in northern Honan has been found underlying a black pottery which is like that of Szechwan Class D.

COMPARISON WITH NEIGHBOURING REGIONS

Before summing up this discussion on the prehistoric pottery of Szechwan, let us follow the two routes of communication out of this region into the North China plain and the routes which lead down into South China, Indo-China and the Malay peninsula, and see what light a comparison of Szechwan pottery with that of neighbouring regions may throw on the situation which has just been outlined.

The prehistoric pottery of North China and Manchuria has recently been carefully studied by Dr G. D. Wu. In his excellent work, *Prehistoric Pottery in China* (**246**, 154), he groups the pottery into six classes, which are given in Table 10.

TABLE 10. The Six Classes of North China Pottery (according to G. D. Wu)

Class	Colour	Material	Thickness	Technique	Surface	Decoration	Shape
I	Red	Fine	Medium	Hand-modelled	Polished	With or without painted designs	Bowls, basins, jars
II	Black	Fine	Thin	Wheel-made	Burnished	Plain	Bowls, basins, jars, *Ting*, beakers with ears and handles
III	Grey	Coarse	Thick	Moulded	Untouched	Plain	Water-jars with painted or round base, open pots, *Tou*, *Min*, *Li* and three other bronze shapes
IV	Brown or black	Coarse	Thick	Wheel-made	Smoothed	Plain or decorated	*Yen* and other hollow-legged vessels
V	White	Fine	Thick	Beaten	Smoothed	Plain or decorated	*Min*
VI	Grey	Coarse	Thin	Hand-made	Smoothed	Modelled in relief	Deep jars

Technically, Class A of Szechwan seems to have the characteristics which are typical of Class III in North China. They are both generally grey in colour, coarse in material, and hand-modelled, with occasional beater work (**246**, 37–8). The wares are generally thick, with plain, untouched or cord-marked surfaces. Some sherds of Class A, which may be of a later date, bear a resemblance to Class IV, which is mostly wheelmade. Class A of Szechwan was the most dominant ware in the region, while Class III of North China has been found widely distributed, with closely related wares occurring also in Manchuria, Mongolia and a large part of South China (**246**, 156).

Most of the prehistoric pottery of Indo-China seems to fall also into this class. In Tonkin, Annam and Laos, potsherds of this sort have been found, mostly in the upper neolithic level (**303**, 35). They are coarse and are decorated with cord-marked (**278**, Pl. 2; **281**, Pl. 6), comb-marked (**274**, Pl. 4; **278**, Pl. 3–4), stamped (**281**, Pl. 5) or incised (**274**, Pl. 2) patterns, and in several cases with perforations (**274**, Pl. 2). The ceramic art of Indo-China seems to have entered upon the scene at the same time as the polished stone tools, probably in the later part of the Indo-Chinese neolithic age.

The same situation seems to have prevailed in the Malay Peninsula as well. In general, most pottery here has been found associated with polished stone tools. In the excavation of Gua Debu, an undisturbed rock shelter at Baling, Kedah, a highly polished axe and some potsherds have been found in a level of chipped tools, and Collings, the excavator, suggests (**324**, 10) that the Gua Debu people might have obtained these objects from their neighbours who had a more advanced culture than their own. The dominant pottery of the Malay Peninsula consists of various types of coarse ware (**324**, Pl. 11, 15; **325**, Pl. 24–5), which also resemble those of Class A of Szechwan, but the fine yellow ware belongs to a different ceramic complex, which will be discussed presently in connexion with Class C.

In examining the association of pottery and stone implements along the Yangtse, in Table 4, the same situation seems to have prevailed also in Szechwan. Here practically all the sites in which pottery has been found contain polished stone tools also (whether or not accompanied by chipped stone tools) and almost no pottery has been found in sites which contain only chipped stone tools.

Class B of Szechwan seems to resemble Class VI of North China in several respects, namely the colour, the technique and the surface treatment. In North China, this ware has only been found at Pan-shan in Kansu (**246**, 156), which lies adjacent to north-west Szechwan. But other characteristics of the Szechwan sherds distinguish them from this coarse Pan-shan ware. Type 12 and some other types of Class B may possibly be the grey variation of the Lung-shan black ware, which will be discussed in connexion with Class D. The characteristic *tou* vessel of the Shantung ware is present in the Szechwan pottery too.

Class C of Szechwan is identical in almost every detail to Class I of North China, where it has a wide distribution over practically the whole plateau, with its eastern boundary of distribution coinciding with the boundary of the primary loess (**246**, 156). Not a single sherd of this ware, which Wu calls 'Red Pottery', and which is often referred to as 'Yangshao Pottery' has yet been found in Shantung. The excavation by K. Hamada of the Red Pottery dwelling site at Hung-shan-hou, in Ch'ih-fêng, Jehol, has established that this famous ware was present in Inner Mongolia (**206**). The discovery of similar pottery, with typical painted designs, in several districts in Sinkiang or Chinese

Turkistan by the Swedish Expedition, headed by Sven Hedin, has extended the boundary of the Red Pottery further west in China (211, 25; 36–7). The tracing of some cultural relationship between North China and western Asia in ancient times, a theory championed by many archaeologists, may be possible. The penetration of painted pottery into Szechwan, which lies not far south of the chief route of international communication from Loyang to Tun-hüang, should have been expected, but it is interesting to find that specimens of this ware have come into this marginal area not only from the north, by the upper Min valley, but also from the east, up the Yangtse.

The painted potsherd (324, Pl. 7. 23) from the undisturbed rock-shelter, Gua Debu, at Baling, in the Malay Peninsula, found associated with highly polished stone tools, seems to belong to another ceramic complex. 'It is of fine yellow ware with fine sand tempering. The outside has a design painted in red. The inside shows the marks of hand moulding' (324, 9).

The ware of Class D of Szechwan corresponds technically in every detail to the typical black ware first discovered in China at the Ch'êng-tzŭ-yai site near Lung-shan village in Shantung. Wu, the discoverer of the site (246, 23), reserves the term 'Lung-shan ware' for the black pottery found at this site and the term 'typical Lung-shan ware' for the same type of pottery found at any site other than Ch'êng-tzŭ-yai. Class D of Szechwan may be called a typical Lung-shan ware and is evidently identical to the Class II of North China, where its area of distribution is different from that of the red pottery of Class I. According to Wu (246, 156), the Black Pottery culture seems to cover the whole great North China plain, with its influence extending as far south as the Huai valley and Hang-chou Bay. It occupies a region mostly free from the influence of Red Pottery. On the other hand, the Black Pottery culture did not establish itself in the plateau area. In the western section of the plain, especially northern Honan, the Black Pottery directly succeeded the Red Pottery. A few black sherds have been noticed among the pottery finds from Hsi-yin in southern Shansi, a region which was probably in constant communication with western Honan in ancient times. The discovery of the black ware together with the red at the mouth of the Yangtse gorges indicates that the contact between these two cultures must have extended into north-western Hupei and evidently into Szechwan.

Although the paste of Class E of Szechwan is similar to that of the white pottery found in Honan, especially the well-known ware unearthed from the

Shang-Yin levels of Anyang, yet one must not confuse this ware with the Shang pottery of North China, which Wu groups in Class V. The technique of the two wares is completely different. The North China white pottery (246, 42) is generally thick and was either made by the beater method or by hand, while the I-ch'ang sherd is wheel-made. The Anyang ware is decorated with engraved designs of the typical conventional Shang style, while the I-ch'ang specimen bears a stamped textile pattern, which is akin to the designs which appear on the stamped fine grey ware (Type 14). Class V of North China has been found not uncommonly in northern Honan. Its earlier stages have, however, appeared over a wider area, in Shansi, Honan and Shantung (246, 156). It is true that thin fragments of pottery have been present with Class V specimens, yet it seems, for the present, too far-fetched to maintain that the Szechwan specimens belong to the same culture as Class V of North China.

In technique of manufacture and in ornamentation, Class F of Szechwan resembles in every detail Class E of the same region and it does not seem to have any similarity to the prehistoric wares of North China as analysed by Wu. It seems likely that these two classes of pottery represent a second wave of intrusion from a highly developed culture in the middle or lower Yangtse, or elsewhere in South China.

CONCLUSIONS

From the facts which have been outlined in the above discussion of the prehistoric pottery of Szechwan, there arise three important conclusions:

(1) Classes A and B are probably the native wares, belonging to one ceramic complex of long duration, but Class A has been found distributed far and wide in eastern Asia.

(2) This ceramic complex seems to have been associated more with the polished stone tools than with the other stone industries in Szechwan. The same has also been found in the prehistoric sites of Indo-China and in the Malay Peninsula.

(3) Classes C, D, E and F are probably imports into Szechwan. The first two classes came from North China, while the origin of the other two is so far unknown.

CHAPTER V

REVIEW OF SZECHWAN PREHISTORY

In the summary of the study of Szechwan stone implements, I divided the prehistoric period of the province into four stages. This is, of course, hypothetical and tentative in nature and should be subjected to revision after more extensive excavations. We have arrived at this hypothesis from the data we have at present: the typological study of the stone tools, their distribution in the four river valleys in the province, their association with pottery, their likeness to specimens from other parts of eastern Asia, the classification of the prehistoric sites along the Yangtse and the very faint stratigraphy at the Tai-hsi site, in Wu-shan.

The first two stages of prehistoric culture in this region belong probably to the mesolithic and early neolithic periods. The posited first stage is characterized by the use of chipped stone tools, many types of which are possibly late survivals of a chopping-tool technique, first developed during the palaeolithic period in eastern Asia.

Some time after the beginning of this stage, there arose a new technique in stone industry which was responsible for the development of the chipped-and-polished stone implements that were used side by side with the chipped tools.

Stages III and IV of Szechwan prehistory belong probably to the late neolithic and aeneolithic periods. In the former stage, chipping and edge-polishing techniques of the lithic industry still survived as the art of pecking was introduced. Our data, considered as a whole, do not suggest a long duration of the pecking industry.

The fourth and last stage marked the domination of a full polishing industry in the Min and Yangtse valleys while the Ta-tu and Ya-lung regions still retained the chipped industry. Pottery in the two western valleys has been found associated with chipped stone tools, but in the Yangtse it has been reported almost always associated with polished stone tools. Along this river, native pottery of Classes A and B has been found associated with potsherds of Classes C, D, E and F, which are probably all imported products.

Stage IV seems to have had a long duration in comparison with Stage III, and future investigation may allow us to divide this last stage of prehistoric culture in Szechwan into several sub-stages.

A few types of the polished stone tools of Szechwan, such as the vertical-grooved axe, the narrow-bit chisel and others, have been recognized as probably belonging to a cultural stage that may be represented by the cultural stratum of Hanchou. I am inclined to think that this stratum at Hanchou is probably somewhat earlier in date than the ceremonial structure of the same site. The typical Chou ceremonial jade implements found in large numbers in the structure suggest that it is probably early Chou in date or about 1000 B.C.

Archaeologically, for the several hundred years of the middle and late Chou periods that followed the period represented by the Hanchou culture, Szechwan is something of a blank. We need material to fill this gap that precedes the Ch'in-Han period.

A considerable body of archaeological data for this latter period (Ch'in-Han) has already been accumulated. In reporting the prehistoric sites of Szechwan, I have mentioned in passing the ruins of a Han dynasty fort found by Nelson at Tai-hsi, Wu-shan, and some remains of a city of the same date found by Graham at Han-chou. These are by no means the only archaeological sites in the province which actually belong to this period. The building of cities, which signifies the establishment of a Chinese population in this region, dates back to the year 310 B.C. (65, 3. 3 A), when Chang Yi, the great Ch'in general, erected the walls of Chengtu. Many cities in Szechwan were built in the Han dynasty, for example, the city of P'o-tao, built in 183 B.C. (65, 3. 4 B) and the city of Wu-yang, 131 B.C. (65, 3. 10 A). During the centuries of Chinese penetration, military stations or forts were established all over the province at strategic points. In addition, many other relics of the Han Period, literally hundreds of them, have been found and recorded. These include stone and brick pillars, stone and brick chambered graves, elaborate cave tombs, sculptures of various styles, stone monuments with inscriptions recording deeds of past heroes and many other remains. All these serve to confirm the literary accounts of this region for the early historical period.

The validity of the four stages of culture in prehistoric Szechwan becomes more evident when we compare the industries which characterize them with cultural remains from other parts of eastern Asia (see Table 6). In this comparison, we eliminate Japan and Kamchatka, because the neolithic culture of the island world of the Far East is considerably later in date than that of the continent and some of the known sites of Kamchatka which show a neolithic culture may be, as far as dates go, only a few hundred years old.

From the data available at present it seems likely that, during the palaeolithic period, all eastern Asia was dominated by a culture characterized by the use of chopping tools, which were made of entire pebbles and flakes. This is evident in North China and Siberia, and probably also in South China and Indo-China.

The palaeolithic culture with its chopping tool industry probably continued without any fundamental changes after the close of the Pleistocene; so it seems possible that a mesolithic stage existed in this part of the world.

It was probably during the mesolithic stage that the microlithic culture began to spread across the steppe region of central Asia and Mongolia. Specimens from the prehistoric sites in southern Siberia, Sinkiang, Mongolia and a part of Manchuria show similar characteristics: microlithic implements, perfection of technique in flint specimens, arrowheads and potsherds decorated by impressions of textile fabrics. The differences between the artifacts of these regions are not large enough to denote anything but local variations inside the same culture, which may be called the Gobi culture. Dating of this culture is difficult. In southern Siberia, where there is some stratigraphy, the culture occurs in mixed form. The desert sites, unfortunately, are situated on the eroded Gobi surface and almost no sites have been reported from which we can determine the cultural reference.

It is interesting to note that the microlithic culture area in eastern Asia did not extend into northern Siberia or the region south of the Yin-shan range in North China or east of the Hsing-an mountains in Manchuria. In fact, the area forms one of the easternmost links of the microlithic culture which covered the whole Eurasian and Afrasian steppe and desert zone.

It is evident that the microlithic culture enjoyed its popularity for a long time and prevailed into the late neolithic and aeneolithic periods in this region. In the Mongolian provinces of Ninghsia, Suiyüan, Chahar and Jehol microlithic implements have been found associated with polished stone tools of late neolithic date. In this common zone, these two industries probably influenced each other to a great extent. Szechwan lies far south of this zone and its prehistoric remains show nothing in common with the microlithic culture.

The mesolithic and early neolithic periods of North China proper are still a blank. Large quantities of chipped stone artifacts have been reported from Suiyüan, Chahar, Jehol, Fêngtien and Kirin, but only a few from Shensi,

Hopei, Honan and Shantung, and these are surface finds which have not been adequately described. It is most interesting to note that no chipped-and-polished stone implements have yet been found on the North China plain.

It is not until the late neolithic period that we begin to have precise information for this region. A number of sites have been reported and some of them have actually been excavated. They contain many kinds of pottery and polished stone tools as well as the older types of chipped tools. Polished stone arrowheads began to occur by the thousands. Our present knowledge of pottery in North China dates back only to Hou-kang, Hou-chia-chuang, Ta-lai-tien (246, 170) and Yangshao in Honan, and Hsi-yin-ts'un in Shansi. The stone artifacts of Groups C and D in Szechwan have close parallels in these sites of North China. Among the three types of chipped-pecked-and-polished stone objects of Szechwan that have parallels outside the province, two have been found in North China and Manchuria. 13 out of the 17 types of polished stone tools of Szechwan have parallels in North China and Manchuria. Among the imported pottery of the province, the red wares of Class C and the black wares of Class D have definitely been connected with North China. But no arrowheads have been found in Szechwan so far.

The prehistory of the region south of the Yangtse may be considered almost a blank. But the discovery of the Kwangsi caves, which are probably mesolithic in date, has added something to our knowledge of this region. The culture is characterized by the use of pebble and chipped implements. With the single exception of the decorated grinder, all the 11 types of stone tools from these caves are represented in the Szechwan collection. The Kwangsi cave dwellers did not use any pottery.

The Szechwan stone implements of Groups C and D have also some representation in South China. One type of chipped-pecked-and-polished stone implement of Szechwan has a parallel in Formosa, but the latter is probably of a later date. Among the 17 types of Szechwan polished stone tools, 11 have their parallels in South China. Some black pottery has been found in Hangchou, Chekiang, and the wares of Classes E and F of Szechwan may have had their origin in South China.

When we proceed beyond the southern borders of China into Indo-China, the situation is very clear. The prehistoric culture of Indo-China is represented by the Hoabinhien and Bacsonien series which were characterized first by the use of pebble and chipped stone implements and later on by the typical chipped-and-polished implements or protoneoliths. Among the 41 types of chipped tools of Szechwan, 34 have their parallels in large numbers in Indo-China and of the 11 types of West China chipped-and-polished implements six have numerous duplicates there. The stratigraphy that is lacking in Szechwan is supplied by many sites in Tonkin, in Annam and in Haut-Laos, and this stratigraphy shows that in Indo-China the major classes of stone implements appeared in every case in the same chronological order that we have postulated for Szechwan.

The culture represented by the last two stages of prehistoric Szechwan shows some striking differences, however, from the neolithic culture of Indo-China. No pecking technique, no red pottery and no black pottery have yet been found in Indo-China, and the late neolithic culture of this area is characterized by the highly developed, polished, shouldered celts of Somrong Sen, which are totally absent in Szechwan. However, 14 of the 17 types of Szechwan polished stone implements have their parallels in Indo-China and several types of the Class A pottery of Szechwan occur frequently there. Moreover, the absence of arrowheads in these two regions links them closely to each other and we may regard the differences between them as merely local variations.

The Malay peninsula presents a picture very similar to that of Indo-China.

From the data we have just reviewed above, it seems not unreasonable to conclude that the course of events in prehistoric Szechwan, as we have tentatively outlined it, may serve as a mirror to reflect what probably took place in a larger way in eastern Asia as a whole. In fact, if we leave out of consideration the microlithic culture that prevailed in southern Siberia, Sinkiang and Mongolia—which had a separate development—it seems possible, on the basis of the Szechwan evidence and what has already been established for other areas, to outline with some assurance the major succession of cultures in eastern Asia, from the end of the Pleistocene period to the beginning of historic times. This succession is as follows:

I. Mesolithic period. This is probably represented by: some of the chipped stone tools of Szechwan; some implements of the same group in North China, Sinkiang and Manchuria; the cave deposits of Kwangsi; some of the Hoabinhien and Bacsonien deposits of Indo-China; and some of the 'Sumatra type' deposits of the Malay peninsula.

II. Early neolithic period. This is probably represented by: some of the chipped-and-polished stone implements of Szechwan; some of the implements of the same group from Manchuria; and some of the 'Protoneolithic' deposits of Indo-China and the Malay peninsula.

III. Late neolithic period. This comprises probably two sub-stages: (A) which may be faintly represented by some chipped-pecked-and-polished stone tools found in Szechwan, North China and Manchuria, and (B) which is unquestionably represented by some of the polished stone tools and pottery of Szechwan, remains from some of the late neolithic sites in Manchuria, North China and South China, some of the Somrong Sen deposits of Indo-China and some of the late neolithic deposits of the Malay peninsula.

IV. Aeneolithic period. This is represented by: some of the polished stone implements and pottery of Szechwan; the deposit of the Hanchou cultural stratum; and most of the aeneolithic deposits of Manchuria, North China, South China, Indo-China and the Malay peninsula.

PART II

HAN BURIAL REMAINS IN SZECHWAN

THE KILN SITES OF CH'IUNG-LAI AND
LIU-LI-CH'ANG

SUNG BURIAL REMAINS IN SZECHWAN

CHAPTER VI

HAN BURIAL REMAINS IN SZECHWAN

INTRODUCTION

THE discovery of Han dynasty remains in the province of Szechwan has a long history. Li Tao-yüan (394), commentator of the *Shui ching*, was probably the first to call attention to the tomb stele that stood on the Chengtu plain in the sixth century A.D. These ancient relics, including cave burials, have never failed to interest scholars devoted to epigraphical studies. Careful recording of these remains has been made by celebrated antiquarians, such as Ou-yang Hsiu (403), Chao Ming-ch'êng (356), Hung Kua (380), Wang Hsiang-chih (423) and many others in the twelfth and thirteenth centuries. Local gazetteers of the province (426) also devoted substantial pages to the subject. In the early part of the nineteenth century, Liu Hsi-hai (395), whose *Chin shih yüan* is considered one of the most important works in Chinese archaeology, described thirteen steles and gate-towers of the Han period.

The first foreigner to write on the subject was probably Baber (347), the English traveller. However, he made the mistake of calling a stone coffin, discovered in Chungking in 1877, a water cistern.

In 1908 the Rev. T. Torrance (416, 417), an English missionary stationed in Szechwan, began to take an interest in these caves and burial mounds. He made extensive investigations and started to collect the mortuary objects that came from the burials. This beginning paved the way for the systematic collecting conducted by the West China Union University Museum, Chengtu.

General D'Ollone's visit in 1907 brought a French expedition under the leadership of Segalen (405) into the field. He succeeded in 1914 in locating almost all the monuments recorded in the works of the Sung scholars, and his report on the funerary art of the Han dynasty is a standard work on the subject.

Segalen was followed by a number of foreign archaeologists, notably Bishop (349) in 1916, Torii (414) in 1926 and Bedford (348) in 1936. Bishop and Bedford have published interesting accounts of the Pai-yai-tung near Lo-shan, while the Japanese scholar compared the cave burials along the Yangtse to those of his own country.

More substantial contributions were made by Graham (**368–373**), Curator of the University Museum from 1932 to 1941. He made several excavations and accumulated a rich collection for the Museum. Meanwhile, two other collections were being assembled in Chengtu, one by the Szechwan Museum (**390**) under the capable curatorship of Fêng Han-yi, and the other by the Hsi-ch'êng Museum. With three rich collections in one city, Chengtu has become the centre of study on this subject.

Then came the war in 1937, causing a great migration back into West China. Subsequent road building and air-field construction brought to light many important finds. Expeditions and excavations were conducted by leading archaeologists in many districts: Fêng Han-yi in Li-fan; Wei Chu-hsien, Kuo Mo-jo (**389**) and Ch'ang Jên-hsia (**352–355**) in Chungking; Shang Ch'êng-tsu and Huang Hsi-Ch'êng (**379**) in Hsin-tsin; Wu Gin-ding (**404**) in P'êng-shan; Jên Nai-hsiang (**386**) in Lu-shan; and Yang Chi-kao (**425**) in the Min and Chia-ling valleys. The province is rich in Han remains, and new tombs and caves are constantly being discovered. In the spring of 1948, a brick tomb was found in Chungking, two of whose bricks have an inscription reading: the fourth year of Yên-kuang, or A.D. 125.

The University Museum has tried to keep a record of all discoveries and, whenever possible, to preserve the material unearthed. Some of the more important and interesting specimens are described below. The various types of remains and the districts in which they were found are listed in Table 11.

BRICK TOMBS AND BURIAL CAVES

A traveller in Szechwan notices at once square openings on the hillsides and on the cliffs along the river banks. Natives inform him that these are Man-tzŭ-tung 蠻子洞 or aboriginal caves. They are, in fact, ancient tombs and are widely distributed throughout the province. Along the Yangtse river from the Hupei border across Szechwan to the foot of the Tibetan highlands, in the Chia-ling valley from Chungking up to the southern slope of the Ch'in-ling mountains, and in the basin of the Min river from Lu-hsien and I-pin up to Kuan-hsien and Li-fan, thousands of these caves can be seen. They are most numerous at Lo-shan, P'êng-shan and Hsin-chin, to the west of Chengtu. The caves are cut in the solid rock (Pls. 16–18) and are usually located high up on the face of a precipice.

TABLE 11. Types of Han burial remains, and districts in which found

Name of Districts	Type of Remains						
	Brick tomb	Tomb stele	Gate-tower	Stone animal	Stone coffin	Cave burial	Dwelling site
昭化 Chao-hua	1	—	—	—	—	—	—
成都 Chengtu	5	—	1	—	—	—	—
夾江 Chia-chiang	—	—	1	—	—	—	—
犍爲 Chien-wei	—	—	—	—	—	M	—
渠縣 Chü-hsien	2	2	7	4	—	—	—
重慶 Chungking	M	—	1	—	3	M	—
新津 Hsin-tsin	M	—	—	—	—	M	—
新都 Hsin-tu	M	—	1	—	—	—	—
宜賓 I-pin	2	—	—	—	—	—	—
閬中 Lang-chung	—	—	—	—	—	M	—
理番 Li-fan	3	—	—	—	—	—	—
樂山 Lo-shan	M	—	—	—	—	M	—
瀘縣 Lu-hsien	—	—	—	—	2	—	—
蘆山 Lu-shan	2	2	—	3	1	—	—
綿陽 Mien-yang	—	1	—	—	—	M	—
彭山 P'êng-shan	M	—	—	—	—	74	1
德陽 Tê-yang	—	—	1	—	—	M	—
梓潼 Tze-t'ung	1	—	3	—	—	—	—
資中 Tzŭ-chung	—	—	—	—	—	M	—
萬縣 Wan-hsien	1	—	—	—	—	—	—
雅安 Ya-an	1	1	1	3	—	—	—

A great number of these caves were opened and robbed of their contents long ago and have stood empty throughout the centuries. They are consequently convenient shelters for human beings as well as for wild animals. A set of caves near Lo-shan was used as a retreat in summer by Sung scholars of the twelfth century, who left a written record of their trips on the walls (**380**). Buddhist priests in one or two places appropriated caves for themselves and gave new names to those they occupied, such as Ku-fo-ssŭ 古佛寺 or Monastery of the Ancient Buddha; and Buddhist sculptures may be found side by side or superimposed on the original carving (Pl. 18. 3, 4). Some may have been occupied by the aboriginal tribes that invaded the Red Basin in later periods, and this probably accounts for the name Man-tzŭ-tung. But there are still hundreds of others, partly open or half-silted up, which could be profitably investigated.

From time immemorial, the Chinese have been greatly preoccupied with the interment of the dead. They have adopted many styles of grave construction, but, so far as we know, it was in Szechwan that the cave burial was most fully developed. It is very clear that these caves were originally tombs of the later Han dynasty in the first two centuries after Christ, as we shall see later in this chapter.

The people of Szechwan during this period had another way of disposing of their dead. This was by constructing a brick vaulted chamber, placing the coffin in it and erecting a dirt mound over it; on the surface of the ground, walls and gates, stone animals and tablets were erected to denote the burial. Many such stone monuments and tomb structures on the surface of the ground have been reported over the whole area of the province, and hundreds of vaulted chambers underground have been carefully excavated by archaeologists in recent years. There is enough evidence to show that the cave burials and the brick tombs are contemporaneous in date.

We know that since the fifth century B.C. the kings of the feudal states began constructing their tombs while they were still living. The custom was closely followed by later emperors, and the Han monarchs went so far as to decree that one-third of the national income should go to the building of their permanent resting place. They went into it on a grand scale, following an elaborate plan carefully prepared by court architects.

According to a chapter on rituals in the *Hou han shu* 後漢書 (**365**), a royal tomb covers an area of 700 *mou*; 100 *mou* are devoted to the grave-pit, which is 130 ft. deep. The pit itself is outlined by a wall and covered with a mound 120 ft. high. The royal coffin is placed in a chamber 20 sq. ft. by 17 ft. high. From the chamber four passages are constructed leading to four doors in the four directions. In these galleries are deposited a chariot, six horses, weapons, silk fabrics, gold and jade utensils, rice and grains, domestic animals, sacrificial vessels, funerary objects and other valuable articles for the royal spirit. In the galleries there are also false-doors, with swords, bows and arrows, and traps which go into action automatically at the approach of an intruder. The tomb is of stone construction in which are stone beds and screens. The walls are decorated with scenes.

The mound on the surface of the ground, the history continues, is round or square in shape, made of a mixture of earth, sand, lime and vegetable fibres, and more than 100 ft. high. A thick wall surrounds the mound with four openings in the four directions. In front of each entrance is a stone temple for holding sacrificial ceremonies, which is connected to the front gate by a road called *Shên-tao* 神道, the 'spirit's way'. The gate, also of stone, is a tower of three stories. There are human and animal figures in front of the temples as well as in front of the gate. A stone stele stands in front of the tomb, and there is a porter's gate beyond the tower which marks the limit of the royal cemetery.

It is also recorded that royal maidens of lower rank could be buried outside the porter's gate, while important officials could be interred near it.

This was the general plan of a royal tomb in the Han dynasty, and students of Chinese archaeology may verify this record with the series of Han royal tombs still to be seen on the hillsides of Sian and Loyang (346).

The belief in a future existence was not a monopoly of the royal family. People of all ranks, high and low, rich and poor, cherished the same faith. This gave rise to many social customs which furnished a background for tomb building. It is interesting to note that the Han emperors did not refuse to have their tomb plans copied. These structures, therefore, became the fashion of the day and were freely imitated by their subordinates. The tombs of Ho Kuang 霍光 and Tung Hsien 董憲 in Shensi (346), the Han burials in western Shantung (366, 367, 383, 393, 406, 411) and the stone burials of prominent officials of Nan-yang in Honan (412) are typical examples. They are simply royal tombs on a smaller scale, the Han tombs in Szechwan being no exception.

The brick tombs of Szechwan are, as a rule, very carefully constructed. The vault may be one of three types. The simplest one is constructed of large curved bricks with socketed joints forming a round arch. The second type is built with wedge-shaped bricks, which naturally make a curved arch when laid on top of each other with the thicker end of the bricks to the outside. The last may be called a 'Gothic arch', as it is supported by a frame of slightly curved and wedge-shaped stone slabs, on which are laid elongated bricks with socketed joints (Pl. 21).

The tomb is usually rectangular in shape and consists of two compartments. The back compartment serves as the coffin chamber while the front one is the gallery where mortuary objects are deposited. The door of the tomb is sealed with bricks of various sizes.

Originally, there were articles of gold, silver, jade, bronze and iron, besides numerous coins and clay mortuary objects in the gallery and the tomb chamber. But practically all the tombs were rifled many centuries ago, the looters removing all the valuable objects, in most cases, however, leaving the pottery and the bronze and iron objects behind.

When we attempt to study the remains on the surface of the ground, however, we have a more difficult problem. Most of the mounds, as well as the structures which used to mark the burial, have long been levelled to the ground—nowhere can a complete structure be seen. Yet remains of these monuments still exist, here and there, scattered over the vast territory of Szechwan.

Several tomb steles have been reported. The stele of the Chiang Wan 蔣琬 tomb in Mien-yang is only a large fragment of rectangular rock. However, the tomb stele of Kao Yi 高頤 in Ya-an is better preserved (Pl. 20. 5). It consists of two pieces of stone: a flat block carved in bas-relief, serving as the pedestal, and a tall rectangular slab with a round top, as the body. The Fan Min 樊敏 tomb stele at Ya-an (386) is a huge structure with the pedestal in the shape of a turtle—the earliest-known tablet to have such a pedestal. The stele also has a head stone in the shape of a semicircle, which is richly decorated with a dragon design in bas-relief. This may be the forerunner of the decorated head stones in later steles which usually feature a pair of dragons entwined with each other. Lu-shan has the head stone of the Yang T'ung 楊統 stele, which is semicircular in shape and is decorated with two deep grooves.

Remains of the gate-towers are more common, the P'ing-yang tower 平陽闕 of Mien-yang being the most famous of all. It is a structure of two stories, richly decorated with classical designs in low relief. The gate-tower of Fêng Huan 馮煥, a tomb in Chü-hsien, is most interesting because parts of the stone enclosure of the mound may still be found attached to the gate (Pl. 20. 1). This district still possesses seven broken towers, mostly of stone construction (Pl. 20. 3, 4, 6–8). Other remains may also be found in Tse-t'ung, Chia-chiang, Ya-an, Chungking and Tê-yang (**361**).

Some of the stone animals which had guarded the entrance to these tombs have also been found, though mostly weather-worn or badly damaged. Two lions, one crouching animal and a human figure have been found in Chü-hsien; three animals from the Fan Min tomb in Ya-an are still in existence. Two of these animals, still facing each other, are probably in the same position that they occupied centuries ago. A stone lion and goat in Lu-shan probably belonged to the tomb of Wang Hui 王暉 (Pls. 80; 81. 8), the lion having a pair of wings on its shoulders. It is most likely that the famous chimera sculptures of the Six Dynasties have their origin in the Han dynasty. A stone goat and a human head from Hsin-tsin, now in the University Museum (Pls. 81, 82) are good examples of the style and technique of the Szechwan sculptor.

The dating of the brick tombs presents no difficult problem because a number of them are actually dated with inscriptions, either on the bricks or on the stone coffins. The dates range from A.D. 60 to A.D. 226 as follows:

	(A.D.)		(A.D.)
The third year of Yung-p'ing	60	The eighth year of Yüan-ch'u	121
The first year of Chien-ch'u	76	The second year of Yen-kuang	123
The first year of Yung-yüan	89	The fourth year of Yen-kuang	125
The eighth year of Yung-yüan	96	The tenth year of Chien-an	205
The first year of Yüan-hsing	105	The fourteenth year of Chien-an	209
The first year of Yen-p'ing	106	The seventeenth year of Chien-an	222
The first year of Yung-ch'u	107	The fourth year of Chien-hsing	226
The fifth year of Yüan-ch'u	118		

The brick tombs of Szechwan serve to portray the funerary practice and religious belief of the people, to illustrate the artistic style and technique of this period and, more important, to throw light on the caves hewn in the solid rock on the cliffs mentioned above. Furthermore, the strange burial customs of Szechwan can be more readily understood when we have the brick tombs for reference.

The caves of Szechwan vary greatly in size, probably according to the wealth of the owner. It is also interesting to find that a simple cave is merely a replica of a brick burial. Caves of this type may be found in large numbers at P'an-lung-shan 盤龍山, Lang-chung or at Po-hsi 柏溪, near Chungking. The

P'an-lung-shan cave consists of two sections. The inner chamber is about 7 feet square, the gallery about 6 ft., and the arched ceiling about 7 ft. high, spanning both rooms. It is evident that the smaller compartment was meant to be the gallery where the mortuary objects were deposited, and the inner compartment was the coffin chamber. Accurate measurement of the interior of a cave is not always possible, because most of the roofs have collapsed, and silt has accumulated to a considerable depth on the floor throughout the years. At the mouth of the cave, circular door sockets or deep horizontal grooves were cut to receive hinged doors or heavy stone slabs intended to seal the tomb. In many cases earth was piled up against the opening to conceal the burial.

In Chiu-shih-kang 九 石 崗 near Chungking, a series of six caves has been found side by side, above the openings of which there are a series of animals sculptured in low relief. They recall sculpture of the same type characteristic not only of the brick burials in Szechwan but also of the tombs of the same period in other parts of China. An inscription has been found on the side of a door giving the name of the owner as well as the date of burial. These may be taken as corresponding to the stele and the stone animals of a brick burial.

The largest and most ornate caves are those of Pai-yai-tung 白 崖 洞 at Lo-shan. The group consists of four caves that penetrate the cliff to a depth of more than a hundred feet. They are large enough to hold several thousand people at a time (Pls. 16–19).

In front of the caves there is a large open space about 90 feet square. This was cut out of the cliff leaving two square columns in the middle separating the court into two sections. At the entrance to the caves, the surface of the cliff is decorated with architectural designs in low relief. The sculptures represent buildings with bracketed pillars, columns with elaborate capitals, panelling, beam-ends, tiles and so forth. These seem to have been intended to portray the gate-tower and the enclosure that would have stood in front of the usual burial mound.

There are also stone animals at the entrance to guard the tomb, but destructive forces throughout the ages have deformed them almost beyond recognition.

The stone doors which were made to fit into the sockets at the entrance are decorated with a bird design or that of a mask, carved in low relief. The passage that leads into the cave should be considered the 'spirit's way' of the brick burial. It is 40 to 50 ft. long. At the end of the passage, there is another opening with a horizontal groove to receive a stone slab to seal it. This may be taken either as a false door or as the inner gate of the brick tomb. Inside this gate, the gallery continues into an elaborately carved coffin chamber with multiple recesses and side apartments. The walls, the coffins and the side apartments in the chamber are also decorated with designs in low relief, possibly the same as a royal tomb chamber.

The ceiling of the caves is about 7 ft. high, but no decoration has been noted. The floor of each of the caves usually rises slightly towards the interior, thus allowing the water which seeps through the cave walls to drain outside.

Other groups of large caves may be found at Shih-tzǔ-wan 柿 子 灣 near Lo-shan, at P'êng-tzǔ-hao 彭 子 浩 in Mien-yang and in Chien-wei. They all have been found to follow a general plan of construction, consisting of at least six essential parts, the stele, the outer gate, the spirit's way, the inner gate, the gallery and the coffin chamber.

The mortuary objects recovered from these caves are not essentially different from those found in the brick burials. In many cases, bricks were used in large numbers in the construction of the inner compartments of the caves. The designs carved on the doors and the walls, and on the stone coffins and cabinets (Pls. 70–78), usually chiselled out of the solid rock, were of the same subject matter and in the same style as those used to decorate the brick tombs, though on a larger scale. However, we noticed one exception, and that was the presence of a considerable number of large cylindrical pottery tubes, which were sections of a pipe line that had been constructed in the cave for drainage. The pipe is covered with cord-marks (**417, 94–5**).

Some of the caves are dated with inscriptions on the walls or on the bricks. They range from A.D. 102 to A.D. 181, as follows:

	(A.D.)		(A.D.)
The fourteenth year of Yung-yüan	102	The fourth year of Hsi-p'ing	175
The third year of Yung-chien	128	The fifth year of Hsi-p'ing	176
The fourth year of Yung-shou	158	The third year of Kuang-ho	181
The fifth year of Yên-hsi	162		

From the data we have just presented, it seems reasonable to conclude that the cave burial of Szechwan developed out of the brick tomb. The construction of the cave tombs began half a century after the introduction of the brick burial. It is very clear that the latter type was a part of the whole cultural-complex that flourished in China during that time. Brick tombs of this type have been found in every province of the great Han empire (**351, 378, 384, 385,**

408, 412, 419, 420, 421, 422), including Korea (401, 407, 376, 387), Manchuria (374, 375, 377, 381, 396, 399, 400, 410, 415, 427), Mongolia (388, 397, 398, 418, 428) and Indo-China (382, 402). Szechwan is but a western branch of this great Han culture.

However, the cave burial seems to be of an alien nature. The excavation of caves in solid rock for the preservation of the dead has not been found in other parts of the eastern Asiatic continent. Did the people of Szechwan invent this novel idea themselves or did they import it? This is a problem that challenges archaeologists who are interested in this field.

BURIAL REMAINS

The Han remains in Szechwan may be classified into three groups according to material: pottery, stone and metal.

The majority of the pottery is grey in colour, ranging from very dark to light. Very often the surface has been discoloured or covered up by reddish sand and dirt or limestone encrustment (Pl. 36, 6). Some of the vessels were well fired, resulting in a light brick-red or yellow colour which is probably due to the presence of iron in the clay. The surface of the pottery is smooth on the whole. Some of the pots are white-slipped, painted or polished in black, a few are washed in yellow, and, more rarely, some are covered with a greenish lead glaze.

The smoothness of the surface seems to have been achieved in two ways: one, by smoothing it with a wet hand, and the other by rubbing it with a smooth object, possibly a pebble. Neither of these processes seems to have been done with the help of a wheel, and the marks on the surface indicate that polishing was applied from various directions. Some of the vessels reveal other forms of surface treatment, such as cord-marking—especially on cooking utensils—impressions with finger-nails, incisions with pointed tools, and stamped designs in bas-relief.

The Han pottery is of a fine paste. It does not seem to have undergone a high temperature in firing and is rather soft. For the making of utensils and figurines, the paste apparently included no foreign material for tempering, but in the case of coffins and cooking vessels, the paste is tempered with particles of sand, and the pottery is always better baked.

The potters were comparatively advanced in their art. Three basic techniques are distinctly noticeable in the ware: wheel-making, shaping in a mould and modelling by hand. The wheel was used to produce bowls, cups, vases, pots and other food receptacles, and sacrificial vessels. Figurines, animals, bricks and tiles, houses and rockeries were usually shaped in moulds. A simple small object was usually cast in one piece, while larger articles were made in parts and assembled afterwards. Modelling was very common, and experienced masters produced excellent pieces of sculpture in clay. The weasel shown on Pl. 39 was first modelled, then scraped into the desired form. This technique has resulted not only in portraying the moving rhythm of the body, but also the tension of the muscles. Many of the oval-shaped *yü-shang* cups were made by gouging out and scraping a lump of clay (Pl. 54. 1–3).

Grave pottery was made for the purpose of accompanying the dead into the other world, and the vessels, mostly models, represent practically everything that might have been used in the lifetime of the deceased. They are classified as follows:

COOKING VESSELS (Pls. 52–53)

Tsao 竈, stove; *kuo* 鍋, boiler; *fu* 釜, cauldron; *tsêng* 甑, steaming vessel.

CONTAINERS (Pls. 48, 51)

Lei 罍, large beverage holder; *hu* 壺, pot; *tun* 敦, small container; *p'ing* 瓶, vase; *p'ou* 瓿, jar; *t'an* 罎, beverage holder; *kuan* 罐, drinking vessel; *i* 匜, ewer.

DRINKING AND EATING VESSELS (Pl. 54)

Tsun 尊, goblet; *pei* 杯, cup; *yü-shang* 羽殤, oval-shaped wine cup; *min* 皿, food receptacle; *yu* 卣, wine vessel; *po* 鈢, rice vessel; *wan* 盌, bowl.

SACRIFICIAL VESSELS (Pls. 48–51)

Ting 鼎, tripod; *hsien* 甗, steaming vessel; *tou* 豆, food receptacle; *têng-t'ai* 燈台, lamp; *po-shan-lu* 博山爐, incense burner; *ch'in* 琴, lute; *chung* 鐘, bell; *to* 鐸, small bell; *chang-tso* 杖座, banner stand?

ARCHITECTURAL MATERIAL (Pls. 25–33; 44–47)

Tile, usually with a disc at the end; brick, in various sizes and with decoration; pipe, for drainage, with cord-marks; house, several types; tower, several types; pond, with bridge, snail, fish, ducks, frogs, etc.; rockery, with monkeys and lute-players.

FIGURINES (Pls. 34–37)

Male and female figurines: musician, dancer, warrior, acrobat, etc.

ANIMALS (Pls. 28–46)

Dog, pig, cow, goat, rabbit, hen and chickens, rooster, duck, pigeon, tiger, monkey, goose, dragon, snail, turtle, frog, fish, weasel, etc.

OTHERS (Pl. 24)

Table, boat, chariot, well-head, coffin, etc.

With the exception of the bricks and the banner stands, the pottery vessels are usually plain and simple in decoration. A few are painted in red or white.

The bricks used in the construction of a Han tomb (Pls. 25–33) are of many varieties. Plain bricks of ordinary shape are used for the floor pavement, but those for the walls and vaulted ceiling vary greatly in shape and in size. These are usually decorated with rich patterns in low relief. However, no large ornamented hollow bricks, so commonly used in North China (**413, 424**) at this time, have been found so far in Szechwan.

The designs on the Szechwan bricks may be classified into five types:

1. Geometrical pattern of straight and curved lines, showing combinations of squares, triangles, rhombus, steps, circles, semicircles and including the coin and the discoidal pi patterns (Pls. 25–26).

2. Floral pattern with twisted branches and leaves; the tree of life or the tree of wealth (Pl. 26. 6–7, 14–15).

3. Animal figures, with phoenixes in symmetrical arrangement, galloping horses, guardians of the four directions; the dragon, tiger, snake-and-turtle and bird; animals of the cycle—rat, cow, tiger, hare, dragon, etc. (Pls. 26. 11–13; 27–28); some are painted in red (Pl. 33).

4. Scenes of daily life, such as cooking, hunting, feasting, processions, acrobatic performances, salt manufacturing, chess-playing, etc. (Pls. 29–31).

5. Inscriptions giving the date of the burial (Pl. 32) or a traditional phrase, such as *yi tzǔ sun*, 宜子孫. 'May you have sons and grandsons!', *yi hou wang* 宜侯王 'May you receive the status of a prince or a marquis!', *fu kuei* 富貴 'Wealth and honour', and so forth.

The pottery of Szechwan illustrates not only the burial customs but also the life and art of the period. Unlike the material unearthed in North China, the collection reveals some special characteristics typical of this region. The three-legged stove (Pl. 55), the rabbit (Pl. 38. 9), the water pipe (417, 94–5), the earthenware coffin (Pl. 24. 3), the banner stand (Pls. 48. 3–4; 49) and several other types have not been found on the northern plain. On the other hand, horse and camel figures, which have been found in large quantities in the north, are almost completely lacking in Szechwan.

Three types of coffins have been found in the Han tombs of Szechwan. A large majority of them were probably made of wood; faint traces of this material have been observed in the graves.

Earthenware coffins are very common. These are generally 6–7 ft. long, 2–4 ft. high and 1–2 ft. wide. The sides are about $\frac{1}{2}$–1 in. thick. The body is in one piece as is also the lid. How the potter managed to construct and fire such a ponderous object without fault in shape or texture is a mystery. They are all plain, with four perforations in the bottom, which might have been meant to keep the body of the deceased dry (Pl. 24. 3).

A number of red sandstone coffins or sarcophagi have also been found in the graves. They are larger in size than the pottery coffins and are richly ornamented with designs in low relief (Pl. 24). The stone coffin of Wang Hui discovered at Lu-shan is a very interesting example (Pls. 22–23). The front of the structure is decorated with a mask on the lid, and a scene of a human figure coming out of a half-opened door is carved on the coffin itself. On the frame of this door is an inscription of thirty-five characters recording that Wang Hui, the *Shang chi shih* was buried there in A.D. 222. 故 上 計 史 王 暉 伯 昭 以 建 安 拾 六 歲 在 辛 卯 九 月 下 旬 卒 其 拾 七 年 六 月 甲 戌 葬 嗚 呼 哀 哉 (386). The coffin faced south, and a dragon is carved on the left wall, a tiger on the right and a snake-and-turtle on the end. Other coffins have been reported to be more elaborately decorated than this, but few have inscriptions.

All the stone sculptures recovered from the brick tombs and burial caves are of red sandstone—very soft, coarse-grained material and a very poor medium for fine carving. It does not take a high polish and is very hard to preserve. With the exception of the tomb stele, the gate-towers and the animals, however, most of the sculptures were found under cover, and, therefore, are better preserved. Technically, they are either in low or high relief or in the round.

Sculpture in low relief is by far the most common of them all. It may be thought of as a translation of painting on to stone. The composition, consisting chiefly of conventionalized human or animal figures, is generally very simple with neither background nor perspective. It is reproduced on the flat

surface of a stone with the background chiselled away. This is done systemati-
cally so that the marks or grooves of chiselling become a pattern of parallel,
horizontal or diagonal lines. In most cases, the scene, either a procession of
human figures or galloping animals, is slightly retouched to give the necessary
details. Most of them are very carefully done (Pls. 24; 70–78), while a few are
crudely carved.

The style and execution of these sculptures is linear in quality, sure and vigor-
ous, similar to those found in Honan and Shantung (**357, 358, 364, 383, 392,
393, 412**). But the composition seems to be closer to the former than to the
latter. The compactness of the Wu Liang Tz'ŭ sculptures does not seem to be
present in Szechwan.

Some excellent examples of Szechwan sculpture in high relief are preserved
on the Fêng Huan stele, the Shên and the P'ing-yang gate-towers (**405**). The
fighting animals, the racing riders, the mask, the dragon, the tiger and the red
bird all fit admirably into the given space. The only specimen of this type in
the University Museum is the fleeing doe reproduced on Plate 79. One senses
at once that a hunter must be very close behind the creature.

There is a monumental effect in the Szechwan sculptures in the round. They
are usually simple but powerful, as for example the animals guarding the
spirit's way (Pls. 80–81), which are in the same tradition as those that guarded
the ancient tombs in Shantung and in Kiangsu. The little stone figurines
unearthed in Suifu (Pl. 81. 3–6) are crude, but they possess an air of shyness that
is compelling. The artist did not even try to remove the chiselling marks on
them. Two figurines in the Szechwan Museum are of the same workmanship,
though they are about 2½ ft. high. The head, reproduced on Plate 82, shows
the same style of execution, but in spite of its badly damaged features, it is
as fresh and powerful as it was centuries ago. The crouching goat (Pl. 81. 9)
represents another style—the use of high relief on sculpture in the round.

Some small pigs carved out of white soapstone or marble have been collected
(Pl. 81. 1–2). They are similar to those commonly found in the Han tombs at
Ch'ang-sha, Hunan (**408, 409**).

Metal articles recovered from the Han tombs of Szechwan present several
interesting problems. Copper and bronze articles and vessels were used as
extensively as those of iron. As a rule, coins, sacrificial vessels, daily utensils
and military equipment were of the former material, while weapons, agricultural tools and craftsmen's implements were of iron.

The types noticed are as follows:

SACRIFICIAL VESSELS AND DAILY UTENSILS (Pls. 55–59; 62–64)

Ting 鼎, tripod; *p'an* 盤, plate; *hsi* 洗, basin; *hu* 壺, pot; *chung* 鍾, vase; *lei* 罍, beverage container; *p'ou* 瓿, jar; *ching* 鏡, mirror; *chiao-tou* 鐎斗, charcoal burner; *hung-lu* 烘爐, wine heater; *yü-shang* 羽殤, oval-shaped wine cup.

WAR IMPLEMENTS AND MILITARY EQUIPMENT (Pls. 61, 68–69)

Ko 戈, halberd; *mao* 矛, lance-head; *tao* 刀, knife; *chien* 劍, sword or dagger; *nu-chi* 弩機, cross-bow mechanism; *tsu* 鏃, arrowhead; *ch'e-shih* 車飾, chariot fitting.

AGRICULTURAL IMPLEMENTS AND CRAFTSMEN'S TOOLS (Pls. 61, 69)

Chui 錐, awl; *tso* 鑿, chisel; *ch'u* 鋤, hoe; *ch'an* 鏟, spade; *lien* 鐮, scythe; *ch'iu* 鍫, branched tool.

OTHERS (Pls. 65–68)

Various types of coins: *wu-shu* 五銖, *pan-liang* 半兩, *huo-ch'uan* 貨泉, *huo-pu* 貨布, *ta-ch'uan wu-shih* 大泉五十, etc.; *ch'ien shu* 錢樹, coin-tree; *tsan* 簪, pin; *ting* 釘, nail.

The metal wares of Szechwan cannot rival the products of North or East China. They are mostly plain and of common types. However, we have found a number of new types, such as the coin-tree (Pls. 66–67), the handled mirror (Pl. 62. 2), the wine heater (Pl. 58. 2) and the animal figure (Pl. 65). These are very elaborately cast. A number of pewter vases with lids of the same material have also been found (Pl. 60. 1). The shape reminds one of the Ming blue-on-white pottery ware.

Three fragments of lacquer, possibly legs of a table, are preserved in the Hsi-ch'êng Museum. The pieces are of plain dark brown lacquer with no decoration. Nothing resembling the beautiful treasures of the Korean and Hunan tombs has yet been found.

CONCLUSION

The material presented in this chapter is of unusual interest because it illustrates the life of the people in a province which had become a great centre of expansion in the Han dynasty. The Ch'in-Han emigrants found the 'Land of the Four Rivers' a paradise for adventure and achievement. A new spirit came over the region. Development took place in every possible direction, and a feeling of expansion filled the air. The newcomers exploited all the natural resources in agriculture, in arts and crafts and in industry. They pushed their borders ever farther back into the hills and mountains, their roads penetrated far and wide, and merchandise flowed in and out in a continuous stream. Energy and power were in the blood of the people, and wealth and prosperity brought leisure and gaiety into their lives.

Art is an expression of life. An observer of these mortuary remains of Szechwan cannot help but feel the dynamic energy of these people. Their daily life, as represented in the pottery, stone and metal objects, included salt-making, mulberry-leaf gathering, circus performance, as well as drinking and feasting, riding and hunting, music and dancing, and processions of many kinds. Their passionate and expressive vitality may be found in the robust curves of a horse, the bulging muscles of a weasel, the jaw of a fighting bear or the charging of a winged dragon. There is power in the grand chariot, wealth in the fancy peacock, romance in the dancing girl, humour in the archaic smile, playfulness in the teasing of a monkey, and leisure and gaiety in drinking and carousing, as well as in chess-playing.

Their spiritual life was as full of activity as their material life had been. The four quarters of their abode were guarded by the red bird, the black warrior, the blue dragon and the white tiger. Their enemy would come face to face with an angry mask as he approached their door. They believed in a supernatural force that would arise at the union of the male and the female, the *yang* and the *yin*, or the sun and the moon. Moreover, they intended to enjoy their life after death and were well provided for the journey into the other world.

The style of the Szechwan mortuary art in the Later Han dynasty is as rich and full as had been the life of the people. In general, the art followed the North Chinese pattern that was developed along the Yellow River. The tomb structures, the mortuary pottery, the stone sculpture and the metal tools and objects are clearly in the North China tradition. But the lively animal style of the Northern Nomads, the simplicity of the north-western highland forms and the playful subject matter seem to have met in the melting pot of Szechwan to create eventually a style that is definitely a school of its own.

CHAPTER VII

THE KILN SITES OF CH'IUNG-LAI AND LIU-LI-CH'ANG

AMONG the men of letters who lived in the province of Szechwan, none is more famous than Tu Fu, one of China's greatest poets. Tu Fu came to Chengtu in A.D. 756 and occupied a straw hut in the western suburb of the city. During his stay in the province, he was very much impressed by the fine porcelain manufactured by the potters at Ta-yi, about 60 miles west of Chengtu. In one of his poems, or rather, a personal note, written probably shortly after 760 to his friend Wei, the poet described this white ware. The verse may be translated freely as follows:

Porcelain manufactured at Ta-yi is light and firm;
When tapped it rings like mournful jade, and its fame has spread in Chengtu.
The white bowls in your house triumph over frost or snow,
Pray have pity on my request and quickly send one to my straw hut.

Throughout the centuries, students of Chinese art have speculated on what the Ta-yi porcelain was like and where the kiln of this beautiful ware might be found, and, so far, they have been unable to locate the site (*see* p. xvi). It is not the custom among scientists to accept poems as data.

THE CH'IUNG-LAI KILN SITE

It was in 1936 that a group of interesting pottery began pouring into the market of Chengtu, and it soon became known that the objects had been unearthed in Ch'iung-lai, about 17 miles to the south of Ta-yi. Although the discovery of the site near Ch'iung-lai does not prove that it was the source of Tu Fu's porcelain, yet the investigation of the remains and the collecting of the ancient wares *in situ* has actually added a new page to the history of ceramic art in West China. Dr Graham (**429**), and Mr Bedford (**430**) and I visited the site in September, 1936, and made a large collection of the material for the University Museum.

The site is situated along the western bank of the river, Ta-nan-ho 大南河 outside the west gate of Ch'iung-lai (see Map 5). It is approximately a thousand feet long and in places four or five hundred feet wide. With the river in front of it, this was an ideal place for a ceramic factory, because there was naturally no transportation problem (Pl. 83. 1). But the plant was abandoned centuries ago, and on the site there is a string of hillocks of debris where the broken pottery and other refuse is probably forty or fifty feet deep. On one of the steep mounds, there stands a Taoist temple built probably many centuries ago (Pl. 83. 2). The villagers and soldiers were digging feverishly into one of the small hills from all sides in search of some not too damaged pieces that they could sell. So insistent was their burrowing that they were endangering the foundations of the crumbling temple on the summit of the refuse heap.

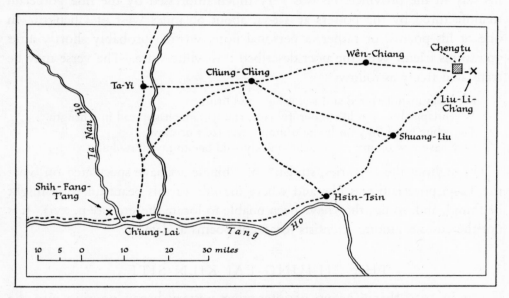

MAP 5. Location of the kiln sites of Ch'iung-lai and Liu-li-ch'ang.

Recent news from Chengtu records the acquisition by the Szechwan Provincial Museum of General T'ang Shih-tsun's 唐 式 遵 collection, which amounts to no less than 20,000 specimens. General T'ang was stationed in Ch'iung-lai while the digging was in progress and was reputed to have obtained and preserved the cream of the Ch'iung-lai ware (**431**).

Local collectors had advanced a theory that the factory was overwhelmed by a flood and abandoned. This is very unlikely. The site is high above the river level, and a flood of such magnitude as to destroy it, would have submerged the whole Chengtu plain lying to the east. Such a disastrous flood is not recorded in history. Besides, the kiln refuse was heaped up in mounds and is not found scattered over a wide area of the countryside, as would be the case if the raging waters of the Ta-nan-ho had overwhelmed the kiln. It seems more likely that it was abandoned through the exhaustion of local raw material. We have found *in situ* lumps of white clay which was not native to the region. This may have been brought in when the local material was getting low.

The kiln did not seem to have had a very long life. Collectors in Szechwan seem to be of the opinion that it was first established in the T'ang dynasty, reached its height towards the end of the period, and was abandoned in the Sung dynasty.

Sherds with inscriptions that give such dates as A.D. 754, 823, and 874–9 have been reported. Coins, mostly of the Wu-shu and K'ai-yüan 開元 types, have been found associated with the sherds.

In the autumn of 1944, a brick tomb of the T'ang period was unearthed on the campus of the National Szechwan University in Chengtu. The structure of the tomb is completely different from those of the preceding Han-Chin period as well as from those of the following Sung and Ming periods. The tomb chamber was constructed of large rectangular bricks, plain in decoration and grey in colour. The chamber was rectangular in shape with square columns on the two sides. It was the tomb of a woman, whose skeleton was found in the grave associated with two pottery jars and two pottery bowls. These wares were the products of the Ch'iung-lai factory. The jars were found on the right of the skeleton near the skull, while the bowls were on the ribs and may have originally been meant to cover the breasts. On removing a bracelet from the wrist, the decomposed brass material broke and in it was found a printed charm, probably in an ancient Tibetan script. A few K'ai-yüan coins were also unearthed and this indicates that the tomb was probably T'ang in date, most likely belonging to the ninth or the tenth century. The tomb is very important because it reveals not only the earliest printed matter found in Szechwan and a strange burial custom in West China, but also a dating for the Ch'iung-lai kiln site.

Moreover, the pottery from Ch'iung-lai is distinctly in the T'ang style and the technique of the potters seems to have followed the T'ang tradition. There- fore, it seems fairly safe to assume that a part of our collection is actually T'ang in date, though the other portion may have been the products of the following dynasty. In the later period, however, the potters still followed established traditions and it is almost impossible, with our present knowledge of the site, to distinguish the earlier from the later wares.

As a whole, the Ch'iung-lai pottery is a monochrome slipped or glazed ware. The white slip, so well-known among the T'ang grave objects, is very evident in the Ch'iung-lai pottery. So many vessels have been covered with white, light yellow or light grey slip and are without glaze, that it seems likely that the potters purposely made slipped wares, some of which are painted with floral designs in grey, yellow, green and brown. Of course, since most of the material was found in the refuse heap, many of these vessels are unglazed because they were defective or not worth glazing.

The glaze is of several colours, predominantly light grey, green, yellow and brown, and rarely dull blue and light purple. Most of the colours are of several shades. The painted floral designs have most frequently been found on a background of light grey. Several vessels are polychrome and they recall the typical tri-coloured ware of the T'ang period.

However, some of the glazes are closer to those of the famous Sung porcelains from other ceramic centres in China. The deep blue or purple glazes, as well as the paler blue, bluish green and bluish grey, sometimes with the small blue or bluish green spots, resemble closely the Honan Chün ware. The grey, green, greenish yellow and light yellow glazes might be relatives of the Lungch'üan ware of Chekiang. The dark brown or dark orange-yellow glazes recall those that are characteristic of the Fukien Chien ware.

Three types of paste have been noticed in the Ch'iung-lai pottery. Crude vessels such as saggars and separators for firing are made of a coarse paste which is tempered with sand. The majority of the products are of a fine paste which varies in colour from grey to yellow and dull red. White paste has also been found in several vessels, but the rareness of this type of material seems to suggest that the paste was not native in origin.

The methods of construction have been found to be wheel-making, mould-shaping and modelling. Large jars and pots might have been made by coiling. The bases of the bowls, jugs, jars, pitchers and vases are generally wide and flat with or without bevelled edges. Bases with rim circles are rare, and when found generally thick and flat. Some of the larger vessels, though rarely, have concave bases. A few bowls have narrow bases with low and thin rims which curve outward from the bases of the bowls. Spouts, handles, legs and other accessories are mostly hand-modelled or mould-shaped. It is interesting to note that in the case of the spout the potters very seldom cut off the tip to produce a beaked tube. Human and larger animal figures and some of the more compli- cated vessels are modelled in parts and assembled for firing.

Firing seems to have been a complicated process at Ch'iung-lai. Vessels were placed one on top of the other separated by separators in a round cylin- drical container or saggar. The separators vary greatly in size and are either three, five, or, very rarely, seven or eight-legged. They left their footprints on the bottom of the lower vessel. The saggars, with round perforations in every direction, probably for air circulation, were in turn placed on top of each other in the kiln for firing.

Some of the vessels may have been fired twice, first with a slip, and later, after the solution of a glaze was applied. The floral ornaments were painted on or under the glaze, and the vessels may or may not have been refired. Most of the pottery is very well baked, and is mostly stoneware, with a hardness not lower than 4. Some of the sherds are as hard as carborundum.

With three kinds of paste and several types of slip and glaze, the Ch'iung-lai kilns produced twenty-two types of stoneware and porcelain. They consist of a large variety of vessels and other articles, which may be classified as follows:

CONTAINERS (Pls. 84–89)

Bowl, cup, saucer, pot, pitcher, powder box, dish, jar, vase, tripod, five- legged bowl, six-legged bowl, etc., in various sizes and shapes.

TOYS (Pls. 89–90)

Turtle, elephant, lion, fowl, fish, dog, horse, dragon, rabbit, cow, rat, monkey, duck, chicken, human figure, marble, rattle, peach, persimmon, etc.

POTTERS' UTENSILS (Pls. 90–91)

Saggar and separator for firing, mould, etc., in various sizes and shapes.

OTHERS

Spindle whorl, lamps, straining jug, grating dish, pestle, Buddhist figure, etc.

It may be of interest to point out that the mould with a pair of phoenix on a lotus flower pattern is commonly portrayed in the T'ang art objects (Pl. 90. 6). The mould of a large deity might have produced a host of armour-clad war- riors that rivalled many of the military guards of a T'ang tomb or the figures of Lokapala in the Buddhist monasteries of this period (Pl. 90. 4–5). On the other hand, the classical shape of a Sung bowl, with a very small base and an out-stretching steep wall, which gives a conical outline when placed upside down, seems to be unknown to the Ch'iung-lai potters.

There were various methods of ornamentation, for example: first, designs were incised on the body of the vessel by means of a sharp tool before it was baked. Second, they were painted on the vessel before or after firing. Third, they were impressed on the inside or on the outside by means of a mould. Fourth, lumps of clay were put on the outside and then moulded into shape. The bowls and pots are mostly painted in floral designs. Some bowls have scalloped pie-rim decoration. The legs of a vessel are mostly headed with a mask. Other impressed patterns are of geometrical combination, dragon, fish, butterfly, galloping animals, phoenix, flying angels, animal figures, human figures, etc. The flying angels that are so freely used to decorate the lids of small round boxes are common T'ang motifs most frequently found on the mirrors and in the Buddhist temples of this period.

There is no doubt, however, that the kiln at Ch'iung-lai continued to operate in the Sung period. Professor Yang reports a small, yellow-glazed *p'an*-saucer which bears a stamped inscription: *Yüan-fu yüan nien Li Ta-hsing tsao* 元符元年李大興造 or 'made by Li Ta-hsing in the first year of Yüan-fu [A.D. 1098]'. On another saucer he found an incised inscription: *Chêng-ho ch'i nien* or '[made in] the seventh year of Chêng-ho [A.D. 1117]' (432).

From the data we have just reviewed, it seems evident that most of the Ch'iung-lai pottery falls into the T'ang and Northern Sung periods, and it may be safe to conclude that the work of the factory ceased when the capital of the Sung dynasty moved to Hangchou, south of the Yangtse.

THE LIU-LI-CH'ANG KILN SITE

The technical development of ceramic art in Szechwan became more apparent when the refuse heaps of another ancient kiln were discovered practically in our backyard. Situated about five miles to the south-east of the city of Chengtu, the kiln site of Liu-li-ch'ang is within easy reach of our museum, and consequently has become a very convenient laboratory for the students. During the war, on account of the shortage of ceramic wares, a pottery kiln was installed at the ancient site, and as the modern technicians practise the age-old techniques of pottery-making with the help of a crude stone wheel and by coiling, and still using a lead glaze solution, visits to the site have become a requirement of our course in archaeology.

The site at Liu-li-ch'ang is roughly circular in shape and has a diameter of about 2000 ft. (Pl. 92. 1). Near the edge of the site is a string of hillocks, roughly conical, which are heaps of burnt clay sherds, discarded vessels and other rubbish from the kilns. Much of the soil between the hillocks is underlaid with sherds. There may have been several kilns operating here at the same time (433).

The fact has been confirmed that the kiln at Liu-li-ch'ang was first established at the end of the T'ang dynasty. Specimens of the ware have been found in the Royal Tomb of Emperor Wang Chien, whose burial took place in A.D. 918.

Szechwan has also yielded many stone and brick tombs which were Sung or Ming in date, and these have been found to contain a rich variety of Liu-li-ch'ang ware. The contents of these later tombs are most interesting, but in this part, I shall limit myself to the material from the kiln site.

Further evidence for the dating of this site may be supplied by objects from the refuse heaps. Some of the sherds recovered are inscribed. A sherd in our museum has on it two characters: 'Lung-hsing', being the years 1163–64 in the Sung dynasty. In several private collections I have come across vessels with such dates as the 7th year of Chêng-ho (1117); the tenth year of Shao-hsing (1140); and the twelfth year of Chia-ting (1219). The Szechwan Provincial Museum has in its collection two dated saucers from the same site. The date of one is 1102, near the end of the Northern Sung dynasty, and the other is dated the thirteenth year of Chih-yüan (1276).

Professor Yang reports a small green-glazed saucer which has two characters: 'Shu-fu' 樞 府. The Shu-fu ware either in white or in pale-bluish glaze is familiar to students of Chinese porcelain. This was manufactured at Ching-tê-chên for the imperial court of the Yüan dynasty. Now we have another Shu-fu ware which was fired by the potter at Liu-li-ch'ang. The design of the Szechwan ceramic is similar to the Kiangsi product, but the paste is red and the glaze green.

It seems evident that the Liu-li-ch'ang kiln enjoyed longer existence than that of Ch'iung-lai. According to the *Hua-yang hsien chih*, a local gazetteer, the kiln at Liu-li-ch'ang was still functioning during the Ming dynasty; it was the official glaze-ware factory of the government.

From the data we have just reviewed, it seems safe to assume that the ceramic industry at Liu-li-ch'ang was first installed at the end of the T'ang dynasty, its products practically monopolized the market of Szechwan in the Southern

Sung period, and it probably continued to produce glazed wares in the Ming period. The devastation brought about by Chang Hsien-chung in the seventeenth century may have been responsible for the destruction of the kiln, when the notorious terror killed practically all the people in this province.

One may be inclined to believe, after a brief observation, that the Liu-li-ch'ang and the Ch'iung-lai wares are closely akin to each other, and the potters of these two centres had been following a common tradition. But in the light of the technique, the style as well as the types, it seems necessary to distinguish the one from the other, because the former belongs to the Sung, the latter to the T'ang tradition. The Ch'iung-lai potters seem to have been more conservative in expression and poorer in technical skill, and their wares are more traditional in type. The manufacturers at Liu-li-ch'ang are more advanced in technique, more creative in types and bolder in style as we shall see presently.

Basically, these two centres followed a common tradition, but being situated near Chengtu, the greatest metropolis of western China during the T'ang-Sung period, the demands of the diverse city population and the keen competition of imported wares might have compelled the city potters to produce wares of new shapes and styles. Most of the well known porcelains from other provinces were being imitated, and hence the materials from Liu-li-ch'ang represent a most heterogeneous development.

As a whole, the Liu-li-ch'ang pottery is a porcellanous stoneware. Most of the vessels are monochrome glazed wares. Brown and green of various shades are by far the most common. The brown-glazed ware varies from orange yellow to yellow orange. The teacups of this ware resemble closely in shape and in colour the Chien-yao and may be taken as imitations of the Fukien ware. However, most of the cups, bowls, vases, pitchers and jugs are much inferior in quality, even to those that were imitated by the Honan kilns.

The green-glazed ware varies from yellow, greenish-yellow, yellow green to green. Some of these are lustrous and seem to be a local relative of the Lung-ch'üan-yao of Chekiang.

White-glazed wares are rare, and blue and grey ones are most unusual. The white glaze varies from a very lustrous to a dull colour. Some of the sherds are actually Ting-yao, possibly imported from Hopei in North China, but the rest are local imitations of the famous Sung porcelain. A few sherds of lustrous bluish-white ware have also been found but they are of the Ch'ing-pai type of material.

There is also a black pottery that may or may not be porcelain. The colour is dull and may be the result of painting with a solution made with soot or Chinese ink. It is used only on ordinary bowls.

But the black paint is very important for the drawing of decorations over the slip and under the glaze, which is mainly white or light yellow. A vessel of this type recalls the beautiful Tz'ŭ-chou ware produced in North China at this period. Some retain the technique of incision so characteristic of this ware.

Polychrome wares are not uncommon in Liu-li-ch'ang. The combination of colour may be brown and white, green and yellow, green and white, but the most dominant ones are of three colours, red, green and yellow, or brown, green and yellow. Poly-glaze is most commonly applied on bowls and vases, and various types of mortuary objects. This recalls the famous tri-coloured glaze of the T'ang period, though the Szechwan material does not have the gay and romantic atmosphere of the T'ang design.

Plain and unglazed wares seem to have been limited to toys, and kiln and kitchen utensils. Slipped wares of yellowish-grey have been found, but they seem to be materials that were defective, and not worth glazing.

Three types of paste have been noted in the Liu-li-ch'ang ware. Crude vessels, such as saggars and separators for firing, toys and some kitchen utensils, are made of coarse paste, which is reddish-brown in colour, and tempered with sand. The majority of the sherds at the site are of a fine yellowish-grey paste, tempered with fine particles of silica. Vessels of white paste have also been found, and they are definitely of two types of clay. The greyish-white one is probably a local material, while the other is pure white kaolin. Two sherds in the Museum are definitely the Ting-yao from North China and the Ch'ing-pai ware from East China, and they should be taken as imported material.

The Liu-li-ch'ang potters seem to have been very keen on imitating the famous wares from other provinces. As we have noticed, vessels that recall the Chien-yao, the Lung-ch'üan, the Ting-yao and the Tz'ŭ-chou wares are very common, but in every case the paste is completely different from the original. This may be due to the fact that the Szechwan potters were unable to secure the right paste and glaze for their work. The closest imitations are those of the Ch'ing-pai wares, which were very finely manufactured and have been treasured by the local collectors as the Shu-yao. The difference between this ware and its prototype seems to lie in the paste. The Kiangsi ware is of a fine and white clay, while the local paste is slightly yellowish and is coarser in texture. As noted above, the Liu-li-ch'ang potter made also a Shu-fu ware, but they failed to produce an exact replica on account of the paste and glaze.

The methods of construction and firing are closely akin to those employed at Ch'iung-lai, but the Liu-li-ch'ang potters were more advanced in their technique. Wheel-making, mould-shaping and modelling were the dominant techniques of construction, and coiling was employed in shaping large vessels. The bases of Liu-li-ch'ang bowls are better developed. In most cases, they have low circular rims with potters' marks on the bottoms, some of which are as follows:

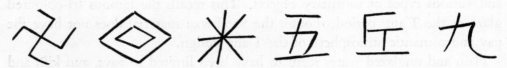

The tip of a spout is neatly levelled, producing a beaked tube. Inscriptions of one character or a whole sentence were sometimes incised on the inner wall of vessels while the paste was still soft and before glaze was applied.

Moreover, the Liu-li-ch'ang potter had a better control of the fire. Sherds from the site maintain a consistent hardness. With the exception of a few sherds, which may have had a decomposed surface and showed a hardness of 3 or lower, the majority of them tested are 6–7 in hardness.

The shapes of the Liu-li-ch'ang ware are probably richer than those produced at Ch'iung-lai, and they may be classified as follows:

CONTAINERS (Pls. 92–95)

Bowl, cup, saucer, pot, pitcher, dish, jar, vase, tripod, five-legged bowl, bottle, bucket, ink slab, funnel, grinder, etc., in various sizes and shapes.

TOYS

Turtle, animal figure, human figure, chessman, whistle, ring, bead, marble, rattle, etc.;

POTTERS' UTENSILS

Saggar and separator for firing, mould, etc., in various sizes and shapes;

OTHERS

Spindle-whorl, Buddhist figure, tomb figure, etc., in various sizes and shapes.

We have found that a number of new shapes were created at Liu-li-ch'ang. It is true that these two kilns produced similar hollow lamps, thick saucers, pitchers with double snouts, grater dishes or grinders, saggars, separators, small human and animal figures, but the differences are even greater. The new shapes of Liu-li-ch'ang are worth noticing: bowls with small bases, fine base rims, big basins, dish pans, small bowls or tea cups, round and rather flat water or wine bottles, ink-slabs, chessmen, slender and tall jars. These are all absent at Ch'iung-lai.

In a way the methods of ornamentation are more accomplished at Liu-li-ch'ang than at Ch'iung-lai. In the latter, sherds with impressed patterns are most common, while in the former, painted sherds are predominant. Painting was done either before or after firing. Incision while the clay was still soft is not unusual. The designs are mostly floral, a few geometrical. Appliqué designs are also more widely used here than at Ch'iung-lai.

To carry the comparison of these two groups of pottery a little further, reference may be made to a chemical analysis of the glaze used in these two centres, done by Professor Kao Yü-ling 高毓靈 of the Chemistry Department of West China Union University (434).

Professor Kao analysed seven types of glaze from Ch'iung-lai and the same number from Liu-li-ch'ang. He came to the conclusion that two specimens of the former contain high percentages of lead oxide, another two contain phosphorus oxide, whereas the other three are feldspathic in nature. Of those from Liu-li-ch'ang, one was found to contain phosphorus oxide and six were of the feldspathic type.

It should be pointed out that Professor Kao did not include a few soft glazed sherds from Liu-li-ch'ang in his analysis. This type of specimen have been found in large numbers at the site as well as in the Sung burials. Similar to that used on the Han and T'ang wares, the soft glaze of Liu-li-ch'ang was produced from lead oxide and fired at a low temperature. There is no reason to doubt that Ch'iung-lai and Liu-li-ch'ang followed the same tradition in glaze manufacture; all the three types of glazes were used in both centres. However, it is also plain that the application of glazes was more specialized at Liu-li-ch'ang than at Ch'iung-lai. In the Chengtu pottery the lead glaze was reserved for the decoration of mortuary objects and architectural materials.

The clay used in pottery-making is a product of feldspar after long weathering, and the paste of a ceramic vessel is generally porous and absorbs moisture.

The glaze is used to fill up the interstices and cover the surface smoothly. The application not only remedies the defects of the paste, but also provides lustre and beauty to the vessel. But, technically, the fusing temperature of the glaze should be lower than that of the paste in order to prevent deformation. Lead glaze fuses at a very low temperature, but it is poisonous. It was widely used in the Han and T'ang periods probably because of its low melting-point since the potters were not very skilful in controlling the fire. The hardness of the Ch'iung-lai pottery ranges from 4 to 9; this shows that the material has been fired at all sorts of temperatures. The indiscriminate use of lead and phosphorus oxides and feldspathic glazes in this kiln indicates that it belongs to a traditional industry, possibly later T'ang and early Sung in date; whereas the specialized use of lead glaze at Liu-li-ch'ang reveals the fact that the Chengtu potters had already acquired a new technique to produce the feldspar glaze with satisfactory efficiency. They probably had designed the kiln in such a way that a draft might be induced for quick combustion. Hence, the fire was in better control and they produced ceramic wares with a more constant hardness ranging only from 6 to 7. These are the characteristics of Sung ware.

By chemical analysis of the glazes we arrive at the same conclusion in regard to the dating of these two kiln sites as we have reached on other grounds mentioned above.

A selection of the typical ceramic wares manufactured by these two Szechwan kilns are reproduced in Plates 48–95. They are all specimens preserved in the University Museum at Chengtu, unless otherwise mentioned. The rich variety of the Sung mortuary pottery supplied by the Liu-li-ch'ang kiln is discussed in Chapter VIII below.

SUNG BURIAL REMAINS IN SZECHWAN

IN the last twenty years hundreds of tombs of the Sung dynasty have been examined in Szechwan. They are found practically everywhere, on the hill-sides, in the rice fields, in suburbs of towns, along the roads and the rivers. In 1934 Dr David C. Graham excavated a brick tomb on the West China Union University campus. He brought back from Lo-shan, in 1941, a pottery urn which had been unearthed on a nearby hillside. In the period between 1941 and 1946, I examined four Sung tombs at Liu-li-ch'ang and observed the excavation of three others in the south-western suburb of Chengtu. Additional information regarding the contents of these tombs has been given to us by Dr Fêng Han-yi, Curator of the Szechwan Museum, and by Mr Huang Hsi-ch'êng, founder and Keeper of the Hsi-ch'êng Museum. Dr W. Franke, Mr Chiang Ta-yi and other members of the University have also supplied us with interesting data. In most cases, we made every effort to get possession of the material which was excavated and thus have built up a collection of Sung funerary objects.

It is now evident that the people of Szechwan observed three types of burial customs during the Sung period. Some buried their dead in stone graves, some in brick tombs, while others practised cremation and buried the ashes later in pottery jars. Originally, there may have been a stone of some kind on the surface of the ground to mark the burial, but none of them has survived, although a few burials are still covered by a mound of earth.

The stone grave is the most elaborate of the three types. It is usually constructed on the surface of the ground with four to eight slabs, about six inches thick, lying side by side to form the floor. The stone chamber is built on this floor in a very simple way. First, six or eight stone columns are erected in two rows, three or four on each side parallel to one another at the desired distance. These columns are chiselled with vertical grooves on each side to receive thin slabs of stone forming the walls. Then another series of stone slabs is laid over the walls to form the ceiling. The door, also of stone, opens in the middle with projections at the two ends which go into socket depressions on the floor and ceiling beside the front columns.

A tomb of this type was found to the north of Liu-li-ch'ang and had been used as an air-raid shelter by the owner of the field. The chamber measures 15 ft. long, 5 ft. wide, and about 3 ft. high. Above the door, there is a decorative motif carved on the ceiling slab in the form of a roof. Faint traces of paint were observed on the walls and ceiling, probably remnants of some floral design (Pl. 96).

In Hsin-tsin, some stone tombs are said to have decorated walls and columns carved in low relief with scenes of daily life and other designs. In the Museum collection there are a pair of columns or corner stones and two wall panels from a similar tomb.

The columns are decorated in high relief with a human figure standing on a floating cloud (Pl. 97. 1, 2). One of the figures has a long-necked pitcher in low relief near his shoulder. This recalls the sacred water vessel used for the bathing of the infant Buddha so commonly reproduced in Buddhist paintings and sculptures.

The wall panels are decorated with scenes in low relief (Pl. 97. 3, 4). We see at once that the technique of carving is typical of the Han tradition, but that the subject matter is completely different. The panels show the furniture in a house—a chair and a table on which are flower pots. On one panel a human figure stands beside a chair. The most striking feature of the composition is the prominent place occupied by the chair. It is well known that the ancient Chinese sat on the floor. Chairs and stools were unknown to them even in the T'ang dynasty. Artists have shown Buddhist figures seated on a stool or on a raised altar, but we have no evidence of the common people using this type of furniture before the tenth century. The earliest example of a stool was found in the Royal Tomb of Wang Chien. There, the emperor is shown seated on a stool of semi-lunar shape in a Buddha-like attitude. Even this is quite unconventional for the period; he should have been seated on the floor like the musicians shown in the tomb or like other dignitaries who appear in paintings of the T'ang period. This may indicate that in China the chair was first used by the aristocracy. However, it soon came into fashion in the Sung dynasty in almost all parts of the country. The excavation of the buried city of Chü-lu 鉅鹿 in Hopei province, which was buried by the overflowing of the Yellow River in the Sung dynasty, revealed a series of house furniture including several wooden chairs. Examples now on exhibition in the Historical Museum in Peking are in exactly the same style as those shown in Plate 97, especially in the curved back and the crossed legs.

To return to the stone burial, tombs of this type with two or more chambers constructed side by side are not uncommon. They are usually of equal size. In Lo-shan, a tomb with five chambers has been found, containing originally the bodies of an official and his four wives.

In comparison with those of the Han period, the Sung tombs are very small indeed. They were just big enough to hold a coffin and a series of mortuary objects. This is also true of the brick tombs of the period, which are simply rectangular chambers with vaulted ceilings. The bricks are generally plain and grey in colour, some with dated inscriptions giving also the place of manufacture. The arch is constructed with either plain or wedge-shaped bricks. The door was sealed from the outside with the same type of brick, but in one case, probably through a miscalculation of the mason, fragments of brick and stone were used to block the entrance (Pl. 98). In several cases fragments of plaster with painted designs have been found on the floor, and it seems likely that these were originally wall decorations.

So far, no tomb has been found that had not previously been opened. Traces of wooden fragments have been observed in most cases, which suggest that the coffin was placed in the rear of the chamber with an array of funerary furniture at the front. Pottery objects recovered from these two types of burials have been found to be identical. The majority are of polychrome or tri-coloured glazed ware, while a small group is of plain coarse terra cotta ware.

The number of pottery figures placed in a burial varies greatly. One tomb contained thirty-four pieces, another only five. The material preserved in the Museum may be classified under four categories as follows:

DAILY UTENSILS (Pl. 99. 2–5)

Drum-shaped container, three-legged *lu* or container, two-handled jar, small bowl.

FIGURINES (Pls. 100–106. 1)

Warriors, male figures, standing female figures, kneeling female figures.

ANIMALS (Pls. 106. 2–110)

Dragon, hen and rooster, dog, cow with human body, monkey with human body, pig with wings, turtle, snake with human head.

TOMB GUARDS (Pls. 111–112)

Mask with legs, drum on stand, disc with pedestal.

Coins and mirrors have frequently been found associated with the tomb pottery. The coins are either of bronze or iron and, almost without exception, are of the Sung dynasty with inscriptions of the reignal periods, such as Ch'ung-ning (1102–6), Ta-kuan (1107–10), Chia-ting (1208–24), etc. The iron coins are mainly of the Southern Sung period (Pl. 113).

The series of bronze and iron mirrors presents many interesting problems. The Kuang-chêng mirror (Pl. 114) belonged originally to the Hsi-ch'êng Museum, whose founder, Mr Huang Hsi-ch'êng, reports that the mirror was discovered in a Sung tomb in the neighbourhood of Chengtu in association with some tri-colour glazed pottery figurines. It is black and has a very lustrous surface, usually described as *hei ch'i ku*, meaning 'the material is like black lacquer'. It is thin and has a diameter of 15·0 cm. The knob of the mirror is very small and is fluted. An undecorated band surrounds the knob, with four almond-shaped leaves projecting in the four directions. The leaves are in low relief, each inscribed with a character. The cast inscription reads: *Kuang-chêng yüan nien*, meaning 'the first year of Kuang-chêng'—that is, A.D. 938. The four leaves penetrate into a background of an all-over comma pattern. The basic design is rectangular, composed of eight commas of irregular shape on a ground of lines and granulations. A narrow fluted band separates the rim from the decorated zone. The rim is concave with its outer edge high enough to form a considerable ridge.

Any student of Chinese art can tell at a glance that the mirror is Late Chou in style. The colour, the knob, the rim and, above all, the decorative designs are unmistakably those of the 'Warring States', 'Ch'in', 'Ch'u', 'Huai' or whatever it may be called. Much has been written on this type of mirror. Mr Orvar Karlbeck has rendered a most valuable service in tracing provenance data for this study, and the discussion reached its climax and 'perfection' with Professor Bernhard Karlgren's detailed exposition of 'Huai and Han' (435). The design of the mirror in question falls into Category C, according to Professor Karlgren's classification. In his masterly work, the celebrated sinologue concludes (435, 35): 'Categories C and D, that have granulation-lined bands, interlocked T's and comma pattern as background filling are of pre-Han date—before the third century B.C.' But the mirror in question has an inscription which is definitely A.D. 938.

The evidence for the survival of the comma pattern on post-Han mirrors is augmented by another example found in Tomsk, Russia, which is on exhibition in the Hermitage Museum, Leningrad. This mirror is only 6·5 cm. in diameter, is decorated with four leaves on a background of comma patterns, and has a small knob and a concave rim. The Tomsk example was found associated with a T'ang mirror decorated with the 'sea-animal and grapes' motif (436, 34, Pl. VII).

With the decline of the dynamic T'ang empire, there was a great revival of ancient culture and tradition. Scholars concentrated on classical studies and championed the *Ku-wên* 古文 literary style, while artists and craftsmen copied ancient works of art. This development reached its height in the period of Hsüan-ho (A.D. 1119–1125) when Emperor Hui-tsung of the Sung dynasty ordered the compilation of the famous *Po ku t'u* 博古圖 and attempted to reproduce the masterpieces of earlier dynasties. Hundreds of Sung bronzes, jades and other works of art, clearly in pre-Han and Han style, can be found in museums and private collections all over the world. The Chengtu and Tomsk mirrors are undoubtedly a result of this development. After seeing these interesting examples, we can only conclude that many of the mirrors now ascribed to Huai and Han are actually T'ang and Sung in date.

In the summer of 1945, a brick tomb was discovered by some masons near Ch'ing-yang-kung 青羊宮 to the south-west of Chengtu. I went out to see the excavation and managed to obtain two pottery figurines and some Sung iron coins. A mason told me that they had found an iron disc the preceding day embedded in a deposit of clay and lime-plaster. The disc had an inscription, *Chien-tê ssŭ nien*, and had been sold to a certain Mr Li. It took me several months to locate the mirror and acquire it for the Museum. It is slightly less than 7·5 cm. in diameter and about 4 mm. thick (Pl. 115. 1). Traces of lime-plaster can still be seen on it. The knob is of ordinary size and the perforation is full of the white material. Four characters in low relief are cast around the knob. A small fluting separates the inscribed zone from the rim which is flat.

The mirror is simple, but is extremely interesting historically. It is well known that Emperor Wu of the Han dynasty started the practice of giving a special name to each reign and that these form a series of reignal periods in Chinese history. Every emperor, therefore, had to assign a name to his reign. 'It was in the fourth year of Chien-lung' (A.D. 963), according to Li Yu (437, 10), 'that a recommendation was first made to change the name of the reign. The Emperor T'ai-tsu told the prime minister not to use any of the names of the preceding dynasties, and accordingly, it was changed to Ch'ien-tê.' Some time after this, the emperor came upon a mirror belonging to a lady in his imperial harem, bearing an inscription of 'Ch'ien-tê' on its back. He asked T'ao Ku 陶 穀 a scholar of the Han-lin Academy about it. T'ao replied, 'That was the reignal name in the unofficial Shu 蜀 dynasty'. The lady had actually come from the old Shu kingdom. The emperor was much impressed by the scholar's knowledge and at the same time dismayed at the ignorance of his prime minister. King Wang Yen 王 衍 of the unofficial Shu had adopted this reignal name 'Ch'ien-tê' in the twelfth moon of the fifth year of Chêng-ming for the next year, and it lasted for six years.

The adoption of a local reignal name for the reign of the great Sung Empire was indeed a grave error. The emperor consequently ordered the title to be changed. K'ai-pao, meaning 'the opening of a precious [dynasty]', was adopted for the following year. This was in A.D. 968. In Chinese history, consequently, there are two reignal periods called 'Ch'ien-tê' comparatively close together; the former from 919 to 924, the latter from 963 to 967. It is difficult to tell whether the date of this mirror, the fourth year of Ch'ien-tê, is 922 or 966, but in any case it illustrates an interesting bit of tenth-century history.

Another simple mirror is also made of iron which may have been plated to furnish a reflecting surface. It is 7·5 cm. in diameter and is decorated with a pair of dragons facing a vertical inscription in the centre of the disc. The inscription reads: *Chün yi kuan wei*, meaning 'Your excellency is fit [to occupy] a place in the officialdom' (Pl. 115. 2).

The Ch'êng-an mirror (Pl. 115. 3) came from a brick tomb at Fêng-huang shan 鳳 凰 山 to the north of Chengtu. It was found associated with a group of pottery mortuary objects and an inscribed stone recording the purchase of the ground in the fifth year of Chia-ting, i.e. A.D. 1212. The mirror is about 10 cm. in diameter. It has a very small knob, with a perforation for the cord, surrounded by four galloping animals; they appear to be chasing one another. An incised circle separates these animals from the inscribed band, and the rim is flat with a very high edge.

The inscription reads: *Ch'êng-an san nien shang-yüan jih, shên-si tung yun ssŭ kuan chao, chien chao luh shih Jên,* [signature], *t'i k'uang yun shih Kao,* [signature]. That is 'In the third year of Ch'êng-an, on the day Shang-yüan, [this mirror was] officially made by the Tung-yun-ssŭ of [the province] of Shen-si. The officials who supervised the work were Jên, the Chien-chao-luh-shih [signature]; and Kao, the T'i-k'uang-yun-shih [signature]'. The date is 1198.

At this time China was dominated by two kingdoms, Chin in the north and Sung in the south. History records many a bloody struggle between them, but it also reports a continuous flow of goods over the border. The Ch'êng-an mirror is a good example—a northern product exported to the south. Trade flourished far and wide during this period in spite of the wars, and it is interesting to note that a large collection of mirrors from these two Chinese kingdoms has been discovered in Asia Minor. Included in this series is a Ch'êng-an mirror which might have been made from the same mould as the one found in Chengtu (436, Fig. 6, 32).

Another group of mirrors found in the Szechwan tombs are largely undecorated, bronze in material and irregular in shape (Pl. 115. 4–6). They are usually inscribed with Sung-style characters in rectangular blocks, indicating that they were made in Hu-chou in eastern China. In pre-T'ang periods, a mirror was called *ching* 竟, monosyllabic, but during the Sung dynasty, when the modern Chinese language began to take shape, the 'looking bronze' was either called *ching-tzŭ* 鏡 子 or *chao-tzŭ* 照 子. This is clearly shown by the inscriptions on these mirrors.

Almost all of the post-T'ang tombs in Szechwan contained a copy of the deed recording the purchase of the land so that there would be no dispute regarding its ownership (Pl. 97. 5). Many of these documents have been collected, but a most interesting one was discovered in 1934 in the brick tomb on the University campus. The document (Pls. 97. 6; 99. 1) is translated as follows:

[This is] the fifth day of the eleventh moon of the fourteenth year of Chia-ting in the Great Sung Dynasty [1221], the year cycle being *hsin-ssŭ*, and the day cycle also *hsin-ssŭ*, at the beginning of the month. Deed of the deceased. . . . After birth he lived in the city [of Chengtu], when he died, he was placed in the house, and by consulting a diviner and a fortune teller, this great lucky place is appropriated at . . . village, in the district of Hua-yang. It is the source of fortune, because there is the green dragon to the left, the white tiger on the right, the red bird in front and the black turtle in the rear, and the constellation of Kou-ch'ên 勾 陳 in the centre. All this is transacted according to legal order.

The custom of having the four auspicious animals of the four directions to bring fortune and prosperity to the deceased has been handed down from early historic days. The idea has played a very important role in the mythology and folklore of the Chinese people.

The brick tomb just mentioned contained only burnt human bones, a gravestone, three glazed figurines and two pottery vessels. Some of the bricks are dated 1219, two years before the funeral, so it is evident that the brick-seller of the period kept a stock of his wares and that ordinary people did not order special material for the construction of their tombs. This tomb is exceptionally small and was built to hold only the ashes of the dead. It seems to be an intermediate type between a grave chamber and a cremation burial.

During the Sung dynasty, some of the inhabitants of Szechwan adopted the Buddhist ritual and disposed of their dead by cremation, the ashes being placed in a jar and buried on a hillside, along with one or more pottery vessels containing coins, grain and food. These jars, so far, have never been found in a grave chamber, and the pottery seems to be different from that found at Liu-li-ch'ang or in the brick and stone tombs of the period. In several cases, however, these grave-jars have been found associated with dated stone grave-deeds, which places them in the same period.

These grave-jars are mostly of a plain yellowish stoneware, generally unglazed. The greenish-yellow glaze, sometimes applied on this pottery, however, recalls the material and technique used on the Han-Chin 'proto-porcelain'. The paste is reddish-brown, tempered with sand, and the vessels are usually very crude, constructed either on a wheel or by coiling. Their shape is that of the usual jar, in various sizes, and they are commonly decorated with appliqué material representing a pagoda, a house, or a granary, with a roof on the cover and upper part of the vessel. The grave-jar usually has on its face an incised inscription. Jars decorated with appliqué floral patterns in high relief are not unusual. A few pots and pitchers have also been found associated with these grave-jars (Pls. 116, 117).

More must be learned about the grave-jars *in situ*, not only at the burial, but also at the kiln site. However, in the light of our present knowledge, it seems safe to conclude that there were two kinds of burial customs in Szechwan during the Sung period. Most of the people followed the old tradition and buried their dead in a grave among a profusion of pottery objects, while others adopted Buddhism, practised cremation, and buried the ashes in grave-jars. These two types continued to dominate the burial customs of the Ming period.

The contents of these Sung tombs in Szechwan are of interest in many respects both archaeologically and historically, but I shall discuss only one of these points—the significance of the mortuary objects.

It is not necessary to repeat here that from time immemorial the Chinese have believed in the future existence of man. Thus it was common practice for the relatives and friends of the deceased to bury in his tomb models of his house, servants, domestic animals, implements and utensils, coins and ornaments, so that the outgoing soul might be provided as fully as possible with the things which had surrounded him in life. This practice dates back to the late palaeolithic age and has continued down to the present time. At first, actual utensils and real objects were used. In the latter part of the Chou dynasty (about the sixth to the third centuries B.C.), these were replaced by wooden and straw models. Beginning with the Han dynasty (second century B.C.), pottery models were introduced, the production of which became an outstanding feature of the T'ang period (618–906). Since the Sung dynasty (906–1127), paper models which are burned for the dead have been used. At the present time, these paper models include Indian policemen, automobiles and aeroplanes.

The study of pottery models, called *Ming-ch'i*, has recently become a special branch of Chinese archaeology and has attracted much attention both in China and abroad. It is generally accepted that tomb pottery has undergone three stages of development. Although it is true that Chinese mortuary objects were produced and used long before the Han dynasty, they did not become popular until Emperor Wên (179–156 B.C.) advocated the practice and took the lead in using them for his imperial sanctuary. The Han potters succeeded in making excellent models of houses and utensils. They also made human figures and domestic animals, which at this early stage are simple and clumsy, and generally out of proportion.

The introduction of Buddhism and the occupation of North China by the northern nomads brought in the Graeco-Indian style of sculpture which had great influence on Chinese art during the Six Dynasties (A.D. 317–618). During this time, the tomb figures gradually developed a style more plastic than in former periods and therefore can be said to represent an intermediate stage.

This art reached its height during the T'ang dynasty, and hundreds of T'ang clay figures are preserved in museums all over the world. They represent without doubt some of the best works of art that China has ever produced. With the downfall of the great T'ang dynasty, however, this art disappeared and mortuary figurines went completely out of fashion.

The chronological sequence for tomb pottery, which was widely accepted by archaeologists in the 1920's and 1930's, was arrived at from the study of material unearthed in the northern provinces of Honan and Shensi. Today, as excavations spread over China, we find that the stages of development for these mortuary objects can only be applied to the Yellow river valley. We must recognize other sequences for other areas.

In the spring of 1936, when I was curator of the University Museum at Amoy, I had the privilege of excavating four tombs in the nearby city of Chüan-chou. In the middle ages, this city and seaport was one of the great trading centres of the world, better known to Marco Polo and other traders from the west as Zayton. The tombs yielded a rich collection of mortuary objects now preserved in the Amoy University (438).

The style and decoration of the objects, the construction of the tombs and the ornamentation of the bricks from Chüan-chou are all strikingly similar to those of the Han period in North China. Three *wu-shu* coins found at Zayton, which were in circulation before the T'ang dynasty, might have convinced us that the Zayton tombs were pre-T'ang in date. However, the inscriptions on the bricks clearly indicate that they were manufactured in the T'ang dynasty— to be exact, A.D. 629–630. Thus it is evident that the chronological sequence arrived at from the study of the North China material cannot be applied in Fukien.

The same is true when we come to the material in Szechwan. According to our present knowledge of the subject, the development of mortuary pottery in this province took place in two stages, without an intermediate period such as that of the Six Dynasties in North China. The first is represented by the pottery objects unearthed from the Han tombs, the second by the material of the Sung tombs we have just described. There is no doubt that the technique and style of the wares followed those of North China, but the dates are far later. The first stage might have continued into the Six dynasties or even later, while the North China T'ang style did not become fully developed in West China until the Sung period. The warriors and the male and female figures are typical examples.

However, some local differences can be observed. In the graves of North China, we expect to find figures of horses and camels of every description, as well as human figures with the prominent nose and deep-set eyes of western Asiatic origin, but none of these central Asiatic creatures has been found in the Szechwan Sung tombs. On the other hand, some new types are evident. The crouching or prostrate female figure is very common, reminding us of the sphinx. The pig with spotted wings is most certainly not an importation from North China. The human-headed snake, the standing dragon and the discoidal mask with pedestal are all types unknown in North or East China.

With regard to the last type, the pedestal mask, I am inclined to think that it represents a degenerate form of a Han-T'ang prototype. A tomb guardian in the form of a lion-like creature with one horn can be seen today in practically every collection of Chinese art. In the Han period, this animal was known as *Pi-hsieh* 辟 邪 or *Fang-hsiang* 方 相 and in the T'ang period as *Fang-hsiang* or *Ch'i-t'ou* 魌 頭. As it was used in the tomb to chase away the evil spirits that might infest the burial place, it was always represented as about to charge on any intruder, a creature of ferocious appearance, full of dynamic force. The degeneration of this powerful creature seems to have started in North China where it began to be represented in a sitting or squatting position (Pl. 118). In the T'ang figures, we notice at once a marked reduction in the size of the body and a consequent enlargement of the head and face. It retains the ferocious air of the Han type, but loses its dynamic force and becomes very grotesque in shape. The Sung figures found in Szechwan seem to have carried the process of degeneration to its climax. In one case, the head was reduced to a discoidal mask, and the body to a stand with four legs in a row (Pl. 111. 1, 2). The second figure shows the simplification of the mask and the shortening of the legs (Pl. 111. 3). A third becomes a discoidal drum on a stand, which retains only a small segment of the two front paws (Pl. 112. 1). A fourth figure is represented only by a drum-shaped disc on a stand without any decoration (Pl. 112. 2). Finally, in Plate 112. 3, we see a simple disc on a base decorated with a pair of spirals in low relief. All these examples have indeed lost their original ferocious characteristics. From an artistic point of view, these figures are very poor specimens indeed, but they should be preserved not only to illustrate the degeneration of the once-powerful tomb guardian, but also to give witness to an old proverb:

Much sitting has made the lion small.

BIBLIOGRAPHY

INTRODUCTION

1. GRAHAM, D. C. A preliminary report of the Hanchou excavation, *JWCBRS* **6** (1934), 114–31.
2. CHÊNG, Tê-k'un. *A history of ancient Szechwan* (Chengtu, 1946), 24–30. Cf. Fêng Han-yi, The megalithic remains of the Chengtu plain, *JWCBRS* **16** (1945), 15–22.
3. WEI, Chü-hsien. The culture of Pa and Shu 巴 蜀 文 化, *SWYK*, **3.4** (1941), 1–29.
4. RUDOLPH, Richard C. and WÊN Yu. *Han tomb art of West China* (Berkeley, 1951).
5. YANG, Hsiao-ku. On Szechwan pottery, *Hua-hsi wên wu* 華 西 文 物 **1** (1951), 8–10.
6. GRAHAM, David C. The pottery of Ch'iung-lai and the Liu-li-ch'ang kiln site, *JWCBRS* **11** (1939), 36–53.
7. CH'ÊNG, Ên-yüan. Notes on the Ta-fo-yüan at Ch'iung-lai, *Hua-hsi wên wu* **1** (1951), 11–21.
8. CHÊNG, Tê-k'un. *HJAS* **8** (1945), 235–41. Cf. Chêng, Tê-k'un, The Royal Tomb of Wang Chien, *Sinologica* **2** (1949), 1–11; Fêng Han-yi, Discovery and excavation of the Yung Ling, *Archives of the Chinese Art Society of America* **2** (1947), 11–20; Sullivan, D. Michael, The excavation of a T'ang imperial tomb, *Illustrated London News*, 20 April 1946.

PART I

ARCHAEOLOGY OF SZECHWAN

9. BABER, E. Colborne. *Travels and researches in western China*, Royal Geographical Society, Supplementary Papers, London, **1** (1882) 1, 129–44.
10. EDGAR, J. Huston. Stone implements on the upper Yangtze and Min rivers. *Journal of the North China Branch of the Royal Asiatic Society* **48** (1917), 85–7.
11. EDGAR, J. Huston. Stone age in China, *JWCBRS* **3** (1926–9), 107.
12. EDGAR, J. Huston. Prehistoric remains in Hsik'ang, *JWCBRS* **6** (1933–4), 56–61.
13. DYE, Daniel S. Data on West China artifacts, *JWCBRS* **2** (1924–5), 63–73.
14. DYE, Daniel S. Symbolism of the designs, *JWCBRS* **2** (1924–5), 45, 75.
15. GRANGER, Walter. Palaeontological exploration in eastern Szechwan, *NHCA* **1** (1932), 501–28.
16. NELSON, N. C. Prehistoric man of central China, *NH* **26** (1926), 570–9: reprinted with slight revision under the title, Archaeological reconnaissance in the Yangtse river gorges, *NHCA* **1** (1932), 542–9.
17. NELSON, N. C. *Journal of the Central Asiatic Expedition to the Yangtse river gorges region*, typewritten manuscript, *AMNH*, New York, 1–115.

18. NELSON, N. C. *Central Asiatic Expedition of the American Museum of Natural History to the Yangtze river, Nov. 6, 1925 to April 6, 1926,* 156 photographs (No. 1925–2081), AMNH, New York.

19. NELSON, N. C. Catalogue of specimens from the Yangtze gorge, *Catalogue of Archaeological specimens in the American Museum of Natural History,* Vol. 73; Asia, working copy, 5–23.

20. GRANGER, Walter. A Reconnaissance in Yünnan, 1926–7, *NHCA* **1** (1932), 529–41.

21. NELSON, N. C. *Journal of the Central Asiatic Expedition to the Province of Yünnan,* typewritten manuscript, AMNH, New York, 1–110.

22. NELSON, N. C. *Central Asiatic Expedition of the American Museum of Natural History to the Province of Yünnan, September, 1926 to March, 1927,* 207 photographs (No. 2081–288), AMNH, New York.

23. NELSON, N. C. Catalogue of specimens from Yünnan, *Catalogue of Archaeological specimens in the American Museum of Natural History,* Vol. 73, Asia, working copy, 1–4.

24. HEIM, Arnold. *Minya Gongkar,* Berlin, 1933, 175–6.

25. BOWLES, Gordon T. A preliminary report of archaeological investigations on the Sino-Tibetan border of Ssŭ-ch'uan, *BGSC* **13** (1933), 119–41.

26. GRAHAM, David C. Implements of prehistoric men in the West China University Museum of Archaeology, *JWCBRS* **7** (1935), 47–56.

27. GRAHAM, David C. A late neolithic culture in Szechwan province, *JWCBRS* **7** (1935), 90–7.

28. *Pictures of objects in the West China Union University Museum of Archaeology,* 46 photographs, album copy, Peabody Museum, Harvard University.

29. GRAHAM, David C. A preliminary report of the Hanchou excavation, *JWCBRS* **6** (1933–4), 114–31.

30. DYE, Daniel S. Some ancient Circles, Squares, Angles, and Curves in earth and in stone in Szechwan, China, *JWCBRS* **4** (1930–1), 97–105.

31. BISHOP, C. W. Letter regarding the Hanchou excavation, *JWCBRS* **7** (1935), 132–3.

32. GRAHAM, David C. An expedition to the China Tibetan border, *JWCBRS* **9** (1937), 215–17.

33. ANDERSSON, J. G. Glaciological and archaeological research in the Hsi k'ang, *BMFEA* **11** (1939), 45–73.

GEOGRAPHY AND LOCAL GAZETTEERS

34. TING, Wên-chiang (V. K.) and others. *Chung hua min kuo hsin ti t'u,* Shanghai, 1934 (53 maps); 丁文江等, 中華民國新地圖.

35. CRESSEY, George Babcock. *China's Geographic Foundations,* London, 1934 (pp. 17+436).

36. HOSIE, Alexander. *Report on the province of Szechwan,* presented to both Houses of Parliament by command of His Majesty, *China,* **5** (1904), 1–101; London, 1904.

37. HOSIE. Alexander. *Three years in western China: a narrative of three journeys in Ssŭ-ch'uan, Kuei-chow and Yün-nan,* London, 1897 (pp. 27+302).

38. LEE, C. Y. 李春昱. The development of the upper Yangtze valley, *BGSC* **13** (1933), 107–17.

39. HO, Chin-shên. *Hsia-chiang t'u k'ao*, 1877 (pp. 68); 賀縉紳, 峽江圖攷.

40. LIU, Shêng-yüan. *Hsia-chiang t'an hsien chih*, Peking, 1920 (3 ch. 63 fig.); 劉聲元, 峽江灘險志.

41. YANG, Fang-ts'an and others. *Ssǔ-ch'uan t'ung chih*, 1816 (204 ch.); 楊芳燦 等, 四川通志.

42. KUNG, Hsi-t'ai. *Ssǔ-ch'uan chün hsien chih*, Cheng-tu, 1935 (12 ch.); 龔熙台, 四川郡縣志.

43. LIU, Tê-ch'üan. *K'uei-chou-fu chih*, 1827, supplemented 1891 (36 ch.); 劉德銓, 夔州府志.

44. YANG, Tê-k'un. *Fêng-chieh-hsien chih*, 1893 (36 ch.); 楊德坤, 奉節縣志.

45. KUO, Wên-chên. *Yün-yang-hsien chih*, 1935 (44 ch.); 郭文珍, 雲陽縣志.

46. FAN, T'ai-hêng. *Wan-hsien chih*, 1866 (36 ch.); 范泰衡, 萬縣志.

47. HUA, Kuo-ch'ing. *Lu-chou-chih-li-chou chih*, 1882 (12 ch.); 華國清, 瀘州直隸州志.

48. CH'IU, Chin-ch'êng. *Hsü-chou-fu chih*, 1895 (43 ch.); 邱晉成, 敍州府志.

49. HUANG, Yung. *Lo-shan-hsien chih*, 1934 (12 ch.); 黃鎔, 樂山縣志.

50. HOU, Chao-yüan. *Han-chou chih*, 1812 (40 ch.); 侯肇元, 漢州志.

51. TSÊNG, Li-chung. *Han-chou hsü chih*, 1869 (24 ch.); 曾履中, 漢州續志.

52. LÜ, T'iao-yang. *P'êng-hsien chih*, 1878, new edition 1917 (13 ch.); 呂調陽, 彭縣志.

53. CHÊNG, Ti-shan. *Kuan-hsien chih*, 1886 (14 ch.); 鄭峛山, 灌縣志.

54. CHOU, Tso-i. *Li-fan-t'ing chih*, 1866 (6 ch.); 周祚嶧, 理番廳志.

55. KUNG, Shao-jên. *I-tu-hsien chih*, 1866 (4 ch.); 龔紹仁, 宜都縣志.

56. WANG, Po-hsin. *I-ch'ang-fu chih*, 1864–6 (16 ch.); 王柏心, 宜昌府志.

57. HUANG, Shih-ch'ung. *Kuei-chou chih*, 1900 (17 ch.); 黃世崇, 歸州志.

CHINESE CLASSICS AND HISTORY

58. JUAN, Yüan (1764–1849). *Shang-shu chu su*, 1815 (20 ch.), Nan-ch'ang ed; 阮元, 尚書注疏.

59. JUAN, Yüan. *Tso-chuan chu su*, 1815 (60 ch.), Nan-ch'ang ed; 阮元, 左傳注疏.

60. JUAN, Yüan. *Êrh-ya chu su*, 1815 (10 ch.), Nan-ch'ang ed; 阮元, 爾雅注疏.

61. LEGGE, James. *The Chinese Classics*, Oxford, 1893–5 (7 vol.).

62. SSǓ-MA, Ch'ien (born 145 B.C.). *Shih-chi*, Shanghai, 1894 (180 ch.), T'ung-wên ed; 司馬遷, 史記.

63. PAN, Ku (32–92), *Han-shu*, Shanghai, 1894 (100 ch.), T'ung-wen ed; 班固, 漢書.

64. TING, Ch'ien (1843–1919). *Geographical notes on the Hsi-nan yi chuan*, *Han-shu*, Hang-chou 1915 (1 ch.); 丁謙, 漢書西南夷傳地理攷證.

65. CH'ANG, Ch'ü (Chin 晉 dynasty). *Hua-yang-kuo chih*, Shanghai, 1934 (12 ch.), *Ssǔ pu pei yao* ed; 常璩, 華陽國志.

66. FU, Sung-mu. *Hsi-k'ang chien shêng chi*, Nanking, 1932 (p. 254); 傅嵩炑, 西康建省記.

67. JÊN, Nai-ch'iang. *Hsi-k'ang t'u ching*, Nanking, 1933 (pp. 246); 任乃強, 西康圖經.

ARCHAEOLOGY OF SIBERIA

68. BAYE, Joseph, Marquis de et VOLKOV, Th. Le gisement paléolithique d'Aphontova-Gora près de Krasnoïarsk, *L'Anthropologie* **10** (1899), 172–8.

69. ABBOTT, W. J. Lewis. Stone implements from the frozen gravel of the Yenisei, *Man* **4** (1904), 145–7.

70. PETRI, Bernard E., Neoliticheskiia nakhodki na beregu Baikala, *Publications de L'Academie Impériale des Science de St.-Pétersbourg* **3** (1916), 113–32.

71. TORII, Ryūzō 鳥居龍藏. On the prehistoric age of Siberia, *JAST* **35** (1920), 1–22, 33–46.

72. ŌYAMA, Kashiwa 大山柏. On some archaeological objects from Siberia, *JAST* **35** (1920), 147–53, 274–5.

73. MERHART, G. von. The palaeolithic period in Siberia, *AA* **25** (1923), 21–55.

74. BREUIL, H. Pierre taillé présumée paléolithique de Skotovó (Sibérie orientale), *L'Anthropologie* **35** (1925), 404–5.

75. PETRIE, Bernard E. *Sibirskiĭ paleolit*, Atlas Risunki ispolneny M. M. GERASIMOVYM, Irkutsk, 1927 (20 pl.).

76. PETRIE, B. E. *Dalekoe proshloe pribaĭkal'ia Izdanie Vtoroe ispravlennoe i dopolnennoe*, Irkutsk, 1928 (pp. 73).

77. MERHART, G. von. Siberien. B. Neolithikum, *RV* **12** (1928), 57–71.

78. JOCHELSON, W. *Archaeological investigations in Kamchatka*, Carnegie Institution, Publication 388, 1928 (23–36, 37–40).

79. SCHNELL, Ivar. Prehistoric finds from the island world of the Far East, now preserved in the Museum of Far Eastern Antiquities, Stockholm, *BMFEA* **4** (1932), 15–104.

80. MONTANDON, George. Instruments néolithiques et poteries de la region de Vladivostok comparés aux objets similaires de Suisse, *ASAG* **5** (1932), 222–30.

81. AUERBAKH, N. K. and SOSNOVSKIĬ, G. P. *Materialy k izucheniiu paleolitcheskoĭ industrii i usloviĭ ee nakhozhdeniia na stoianke Afontova Gora*, Trudy, Akademii nauk SSSR, and Komissii po izucheniiu chetvertichnogo perioda, Leningrad, **1** (1932), 45–114.

82. GOLOMSHTOCK, E. A. Anthropological activities in Soviet Russia, *AA* **35** (1933), 301–27.

83. SOSNOVSKIĬ, G. P. *Sledy prebyvaniia paleoliticheskogo cheloveka v Zabaĭkal'e*, Trudy, Akademii nauk SSSR, and Komissii po izucheniiu chetvertichnogo perioda **3** (1933), 23–39.

84. NAKAYAMA, Eiji 中山英司. Neolithic remains from the western coast of Kamchatka Peninsula, *JAST* **48** (1933), 63–71.

85. NAKAYAMA, Eiji. Neolithic remains from the western coast of Kamchatka Peninsula, *JAST* **49** (1934), 375–88.

86. PANICHKINA, M. Z. O datirovke nahodki u st. Innokentievskoy na Amure, *Sovietskaya Etnografiya* **4–5** (1935), 211–16.

87. LEV, D. Novye Arkheologicheskie Pamiatniki Kamchatki, *Sovietskaya Etnografiya* **4–5** (1935), 217–24.

88. GERASIMOV, M. M. Raskopki paleolitncheskoĭ stoianki v sele Mal'te, *Paleolit SSSR* **118** (1935), 78–124.

89. SOSNOVKIĬ, G. P. Posdnelaleolitcheskie stoianki Eniseĭskoi doliny, *Paleolit SSSR* **118** (1935), 152–218.

90. BABA, O. 馬場修. Archaeological investigations in the Shimushu Islands (Kurile Is.), *JAST* **49** (1934), 39–63; **51** (1935), 91–115.

91. FIELD, Henry and PROSTOV, Eugene. Recent archaeological investigations in the Soviet Union, *AA* **38** (1936), 260–90.

92. GORODTSOV, V. A. Urtuiskaia mikroliticheskaia stoianka v basseine r. Amura, *Sovietskaya Arkheologiya* **1** (1936), 105–12.

93. OKLADNIKOV, A. P. K Arkheologicheskim Issledovaniyam v 1935 na Amure, *Sovietskaya Arkheologiya* **1** (1936), 275–8.

94. FIELD, Henry and PROSTOV, Eugene. Archaeology in the Soviet Union, *AA* **39** (1937), 457–90.

95. FIELD, Henry and PROSTOV, Eugene. Archaeology in the U.S.S.R., *AA* **40** (1938), 653–79.

96. FIELD, Henry and PROSTOV, Eugene. Archaeological researches in the U.S.S.R., 1938–1939, *AA* **42** (1940), 211–35.

97. FIELD, Henry and PROSTOV, Eugene. Archaeology in the Soviet Union, *Antiquity*, December, 1940 (404–26).

98. OKLADNIKOV, A. P. Buret, novaia paleoliticheskaia stoianka na Angare, *Sovietskaya Arkheologiya* **5** (1940), 290–3.

ARCHAEOLOGY OF JAPAN AND KOREA

99. MORSE, Edward S. Shell-mounds of Omori, *MUT* **1.1** (1879), 1–36, 18 pls.

100. IIJIMA 飯島 Isao and SASAKI 佐佐木 Chūjirō, Okadira shell mound at Hitachi, *MUT* **1.1** (1883). Appendix 1–7, 11 pls.

101. KANDA 神田 T. Notes on ancient stone implements, etc., of Japan, Tokyo, 1884 (pp. 8, pls. 24).

102. MUNRO, N. G. *Prehistoric Japan*, Yokohama, 1911 (pp. 17+705).

103. HAMADA, Kōsaku 濱田耕作. Report upon the excavation of a neolithic site at Kōmura, near Dōmyōji, in the Province of Kawashi, *RARKU* **2** (1918), 1–48.

104. UMEHARA, Sueji 梅原末治. Notes on neolithic sites at Takayasu and at Kishi in the Province of Kawachi, *RARKU* **2** (1918), 49–60.

105. MATSUMURA, A. 松村瞭. The shell-mounds of Ogido in Riu-kiu, *PAI* **3** (1920), 1–70.

106. HAMADA, Kōsaku. Second excavation at Kô, a neolithic site in the Province of Kawachi, *RARKU* **4** (1920), 1–34.

107. HAMADA, K. and others. Excavation of the shell-mound at Tsu-kumo, a neolithic cemetery in the Province of Bitchu, *RARKU* **5** (1920), 1–28.

108. HAMADA, K. and others. Excavation of the Todoroki shell-mound in the Province of Higo, *RARKU* **5** (1920), 65–79.

109. HAMADA, K. and SHIMADA, S. 島田貞彦. Excavation of the shell-mound at Idzumi, in the Province of Satsuma, *RARKU* **6** (1921), 1–12.

110. HAMADA, K. A prehistoric site at Ibusuki, *RARKU* **6** (1921), 29–48.

111. ŌYAMA, K. Study of the shell-mounds at Iha, Loochoo Islands, *JAST* **36** (1921), 1–29.

112. TORII, R. *Prehistoric and protohistoric periods in upper Iida*, Tokyo, 1925 (pp. 18+290+ 15, 60 pls.).

113. NAKAYA, Jūjirō. *The stone age of Japan*, Tokyo, 1929 (pp. 580); 中谷治宇二郎, 日本石器時代提要.

114. KOHNO, Isamu. 甲野勇. Mitteilungen über die Ausgrabung der Musshelhaufen von Nakazuma beim Dorf Komomma, Provinz Ibaraki, *SZ* 1 (1929), 37–56.

115. SHIMADA, S. Studies on the prehistoric site of Okamoto, Suku, in the Province of Chikuzen, *RARKU* 11 (1930), 1–78.

116. SANO, Buyū 佐野武勇. Stone implements from the plain about the southern foot of Mt Fuji, *JAST* 45 (1930), 288–94.

117. MOROZUMI, Moriichi 兩角守一. Untersuchung von prä- und protohistorischen Funden in der Umgebung von Suwa unter Begleitung Seiner Kaiserlichen Hoheit Prinz Fushimi, *SZ* 2 (1930), 58–72.

118. MIYASAKA, Mitsuji 宮坡光次. Die Steinzeiliche Fundstation von Ichi-ohji bei Korekawa, nordost Japan, *SZ* 2 (1930), 377–57.

119. ŌYAMA, Kashiwa. Korekawa-Funde vom Korekawa, einer charakterischen steinzeitlichen Station von Kame-ga-oka Typus der Nord-Ost Jomon-Kultur, *SZ* 2 (1930), 235–81.

120. OGATA, J. 尾形順一郎 and MATSUSHITA, T. 松下胤信. Über dem Muschelhaufen Tohzenji bei Yokohama, No. 3, *SZ* 2 (1930), 381–94.

121. HIGUCHI, Kiyoyuki 樋口清之. Über die neu gefundenen Muschelhaufen Mori unweit von Takada, Prov. Bungo, Kyūshū, *SZ* 3 (1931), 18.

122. IKEGAMI, Keisuke 池上啓介. Kulturreste von der Fundstation Nogawa, Province Musashi, *SZ* 3 (1931), 188–91.

123. HIGUCHI, Kiyoyuki. Neu gefundene steinzeitliche Reste aus der Prov. Iyo, Insel Shikoku, *SZ* 3 (1931), 253–4.

124. SCHNELL, Ivar. Prehistoric finds from the island world of the Far East, *BMFEA* 4 (1932), 15–104.

125. YAWATA, Ichirō 八幡一郎. The Stone Age site at Ubayama Shimosa, *PAI* 5 (1932), 1–72, pls. 25.

126. YOKOYAMA, Shōsaburō 横山將三郎. Ausgrabungsbericht ueber den Muschelhaufen Tôsandô auf der Insel Maki-no-shima, Sued-Korea, *SZ* 5 (1933), 4, 1–49.

127. HIGUCHI, Kiyoyuki. Uebersicht über die Funkstationen im Kreis Kita, Province Ehime, *SZ* 5 (1933), 77–96.

128. HAYASHI, Kwaiichi 林魁一. Ueber die Fundstationen in der Umgebung von Takayama, Prov. Gifu und die Dort gefundenen Gegenstände, *SZ* 5 (1933), 97–109.

129. ŌYAMA, Kashiwa and OBARA, Kazuo 小原一夫. Kulturreste aus dem Muschelhaufen Omonawa No. 1, Insel Toku-no-Shima, Ryukiu Archepel, *SZ* 5 (1933), 301–8.

130. AKABOSHI, Naotada 赤星直忠. Fundstationen Hiratoyama, bei Oofuna-Machi, Prov. Sagami, *SZ* 6 (1934), 15–28.

131. TAKASHIMA, Tokusaburō 高島德三郎. Ueber die Funde von Uenodai, Militärübungsplatz Toyama-no-hara, Tokio, *SZ* 6 (1934), 46–51.

132. SHICHIDA, Tadashi 七田忠志. Ueber die ornamentierte Yayoi Keramik aus Senjôgatani, Prov. Saga, *SZ* 6 (1934), 99–103.

133. IKEGAMI, Keisuke. Steinzeitlichen Funde vom Tendô-yama, Prov. Mie, *SZ* **6** (1934), 105–10.

134. IKEGAMI, Keisuke. Die steinzeitlichen Funde Yayoika beim Dorf Nagamura, Prov. Tochigi, *SZ* **6** (1934), 115–16.

135. TANAKA, Y. 田中幸夫. On stone implements of Okitsumiya, in the Province of Chikuzen, *KZ* **25** (1935), 108–19.

136. GOTŌ, Juichi 後藤壽一. A report of the excavation of pit graves at Ebetsu, Hokkaido, *KZ* **25** (1935), 298–327.

137. YAWATA, Ichirō. Notes on microliths from Hokkaido, *JAST* **50** (1935), 128–30.

138. AKABOSHI, Naotada. Bericht über die steinzeitlichen Fundstation Tado bei der Stadt Yokosuka, Prov. Kanagawa, *SZ* **7** (1935), 267–96.

139. HAYASHI, Kwaiichi. Prehistoric remains from Kōkuchi, Gifu Province, *JARS* **3** (1935), 13–21.

140. HAYASHI, Kwaiichi. Sites and relics of the Stone Age found at Asahimura, Hida, *JAST* **51** (1936), 164–75.

141. KASAHARA, Ugan 笠原烏丸. A neolithic site containing the Kammkeramik found at Seikori, northern Korea, *JAST* **51** (1936), 183–97, 256–67.

142. HIGUCHI, Kiyoyuki. Bericht über den Muschelhaufen Tsutajima, bei ber Insel Ko-Tsutajima, nahe der Stadt Nio, Gau Sanuki, Insel Shikoku, *SZ* **8** (1936), 1–22.

143. IKEGAMI, Keisuke. Die steinzeitliche Siedelung Tsukinokizawa bein Dorf Karino, Prov. Tochigi, No. 2, *SZ* **8** (1936), 23–44.

144. MATSUMOTO, Kichiji 松本吉治. Jomonfunde Kawayama beim Dorf Miyakoda, Kreis Inasa, Prov. Shizuoka (Mittel-Hon-do), *SZ* **8** (1936), 284–308.

145. IKEGAMI, Kichiji. Neueres Steinmateriae vom Gau Hida, *SZ* **8** (1936), 311–12.

146. MIMORI, Sadao 三森定男. Ona prehistoric site in the Kagawa Province, *JARS* **4** (1937), 337–73.

147. SERIZAWA, Chōsuke 芹澤長介 and others. On the Jomon pottery and stone implements from Ōhitō and Suruga, Shizuoka Province, *JARS* **5** (1937), 1–25.

148. MITOMO, Kokugorō 三友國五郎. Stone implements from Fukuoka, *JARS* **5** (1937), 46–59.

149. GOTŌ, Juichi. Sites of dwelling with stone-paved floor at Haketa, Musashi Province, *KZ* **27** (1937), 429–62.

150. GOTŌ, Juichi. Prehistoric sites and relics found in Sapporo, Hokkaido, *KZ* **27** (1937), 585–619.

151. ŌYAMA, Kashiwa. Der Ausgrabungsbericht über den Muschelhaufen Kasori, beim Dorf Miyako, Prov. Chiba, *SZ* **9** (1937), 1–68.

152. AKABOSHI, Naotada. Wieder über den Muschelhaufen Kayama, *SZ* **9** (1937), 114–18.

153. SAITŌ, Fusatarō 齊藤房太郎. Yayoi-Steinbeile vom Azumadai bei Yokohama, *SZ* **9** (1937), 119.

154. ŌYAMA, K. and others. Ausgrabungsbericht über die Muschelhaufengruppe Takaku-Neka, beim Dorf Funashima, Prov. Ibaraki, *SZ* **9** (1937), 191–224.

155. ŌYAMA, K. and others. Ausgrabungsbericht über den Muschelhaufen Ichinomiya, bei der kleinen Stadt Ichinomiya, Prov. Chiba, *SZ* **9** (1937), 239–74.

156. AKABOSHI, Naotada. Ausgrabungsbericht über den Muschelhaufen Yoshii, beim Halbinsel Miura, Prov. Kanagawa, *SZ* **9** (1937) 299–337.

157. HAYASHI, Kwaiichi. Ueber die steinzeitlichen Funde beim Dorf Kamitakara, Gau Hida, *SZ* **9** (1937), 338–50.

158. SAKAZUME, Nakao 酒詰仲男 and SERIZAWA, Chōsuke. Relics found in the kitchen midden of Aratate in Yokohama, *KZ* **28** (1938), 93–108.

159. GOTŌ, Juichi. Neolithic site of Temiya, Hokkaido, *KZ* **28** (1938), 806–29.

160. ARIMITSU, Kyōichi 有光教一. Prehistoric relics from Kôgendô, Chôsen, *KZ* **28** (1938), 709–29.

161. YAWATA, Ichiro. Cylindrical axes with pointed butt of prehistoric Japan, *JAST* **53** (1938), 25–9.

162. INŌ, Tentarō 稲生典太郎. Steinwerkzeuge von der Nordküste Hokkaidōs und der Insel Süd-Chishima am Ochotskischen Meers *SZ* **10** (1938), 9–21.

163. NAKAGAWA, Naosuke 忠川直亮. Der Siedlungsfund Aradate bei Yokohama, *SZ* **10** (1938), 22–37.

164. MIYAZAKI, Tadasu 宮崎糺. Ueberreste der Steinzeit in der Gegend von Ninomiya, Nishitamagun, Tokyo-fu, *SZ.* **10** (1938), 66–85.

165. HORINO, Ryōnosuke 堀野良之助. Zahlreiche Ueberreste der Steinzeit bei Ekoda, *SZ* **10** (1938), 89–92.

166. HIGUCHI, Kiyoyuki. Ueber den Muschelhaufen Minamikusaki, bei der kleinen Stadt Nio, Prov. Ehime, Insel Shikoku, *SZ* **10** (1938), 186–202.

167. MUTŌ, Tetsujō 武藤鉄城. Ausgrabungsbericht über die Fundstation Fudanoki, beim Dorf Kamiyo, Prov. Akita, *SZ* **10** (1938), 203–9.

168. KUROKAWA, Sakuma 黒川作間. Stone Age sites in the Shibayamagata, Ishikawa Prefecture, *KZ* **29** (1939), 47–53.

169. OKAZAKI, Takashi 岡崎敬. Neolithic sites along the upper Onga river in northern Kyūshū, *KZ* **29** (1939), 125–35.

170. HAYASHI, Kwaiichi. On some artifacts from the Stone Age sites in Hida District, *JAST* **54** (1939), 162–5.

171. SAKAZUME, Nakao. General view of Stone Age sites in Imbagun, Chiba-ken, *JAST* **54** (1939), 305–56.

172. WAJIMA, Seiichi 和島誠一. A report on the neolithic sites around Lake Inba, Saitama-ken, *JAST* **54** (1939), 469–83.

173. ŌYAMA, Kashiwa. Klassifikation der Steinzeitlichen Kulturreste, I. Lieferung, Die Steinwerkzeuge, *SZ* **11** (1939), 1–200.

174. YAMAMOTO, H. 山本博. The Yayoi type relics excavated in the river bed of the Yamato-gawa, Kawachi Province, *KZ* **30** (1940), 776–803.

175. YAJIMA, S. 矢島清作. The Stone Age dwelling sites at Mayezawa, Kurume-mura, Musashi Province, *KZ* **30** (1940), 804–16.

ARCHAEOLOGY OF MANCHURIA, MONGOLIA AND SINKIANG

176. SMITH, R. A. The Stone Age in Chinese Turkestan, *Man* **11** (1911), 81–3.

177. ANDERSSON, J. C. The cave-deposit of Shakoutun in Fêngtien, *PS* D1.1 (1923), 1–47, 12 pls.

178. LICENT, E. and TEILHARD DE CHARDIN, P. Notes sur deux instruments agricoles du Néolithiques de Chine, *L'Anthropologie* **35** (1925), 63–74.

179. NELSON, N. C. The dune dwellers of the Gobi, *NH* **26** (1926), 246–51.

180. BERKEY, Charles P. and NELSON, N. C. Geology and prehistoric archaeology of Gobi Desert, *American Museum Novitates* **222** (1926), 11–14.

181. YAGI, S. 八木奘三郎. *Manshū kōkogaku* or the archaeology of Manchuria, Tokyo, 1928 (pp. 13 + 7 + 621).

182. HAMADA, K., *Pi-tzǔ-wo* 貔子窩. *Prehistoric Sites by the River Pi-liu-ho, South Man-churia*, *AO* A **1** (1929), 16 ch., 2 supplements.

183. LICENT, E. Les Gisements néolithiques representes au Musée Hoangho-Paiho de Tientsin, Japanese translation by MATSUMOTO, H. 松本廣信, *JAST* **46** (1931), 35–46, 90–102, 127–37.

184. LOUKASHKIN, A. S. New data on neolithic culture in northern Manchuria, *BGSC* **9** (1931), 171–81.

185. TEILHARD DE CHARDIN, Pierre. Some Observation on the archaeological material collected by Mr. Loukashkin near Tsitsihar, *BGSC* **9** (1931), 183–93.

186. KOMAKI, Saneshige 小牧實繁 and others. On the Neolithic Sites in Dolonor, Mon-golia, *JAST* **46** (1931), 291–6.

187. EGAMI, Namio 江上波夫. The stone age of south-eastern Mongolia, *KZ* **22** (1932), 228–37, 297–308.

188. TORII, Ryūzō. Restes néolithiques de la Mandchourie méridionale et de la Mongolie orientale, *PAO* **1** (1932), 91–2.

189. LICENT, E. *Les Collections néolithiques du Musee Hoangho Paiho de Tientsin*, 2 vols., 98, 113 pls. Publications du Musée Hoangho Paiho de Tientsin 14; Tientsin, 1932.

190. TEILHARD DE CHARDIN, P. and YOUNG, C. C. 楊鍾健. On some Mesolithic (and possibly Palaeolithic) finds in Mongolia, Sinkiang and West China, *BGSC* **12** (1932), 83–104.

191. LIANG, Ssǔ-yung 梁思永. A prehistoric site at Ang-ang-hsi, *CYYY* **4.1** (1932), 1–44.

192. KOMAI, K. 駒井和愛. A neolithic site in Manchuria, *KZ* **24** (1934), 11–16.

193. EGAMI, N. and others. A neolithic site at Shuang-ta-tzǔ-shan near Port Arthur, Manchuria, *JAST* **49** (1934), 1–11.

194. MIKAMI, T. 三上次男. A prehistoric site in J'uan-shan-tzǔ, Kirin Plains, Manchuria, *JAST* **49** (1934), 235–6.

195. YAWATA, I. Contribution to the prehistoric archaeology of southern Jehol, *RFSEM* **6.1** (1935), 1–106.

196. KOMAI, K. and MIKAMI, T. Stone implements from San-ling-tun, Pin-chiang Pro-vince, Manchoukou, *KZ* **26** (1936), 487–96.

197. YAWATA, I. Neolithic sites in Chao-yang-hsien, Jehol, *KZ* **26** (1936), 685–700.

198. MIZUNO, Seiichi 水野清一 and KOMAI, K. Neolithic sites at Shih-pei-ling and Tieh-ling, Manchuria, *JAST* **51** (1936), 405–15.

199. TOKUNAGA, Shigeyasu 德永重康 and NAORA, Nobuo 直良信夫. Palaeolithic artifacts excavated at Ho-chia-kou in Ku-hsiang-tung, Manchoukuo, *RFSEM* **6.2** (1936), 1–107.

200. EGAMI, N. and MIZUNO, S. *Inner Mongolia and the region of the Great Wall* 內蒙古長城地帶, *AO* B**1** (1936). Part 1, 1–62.

201. LIANG, Ssǔ-yung. Neolithic finds made in the Province of Jêhê (Jehol), *TYKP* **1** (1936), 1–67, I–X.

202. AKABORI, Eizō 赤 堀 英 三 and MIKAMI, T. Ta-miao: prehistoric sites in the north-western part of Jehol, *KZ* **27** (1937), 281–303.

203. SHIMAMURA, K. 島 村 孝 三 郎 and KOBAYASHI, T. 小 林 知 生. Neolithic site of Szǔ-tao-tsing-tzǔ, Ch'ih-fêng, *KZ* **28** (1938), 258–65.

204. KODAMA, S. 兒 玉 重 雄 and MARUOKA, Y. 丸 岡 良 郎. Prehistoric sites in the neighbourhood of Ch'êngtê, Jehol, *KZ* **28** (1938), 277–280.

205. SHIMADA, S. Relics of Stone Age from Khailar, *KZ* **28** (1938), 548–50.

206. HAMADA, K. *Hung-shan-hou, Ch'ih-fêng* 赤 峯 紅 山 後 *AO* A6 (1938), 7 ch. 3 supple-ments; Tokyo, 1938.

207. NELSON, N. C. Archaeology of Mongolia, *Compte-rendu de la deuxième session of the Congrès International des Sciences Anthropologiques et Éthnologiques, Copenhague,* 1938 (259–62); Copenhagen, 1939.

208. AKABORI, Eizō. A few additional findings from Djalai-nor deposit, north Manchuria, *JAST* **54** (1939), 93–8.

209. OKUDA, Naoshige 奧 田 直 榮. Note on the prehistoric artifacts from Sunghuaching, north Manchuria, *JAST* **54** (1939), 459–63.

210. YAWATA, I. Additional notes on some prehistoric relics in northern Manchuria, *JAST* **54** (1939), 464–6.

211. BERGMAN, Folke. *Archaeological researches in Sinkiang; report of the Sino-Swedish Expedition,* Publication 7.1 (1939), 13–37.

212. YAWATA. Contribution to the prehistoric archaeology of northern Jehol, *RFSEM* **6.3** (1940), 1–114.

ARCHAEOLOGY OF NORTH CHINA

213. WU, Ta-ch'êng. *Ku yü t'u k'ao,* Shanghai, 1889 (pp. 144); 吳 大 澂, 古 玉 圖 攷.

214. LAUFER, Berthold. *Jade, a study in Chinese Archaeology and Religion;* Publication 154, Field Museum of Natural History; Chicago, 1912 (pp. 370, 68 pls. and 204 figs.).

215. ANDERSSON, J. G. Stone implements of neolithic types in China, *China Medical Journal* **34.4** (1920), 40–6.

216. POPE-HENNESSY, Una. *Early Chinese Jades,* London, 1923 (pp. 149, 64 pls.).

217. ANDERSSON, J. G. *An early Chinese culture,* Peking, 1923 (pp. 68 + 46 + 15, 16 pls.).

218. ANDERSSON, J. G. Preliminary report on Archaeological research in Kansu, *MGSC* A. **5** (1925), 10–19.

219. TEILHARD DE CHARDIN, P. Fossil man in China and Mongolia, translated by C. D. MATTHEW, *NH* **26** (1926), 238–45.

220. BREUIL, H. Le Paléolithique de la Chine, Troisième Partie, Archéologie, *Archives de L'Institut de Paléontologie Humaine, Mémoire* **4** (1928), 103–38.

221. BARBOUR, George B. The Geology of the Kalgan area, *MGSC* A6 (1929), 1–148.

222. TEILHARD DE CHARDIN, P. and YOUNG, C. C. Preliminary observations on the Pre-loessic and Post-pontian formations in western Shansi and northern Shensi, *MGSC* A8 (1930), 1–35.

223. LI, Chi 李 濟. Report of the Anyang excavation, Autumn season, 1929, *Preliminary reports of excavations at Anyang;* 安 陽 發 掘 報 告, Part 2 (1930), 219–52.

224. KOMAKI, Saneshige and others. Neolithic cave deposit near Kalgan, North China, *JAST* **46** (1931), 319–23

225. MIZUNO, Seiichi. On the neolithic age of China, *KZ* **22** (1932), 663–70.

226. HSÜ, Chung-hsü, *P'iao-shih pien chung t'u shih*, Peiping, 1932 (pp. 13, 24 pls., 24); 徐中舒, 鳳氏編鐘圖釋.

227. FU, Chên-lun, Yen Hsia-tu fa chüeh pao-kao, *KHCK* **3** (1932), 175–182; 傅振倫, 燕下都發掘報告.

228. BISHOP, C. W. The neolithic age in northern China, *Antiquity* **7** (1933), 389–404.

229. TEILHARD DE CHARDIN, P. and PEI, Wên-chung. The lithic industry of the Sinanthropus deposits in Choukoutien, *BGSC* **11** (1932), 315–64.

230. BLACK, Davidson, and others. Fossil man in China, *MGSC* A**11** (1933), 1–158.

231. WHITE, William Charles. *Tombs of old Lo-yang*, Shanghai, 1934 (pp. 14 + 117, 187 pls.).

232. ANDERSSON, J. G. *Children of the Yellow Earth*, London, 1934 (pp. 21 + 345 + 147, 32 pls.).

233. YOUNG, C. C. and PEI, W. C. On a collection of Yangshao cultural remains from Mienchihhsien, Honan, *BGSC* **13** (1934), 305–18.

234. PEI, W. C. A preliminary report on the late-palaeolithic cave of Choukoutien, *BGSC* **13** (1934), 327–58.

235. PEI, W. C. Report on the excavation of the locality 13 in Choukoutien, *BGSC* **13** (1934), 359–67.

236. TEILHARD DE CHARDIN, P. and PEI, W. C. New discoveries in Choukoutien, 1933–4, *BGSC* **13** (1934), 369–94.

237. LI, Chi and others. *Ch'êng-tzŭ yai* 城子崖, *Archaeologia Sinica* **1** (1934) (pp. 27 + 105, 54 pls.).

238. WHITE, W. C. Sacrificial knives and weapons from ancient China, *The Illustrated London News*, April 20, 1935.

239. LIU, Chieh. *Ch'u ch'i t'u shih*, Peiping, 1935 (pp. 42 + 2, 9 pls., 42 figs.) 劉節, 楚器圖釋.

240. LIANG, Ssŭ-yung, Hsiao-t'un, Lung-shan and Yang-shao. *Studies Presented to Ts'ai Yüan-p'ei on his Sixty-fifth Birthday* **2** (1935), 555–65.

241. EGAMI, N. and MIZUNO, S. *Inner Mongolia and the Region of the Great Wall*, *AO* B**1** (1936), Part 3, 1–40.

242. LIU, Yao 劉燿, Report on the excavation of the prehistoric site at Ta-lai-tien, Hsun Hsien, Honan, *TYKP* **1** (1936), 69–90, I–IX.

243. KUO, Pao-chün 郭寶鈞. Preliminary report on the excavations of the ancient cemetery at Hsin Ts'un, Hsun Hsien, Honan, *TYPK* **1** (1936), 167–200, I–XII.

244. LI, Ching-tan 李景聃. Report on the preliminary investigation of the Ch'u tombs at Shou Hsien, Anhui, *TYKP* **1** (1936), 213–279.

245. HUANG, Chün. *Yeh chung p'ien yü*, Anyang Antiquities B Peiping, 1937 (pp. 49 + 51) 黃濬, 鄴中片羽二集.

246. WU, G. D. 吳金鼎. *Prehistoric Pottery in China*, London 1938 (pp. 11–180, 64 pls.).

247. PEI, W. C. On the upper cave industry, *Peking Natural History Bulletin* **13** (1939), 175–9.

ARCHAEOLOGY OF SOUTH CHINA

248. ANDERSON, J. *A report of the expedition to western Yunnan via Bhamo*, Calcutta 1871, Appendix C, 410–15.

249. MIYABARA, A. 宮原敦. The Stone Age site at Suiteiryo, Formosa *JAST*, **41** (1926), 215–17.

250. KOHNO, Isamu. Geschlissene Steinbeile aus Niitakagun, Formosa, *SZ* **1** (1929), 88–9.

251. KOHNO, Isamu. Hacke der Primitiven in Formosa, *SZ* **1** (1929). 96–7.

252. KANO, Tadao 鹿野忠雄. Tabellen der steinzeitlichen Fundorte von Formosa, *SZ* **1** (1929) 401–4; **2** (1930) 63–5.

253. KANO, Tadao. Ueber der Steinwerkzeuze von der Insel Kohto-sho, Formosa, *SZ* **2** (1930), 213–18.

254. HEANLEY, C. M. and SHELLSHEAR, J. L. A contribution to the prehistory of Hongkong and the New Territories, *PAO* **1** (1932), 63–76.

255. BYLIN, Margit. Notes sur quelques objets néolithiques trouvés à Formose, *BMFEA* **4** (1932), 105–14.

256. FINN, D. J. Archaeological finds on Lamma Island, near Hongkong, 13 Parts, *HN* **3** (1932), 226–46; **4** (1933), 55–70, 132–55; **5** (1934), 46–53, 123–45, 197–209, 282–303; **6** (1935), 40–61, 117–31, 240–71; **7** (1936), 37–60, 163–83, 257–68.

257. UTSURIKAWA, N. 移川子之藏 and MIYAMOTO, N. 宮本延人. A neolithic site at Shinjō, Suō County, Taihoku Province, *ND* **2** (1933), 227–36.

258. SAITŌ, S. 西東重義. A neolithic site of Atogolan, Taitō district, east coast of Formosa, *ND* **3** (1934), 187–200.

259. SCHOFIELD, W. Implements of palaeolithic type in Hongkong, *HN* **6** (1935), 272–5.

260. PEI, W. C. Mesolithic (?) Industry of the caves of Kwangsi, *BGSC* **14** (1935), 393–412.

261. WEI, Chü-hsien 衞聚賢. *Report of the excavation at Hangchou*, Shanghai, 1936 (pp. 9–2, 22 pls.) 杭州古蕩新石器時代遺址之試探報告.

262. ZEN, W. T. Discovery of stone age implements near Huchow, *Journal of the North China Branch of the Royal Asiatic Society* **68** (1937), 73–4.

263. LEACH, E. R. Stone implements from Botel Tobago Island, *Man* **38** (1938), 161–3.

264. MAGLIONI, R. Archaeological Finds in Hoifong 海豐, Part I, *HN* **8** (1938), 208–44.

265. HEANLEY, C. M. Archaeology—Letter to the Editor, *HN* **9** (1938), 92–4.

266. BIEN, M. N. 卞美年. Cave and rock-shelter deposits in Yunnan, *BGSC* **18** (1938), 325–47.

267. WEI, Chu-hsien. Remains of prehistoric civilization in south-east China, *HN* **9** (1939), 184–92.

268. KOHNO, Isamu, Notes on the prehistoric artifacts from Uzantō, Formosa, *JAST* **54** (1939), 166–9.

269. MAGLIONI, R. Archaeology, *HN* **10** (1940), 130–3.

ARCHAEOLOGY OF INDO-CHINA AND SIAM

270. MANSUY, Henri. Stations préhistoriques de Somrong-Seng et de Longprao (Cambodge), *BSGI* (1902); translation in Japanese, *SZ* **3** (1931), 194–201.

271. JEANSELME, Dr. Note sur le préhistorique de Luang Prabang (Laos), *HP* **4** (1906), 225–30.

272. MANSUY, H. Gisement préhistorique de la caverne de Pho-binh-gia (Tonkin), *L'Anthropologie* **20** (1909), 531–43.

273. MANSUY, H. Contribution à l'étude de la préhistoire de l'Indo-chine: I. L'industrie de la pierre et du bronze dans la Region do Luang-Prabang, Haut Laos, *BSGI* **7.1** (1920), 1–14.

274. MANSUY, H. Contribution à l'étude de la préhistoire de l'Indo-chine: II. Gisements préhistoriques des environs de Lang-son et Tuyên-quang, Tonkin, *BSGI* **7.2** (1920), 1–10; translation in Japanese, *SZ* **3** (1931), 249–54.

275. PATTE, Étienne, Notes sur le préhistorique Indochinois: I. Résultats des fouilles de la grotte sépulcrale néolithique de Minh-Cam (Annam); translation in Japanese, *SZ* **4** (1932), 182–5. II. Note sur un outil en rhyolite grossièrement taillé provenant du massif du Bac-Son (Tonkin), *BSGI* **12.1** (1923), 1–35.

276. MANSUY, H. Contribution à l'étude de la préhistoire de l'Indochine: III. Résultats de nouvelles recherches effectuées dans le gisement préhistorique de Somrongsen (Cambodge)—Suivi d'un résumé de l'état de nos connaissances sur la préhistoire et sur l'ethnologie des races anciennes dans l'Extrême-Orient meridional, *MSGI* **10.1** (1923), 1–25.

277. PATTE, É. Le kjökkenmödding néolithique du Bau-Tro à Tam-Toà près de Dông-Hói (Annam), *BEFEO* **24** (1924), 521–62.

278. MANSUY, H. and FROMAGET, Jacques. Stations néolithiques de Hang-Rao et de Khé-Tong (Annam), *BSGI* **13.3** (1924), 1–12.

279. MANSUY, H. Contribution à l'étude de la préhistoire de l'Indochine: IV. Stations préhistoriques dans les cavernes du massif calcaire de Bac-Son (Tonkin), *MSGI* **11.2** (1924), 1–39.

280. VERNEAU, R. Les récentes découvertes préhist. en Indochine, *L'Anthropologie* **35** (1925), 47–62.

281. PATTE, É. Notes sur le préhistorique Indochinois: IV. Le kjökkenmödding néolithique du Bau-Tro à Tam-Toà près de Dông-Hói (Annam), *BSGI* **14.1** (1925), 1–33. [cf. 269.]

282. MANSUY, H. Contribution à l'étude de la préhistoire de l'Indochine: V. Nouvelles découvertes dans les cavernes du massif calcaire de Bac-Son (Tonkin), *MSGI* **12.1** (1925), 1–38.

283. MANSUY, H. Contribution à l'étude de la préhistoire de l'Indochine: VI. Stations préhistoriques de Kéo-Phay (suite), de Khac-Kiêm (suite) de Lai-Ta et de Bang-Mac, dans le massif calcaire de Bac-Son (Tonkin); Note sur deux instruments en pierre polie provenant de l'île de Trê (Annam), *MSGI* **12.2** (1925), 1–20.

284. MANSUY, H., et COLANI, Madeleine. Contribution à l'étude de la préhistoire de l'Indochine: VII. Néolithique inférieur (Baconien) et néolithique supérieur dans le Haut-Tonkin (dernières recherches), avec la description des crânes du gisement de Lang-Cuam, *MSGI* **12.3** (1925), 1–54.

285. EVANS, Ivor H. N. An ethnological expedition to south Siam, *JFMSM* **12** (1926), 35–58.

286. COLANI, M. L'âge de la pierre dans la province de Hoa-Binh (Tonkin), *MSGI* **14.1** (1927), 1–86.

287. MENGHIN, Oswald. Zur Steinzeit Ostasiens, *Festschrift publication d'hommage offerte au P. W. Schmidt*, 908–42; Vienna, 1928.

288. HEINE-GELDERN, Robert von. Ein Beitrag zur Chronologie des Neolithikums in Süd-ostasien, *Festschrift publication d'hommage offerte au P. W. Schmidt*, 809–43; Vienna, 1928.

289. COLANI, M. Notice sur la préhistoire de Tonkin. I. Deux petits ateliers; II. Une pierre à cupules; III. Stations hoabinhiennes dans la region de Phu-Nho-Quam (province de Ninh-Binh), *BSGI* **17** (1928), 1–46.

290. COLANI, M. Quelques paléolithes hoabinhiens typiques de l'abri sous roche de Lang-Kay, *BSPE* **26** (1929), 353–84.

291. COLANI, M. Recherches sur le préhistorique indochinois, *BEFEO* **30** (1930), 299–422.

292. FROMAGET, Jacques. Les phénomènes géologiques récentes et le préhistorique indo-chinois, *PAO* **1** (1932), 47–62.

293. COLANI, M. Le protonéolithe, *PAO* **1** (1932), 93–6.

294. COLANI, M. Différentes aspects du néolithique indochinois, *PAO* **1** (1932), 97–100.

295. COLANI, M. Divers modes de sépultures néolithiques et proto-historiques en Indo-chine, *PAO* **1** (1932), 101–2.

296. HEINE-GELDERN, Robert von. Urheimat und früheste Wanderungen der Austronesien, *Anthropos* **27** (1932), 543–619.

297. PATTE, É. Notes sur le préhistorique indochinois: V. Le kjökkenmödding néolithique, de Da But et ses sépultures (Province de Thanh Hoa, Indochine), *BSGI* **19.3** (1932), 1–110.

298. SARASIN, Fritz. Recherches préhistoriques au Siam, *L'Anthropologie* **43** (1933), 1–40.

299. HEINE-GELDERN, Robert von. Prehistoric research in Indonesia, *Annual Bibliography of Indian Archaeology* **9** (1934), 26–38.

300. COLANI, M. Haches et Bijoux, *BEFEO* **35** (1935), 313–50.

301. PATTE, É. L'Indochine préhistorique, *RA* **46** (1936), 277–314.

302. SAURIN, Edmond. Station néolithique à Na Mou, Province de Luang Prabang (Haut-Laos), *CCPF* **11** (1934), 258–66.

303. FROMAGET, Jacques et SAURIN, Edmond. Notes préliminaires sur les formations céno-zoïques et plus récentes de la chaîne annamitique septentrionale et du Haut-Laos, (Stratigraphie, préhistoire, anthropologie), *BSGI* **22.3** (1936), 1–48.

304. COLANI, M. Instruments modernes inchines survivances de types préhistoriques, *CCPF* **12** (1937), 721–35.

305. SAURIN, Edmond. Mésolithique et néolithique dans le Haut-Laos, *CCPF* **12** (1937), 816–23.

306. MATSUMOTO, N. Problems of the shouldered axe, *Shigaku* 史 學 **18** (1939), 483–514.

ARCHAEOLOGY OF THE MALAY PENINSULA

307. WRAY, L. Further notes on the cave dwellers of Perak, *JFMSM* **1** (1905), 13–15.

300. EVANS, I. H. N. On a find of stone implements at Tanjong Malim, *JFMSM* **9** (1922), 257–8.

309. EVANS, I. H. N. A rock-shelter at Gunong Pondok (Perak), *JFMSM* **9** (1922), 267–70.

310. EVANS, I. H. N. A hoard of stone implements from Batu Gajah (Perak), *JFMSM* **12** (1926), 67.

311. EVANS, I. H. N. On a find of stone implements associated with pottery, *JFMSM* **12** (1928), 133–5.

312. EVANS, I. H. N. Further notes on stone implements associated with pottery, *JFMSM* **12** (1928), 143–4.

313. STEIN CALLENFELS, P. V. van and EVANS, I. H. N. Report on cave excavations in Perak, *JFMSM* **12** (1928), 145–60.

314. EVANS, I. H. N. Further excavations at Gunong Pondok, *JFMSM* **12** (1928), 161–2.

315. EVANS, I. H. N. Further notes on a find of stone implements with pottery, *JFMSM* **12** (1929), 175–6.

316. EVANS, I. H. N. On a stone spear-head from Kelantan, *JFMSM* **15** (1930), 1–4.

317. EVANS, I. H. N. On a stone implement from Kinta, Perak, *JFMSM* **15** (1930), 5–6.

318. EVANS, I. H. N. Further notes on stone implements from Pahang, *JFMSM* **15** (1930), 7.

319. EVANS, I. H. N. A search for antiquities in Kedah and Perlis, *JFMSM* **15** (1931), 43–50.

320. EVANS, I. H. N. Excavations at Nyong, Tembeling river, Pahang, *JFMSM* **15** (1931), 51–62.

321. EVANS, I. H. N. A stone spear-head from Pahang, *JFMSM* **15** (1931), 65–6.

322. EVANS, I. H. N. A note on beaked stone adzes, *JFMSM* **15** (1931), 67–8.

323. EVANS, I. H. N. Excavations at Tanjong Rawa, Kuala Selinsing, Perak, *JMFSM* **15** (1932), 79–134.

324. COLLINGS, H. D. Report of an archaeological excavation in Kedah, Malay Peninsula, *BRM* B.**1** (1936), 5–16.

325. TWEEDIE, M. W. F. Report on cave excavations carried out in Bukit Chintamani, near Bentong, Pahang, *BRM* B.**1** (1936), 17–26.

326. STEIN CALLENFELS, P. V. van. An excavation of three kitchen middens at Guak Kepah, Province Wellesley, Straits Settlements, *BRM* B.**1** (1936), 27–37.

327. STEIN CALLENFELS, P. V. van. A remarkable stone implement from the Malay Peninsula, *BRM* B.**1** (1936), 38–40.

328. COLLINGS, H. D. An excavation at Bukit Chuping, Perlis, *BRM* B**2** (1937), 94–119.

329. COLLINGS, H. D. Note on a stone arrow-head from Kedah, *BRM* B**2** (1937), 121.

330. COLLINGS, H. D. A collection of stone tools in the Raffles Museum from the Kuantau District, Pahang, *BRM* B**2** (1937), 124–37.

331. TWEEDIE, M. W. F. Minor excavations carried out in caves in Pahang and Johore, *BRM* B**3** (1938), 154–5.

332. NOONE, H. D. An excavation at Sungai Siput, Perak, *Note présentée au troisième Congrès de Préhistoriens d'Extrême-Orient*, Singapore, 1938.

333. NOONE, H. D. Report on a new neolithic site in Ulu Kelantan, *JFMSM* **15** (1939), 170–74.

334. TWEEDIE, M. W. F. Report on excavations in Kelantan, *JMRAS* **18.2** (1940), 1–22.

MISCELLANEOUS REPORTS ON FAR EASTERN PREHISTORY

335. EVANS, I. H. N. Stone celts from northern Burma, *Man* **28** (1928), 25–6.

336. RIVET, P. Les Oceaniens, *PAO* **1** (1932), 35–46.

337. BEYER, H. Otley. A tabular history of the Philippine population as known at the present time from combined historical, ethnographical and archaeological studies, *PAO* **1** (1932), 129–32.

338. BEYER, H. Otley. Types of archaeological remains in the Philippines, *PAO* **1** (1932), 135–6.

339. PRICE, Willard. *Pacific Adventure*, New York, 1936 (pp. 317, illus. 48).

340. STEIN CALLENFELS, P. V. The Melanesoid civilizations of eastern Asia, *BRM* **B1** (1936), 41–51.

341. The Chase National Bank, *Moneys of the world, an illustrated guide book of the collection*, New York, 1938 (pp. 24).

342. WORMINGTON, H. M. *Prehistoric stone and bone artifacts of Japan*, Anthropology 20 report, Department of Anthropology, Harvard University, 1938 (Manuscripts).

343. CARLETON, E. J., Jr. *The typology of the palaeolithic stone implements of Siberia*, Anthropology 28 report, Department of Anthropology, Harvard University, 1940 (Manuscripts).

344. GEBHARD, Paul. *Post-palaeolithic stone implements from north-eastern Asia*, Honor Thesis, Department of Anthropology, Harvard University, 1940 (Manuscripts in 3 vols.).

345. LIANG, Ssǔ-yung. The Lungshan culture: A prehistoric phase of Chinese civilization, *Quarterly Bulletin of Chinese Bibliography*, Kumming, New Series **1** (1940), 251–62.

PART II

HAN BURIAL REMAINS

346. ADACHI, Kiroku 足立喜六. *Chōan shiseki no kenkyū* 長安史蹟の研究, Tōyō bunko ronsō 東洋文庫論叢, Tokyo, 1933.

347. BABER, E. Colborne. *Travels and research in the interior of China*, London, 1877.

348. BEDFORD, O. H. Han dynasty cave tombs in Szechwan, *The China Journal* **26** (1937), 175–6.

349. BISHOP, C. W. The expedition to the Far East, *Pennsylvania University Museum Journal* **7** (1916), 97–118.

350. CH'ANG, Chü (third century). Hua-yang-kuo chih, Shanghai, 1929, Ch. 3, 8a, b.

351. CHANG, Hsi-lu 張希魯. A new archaeological discovery in south-western China, *Quarterly Bulletin of the Yunnan Association* 雲南旅平學會季刊 **4** (1932), 56–78.

352. CH'ANG, Jên-hsia 常任俠. On the stone sculpture discovered at Sha-p'ing-pa, *Nanking Journal* 金陵學報 **8** (1938), 7–16.

353. CH'ANG, Jên-hsia. The discovery of Han cave tombs and stone gate-tower in Chungking, *SWYK* **2.2** (1940), 43–6.

354. CH'ANG, Jên-hsia. Notes on the Han tombs of Chungking, *SWYK* **3.4** (1941), 41–4.

355. CH'ANG, Jên-hsia. Three types of Han burial found around Chungking, *SWYK* **3.4** (1941), 77–82.

356. CHAO, Ming-ch'êng 趙明誠 (1081–1129). *Chin shih lu* 金石錄, Shanghai, 1934.

357. CHAVANNES, Édouard. *La Sculpture sur pierre en Chine au temps des deux dynasties Han*, Paris, 1893.

358. CHAVANNES, Édouard. *Mission archéologique dans la Chine septentrionale*, Paris, 1909, 1913–15.

359. CHÊNG, Tê-k'un 鄭德坤. *A brief history of Chinese mortuary objects* 中國明器, Peiping, 1933.

360. CHÊNG, Tê-k'un. *A catalogue of Chinese mortuary objects* 中國明器圖譜, Amoy, 1935.

361. CHÊNG, Tê-k'un. *A history of ancient Szechwan* 四川古代文化史, Chengtu, 1946.

362. CHÊNG, Tê-k'un. Archaeological chronology in Szechwan, *Antiquity* **81** (1947), 46–50.

363. CHIN, Ching-an 金靜庵. On the Han tombs of Sha-p'ing-pa, *SWYK* 1 (1939), 709–10.

364. DRAKE, F. S. Sculptured stones of the Han dynasty, *Monumenta Serica* **8** (1943), 280–318.

365. FAN, Yeh 范曄 (398–445). *Hou han shu* 後漢書, the T'ung-wên ed., 1894, Ch. 16, 4a.

366. FAIRBANK, Wilma. The offering shrines of Wu Liang Tz'ŭ, *HJAS* **6** (1941), 1–36.

367. FAIRBANK, Wilma. A structural key to Han mural art, *HJAS* **7** (1942), 52–88.

368. GRAHAM, David C. The ancient caves of Szechwan province, *Proceedings of the United States National Museum* **80.16** (1932), 1–13.

369. GRAHAM, David C. An excavation at Suifu, *JWCBRS* **8** (1936), 88–105.

370. GRAHAM, David C. Notes on the Han dynasty grave collection in the West China Union University Museum, *JWCBRS* **9** (1937), 213–15.

371. GRAHAM, David C. Archaeology in west China, *The China Journal* **26** (1937), 213–15.

372. GRAHAM, David C. Excavation of a Han dynasty tomb at Chungking, *JWCBRS* **10** (1938), 191–92.

373. GRAHAM, David C. Ornamented bricks and tiles from western Szechwan, *JWCBRS* **10** (1938), 191–92.

374. HAMADA, Kōsaku. Archaeological research in south Manchuria, *Tōyō gakuhō* 東洋學報 **3.1**.

375. HAMADA, Kōsaku. *Nan Shan Li* 南山裡, Tokyo, 1933.

376. HARADA, Yoshito. *Lo Lang* 樂浪, Tokyo, 1930.

377. HARADA, Yoshito. *Mu Yang Ch'êng* 牧羊城, Tokyo, 1931.

378. HO, Shih-i 何士驥. The tomb of Chang Ch'ien, *SWYK* **3.10** (1943), 157–67.

379. HUANG (LO), Hsi-ch'êng 黃（羅）希成. The stone coffins of Hsin-tsin, *The Arts and Life* 美術生活, June, 1937.

380. HUNG, Kua 洪适 (1117–1184). *Li shih* 隸釋, Shanghai, 1935.

381. IKEUCHI, Hiroshi 池內宏. *T'ung Kou* 通溝, Tokyo, 1940.

382. JANSE, O. R. *Archaeological research in Indo-China*, Cambridge, 1947.

383. JUNG, Kêng 容庚. *Han Wu Liang Tz'u hua hsiang lu* 漢武梁祠畫象錄, Peiping, 1936.

384. JUNG, Yüan 容媛. The Han stone sculpture of Lin-ch'i, *YCHP* **18** (1935), 203–4.

385. JUNG, Yüan. An ancient tomb found at Hwai-an, *YCHP* **9** (1931), 1929–30.

386. JÊN, Nai-ch'iang 任乃強. On the Han stone sculpture recently discovered at Lu-shan, *K'ang tao yueh k'an* 康導月刊 **4.6–7** (1942).

387. KOIZUMI, A. 小泉顯夫. *The tomb of painted basket and two other tombs of Lo-lang* 樂浪彩篋冢, Seoul, 1934.

388. KOZLOV, P. K. *Northern Mongolia* Leningrad, 1925.

389. KUO, Mo-jo 郭沫若. On the discovery of Han tombs in Chungking, *SWYK* **3.4** (1941), 35–40.

390. K'UNG, Yü-fang 孔玉芳. Notes on the Han stone sculptures and mortuary objects in the Szechwan Museum, *SWYK* **5.3** (1945), 37–46.

391. LAUFER, B. *Chinese pottery of the Han dynasty*, Leiden, 1909.

392. LAUFER B. *Chinese grave-sculptures of the Han period*, London, 1911.

393. LAO, Kan 勞榦. Notes on three western Shantung sculptures of the Han dynasty, *CYYY* **8.1** (1939).

394. LI, Tao-yüan 酈道元 (472–527). *Shui Ching chu* 水經注, Ho-chiao ed., 1928.

395. LIU, Hsi-hai 劉喜海 (eighteenth to nineteenth century). *Chin shih yüan* 金石苑 T'ung-wên ed.

396. MIZUNO, Seiichi. The Han jade carving from Liao-yang, South Manchuria, *Tōhō gakuhō* 東方學報, Kyoto **4. 4** (1933), 444–49.

397. MIZUNO, Seiichi. The brick tombs of Lao Hsi-ying-tzŭ, Jeho, *JAST* 人類學雜誌 **50. 10** (1935), 27–30.

398. MIZUNO, Seiichi. *Pei-cha-tch'eng, Wan-ngan* 萬安北沙城, Tokyo, 1946.

399. MIKAMI, Tsugio. On the Han tomb at Tung-chia-kou, Kwan-tung, *JAST* **48** (1933), 627–35.

400. MORI, O. 森修. *Ying Ch'êng Tzŭ* 營城子, Tokyo, 1934.

401. OBA, T. 小場恒吉. *The tomb of Wang Kuang and another tomb of Lo-lang* 樂浪王光墓 Seoul, 1935.

402. KOBAYASHI, T. 小林知生. On the brick tombs of Indo-China, *JAST* **50. 8** (1935), 1–7; **50. 12** (1935), 22–7.

403. OU-YANG, Hsiu 歐陽修 (1007–1072). *Chi ku lu* 集古錄, *San ch'ang wu chai tsung shu* 三長物齋叢書.

404. Important archaeological discoveries at P'eng-shan, *Quarterly Bulletin of Chinese Bibliography*. New Series 4.12 (1943), 197–98.

405. SEGALEN, Victor. *L'art funéraire en l'époque des Han*, Paris, 1935.

406. SEKINO, T. 關野貞. *The decorations of Han tombs in Shantung* 支那山東に於ける漢代墳墓の表飾, Tokyo, 1916.

407. SEKINO, T. *Archaeological researches on the ancient Lo-lang district* 樂浪郡時代の遺蹟, 2 vols. Seoul, 1925.

408. SHANG, Ch'êng-tso 商承祚. *Ch'ang-sha ku-wu chien-wên chi* 長沙古物見聞記, Chengtu, 1939.

409. SHANG, Ch'êng-tso. Ch'ang-sha ku-wu chih-nan, *SWYK* **4** (1944), 29–34.

410. SHIMADA, Sadahiko 島田貞彥. Notes on the Han tombs of south Manchuria, *Rekishi to chiri* 歷史と地理 **33** (1934) **1** 27–32.

411. SUN, Tsung-wên 孫宗文. Notes on Han tombs, *SWYK* **3.4** (1941).

412. SUN, Wên-ch'ing 孫文青. *Nan-yang Han hua-hsiang hui ts'un* 南陽漢畫像彙存, Nanking, 1937.

413. TING, Shih-hsüan 丁士選. Notes on tomb bricks, *Kao ku* 考古 **6** (1937).

414. TORII, Ryūzō. *South-western China* 人類學上より見たる西南支那, Tokyo, 1926.

415. TORII, Ryūzō. *Ancient remains in Manchuria and Mongolia* 滿蒙古蹟考, Shanghai, 1933.

416. TORRANCE, T. Burial customs in Szechwan, *Journal of the North China Branch of the Royal Asiatic Society* **41** (1910), 57–75.

417. TORRANCE, T. Notes on the cave tombs and ancient burial mounds of western Szechwan, *JWCBRS* **4** (1931), 88–96.

418. TREVER, Camilla. *Excavations in northern Mongolia*, Leningrad, 1932.

419. TS'AI, Han-ch'iung 蔡 寒 瓊. An excavation of a Han tomb in Canton, *The Archaeological Journal* 考 古 學 雜 誌 I (1932), 93–108.

420. TSÊNG, Ch'uan-t'ao 曾 傳 韜. Notes on the Han tomb at Kwei-kang, Canton, *Journal of the Sun Yat-sen University* 國 立 中 山 大 學 研 究 所 月 刊, 1.5.

421. UMEHARA, Sueji. The discoveries of Han remains in Chêng-chou and Yung-chê, Honan, *Tōyō gakuhō* 東 洋 學 報 **19.1** (1931).

422. UMEHARA, Sueji. Notes on the brick tombs of Wu-hu Anhui, *Shina kōkogaku ronsō* 支 那 考 古 學 論 叢, Supplement to Series V.

423. WANG, Hsiang-chih 王 象 之 (twelfth to thirteenth century). *Shu pei chi* 蜀 碑 記, Chin-hua, 1869.

424. WHITE, William C. *Tomb tile pictures of ancient China*, Toronto, 1939.

425. YANG, Chih-kao 楊 枝 高. Notes on the cave tombs of Szechwan, *Hua-wên Monthly* 華 文 月 刊 **6** (1944).

426. YANG, Fang-ts'an 楊 芳 燦. *Ssŭ-ch'uan t'ung-chih* 四 川 通 志 Chengtu, 1816.

427. YAGI, S. *Manshū kōkagaku* 滿 州 考 古 學, Tokyo, 1928.

428. YETTS, W. P. Discoveries of the Kozlóv Expedition, *The Burlington Magazine*, April, 1926, 1–16.

KILN SITES

429. GRAHAM, David C. The pottery of Ch'iung-lai, *JWCBRS* **11** (1939), 46–53.

430. BEDFORD, O. H. An ancient kiln site at Chiung-chou, Szechwan, *The China Journal* **26.1** (1937), 14–15.

431. *Hua-hsi wên wu* **I** (1951), 38.

432. YANG, Hsiao-ku. On Szechwan pottery, *Hua-hsi wên wu* **I** (1951), 8–10.

433. GRAHAM, David C. The Liu-li-ch'ang kiln site, *JWCBRS* **11** (1939), 36–45.

434. KAO, Yü-ling. A chemical analysis of Szechwan pottery glaze, *JWCBRS* **11** (1939), 54–7.

SUNG BURIAL REMAINS

435. KARLGREN, B. Huai and Han, *BMFEA* **13** (1941), 1–125.

436. UMEHARA, S. *Ōbei ni okeru shina kokyō*, Tokyo (1931).

437. LI, Yu 李 攸. *Sung-ch'ao shih-shih*, Wu-ying tien ed. 1776 宋 朝 事 實.

438. CHÊNG, Tê-k'un. The excavation of T'ang dynasty tombs at Ch'üan-chou, southern Fukien, *HJAS* **4** (1939), 1–10.

PLATES

PLATE I

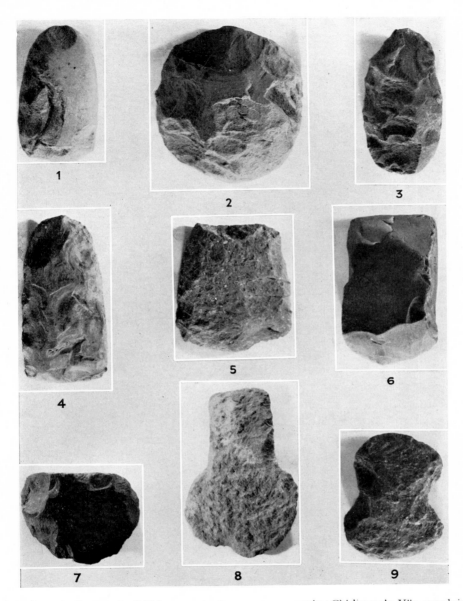

Chipped stone implements. 1. Pebble axe: 112 × 63 × 32 mm.; quartzite; Chi-liang-t'o, Yün-yang hsien; AMNH 383.   2. Discoidal chopper: 135 × 39 mm.; sandstone; Ku-lao-pei, I-tu hsien; AMNH 83. 3. Curved-bit axe: 122 × 71 × 29 mm.; quartzite; Ku-lao-pei, I-tu hsien; AMNH 120.   4. Straight-bit axe: 140 × 65 × 33 mm.; quartzite; Ku-lao-pei, I-tu hsien; AMNH 121.   5. Broad axe: 107 × 92 × 27 mm.; quartzite; Miao-ho, I-ch'ang; AMNH 188.   6. Rectangular axe: 129 × 73 × 39 mm.; quartzite; Huang-ling-miao, I-ch'ang; AMNH 181.   7. Short axe: 94 × 74 × 28 mm.; quartzite; Pei-shih, Wu-shan hsien; AMNH 235.   8. Stemmed axe: 141 × 93 × 21 mm.; quartzite; Ku-lao-pei, I-tu hsien; AMNH 126.   9. Waisted axe: 105 × 80 × 21 mm.; quartzite; Chi-liang-t'o, Yün-yang hsien; AMNH 373.

PLATE 2

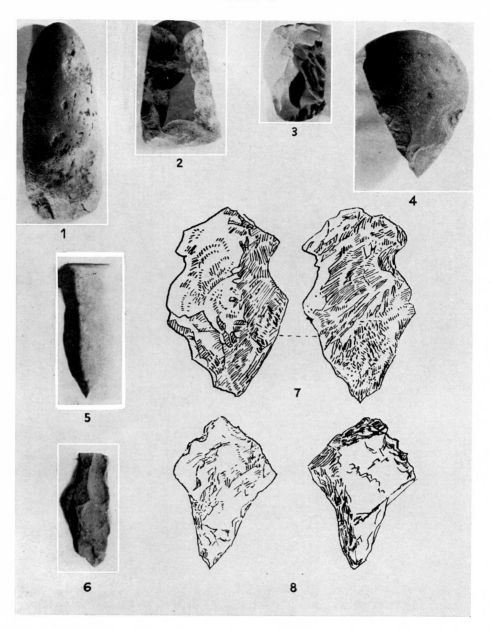

Chipped stone implements. 1. Curved-bit adze: 169 × 61 × 33 mm.; quartzite; Lower Wushan Gorge, Wu-shan hsien; AMNH 215. 2. Straight-bit adze: 107 × 63 × 32 mm.; sandstone; Wu-shan, Wu-shan hsien; AMNH 265. 3. Chisel: 68 × 37 × 19 mm.; quartzite; Pa-yang-hsia, Wan-hsien; AMNH 409. 4. Pick: sub-triangular; 125 × 83 × 38 mm.; quartzite; Ku-lao-pei, I-tu hsien; AMNH 92. 5. Pick: straight-butted; Hsik'ang; **28**, Pl. 41. 1. 6. Pick: stemmed; Hsik'ang; **28**, Pl. 45. 4. 7. Pick: waisted; 142 × 38 mm. Kwan-hsien; **13**, Fig. 7. 8. Pick: point-butted; 113 × 30 mm.; K'ang-ting; **13**, Fig. 20.

200

PLATE 3

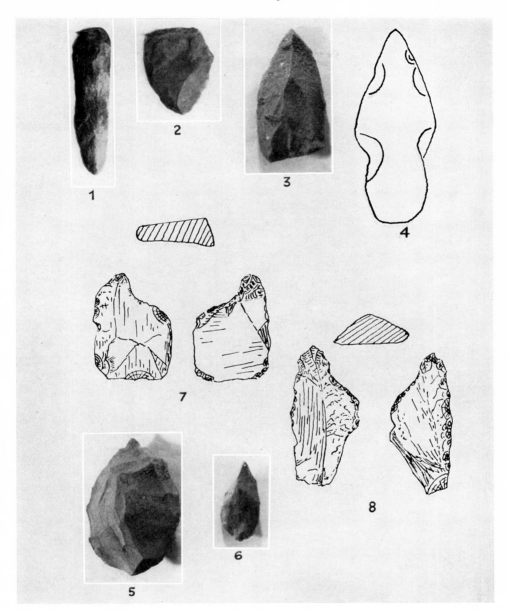

Chipped stone implements. **1.** Pick: elongated; Hsik'ang; **28**, Pl. 40. 3. **2.** Pick: leaf-shaped; Hsik'ang; **28**, Pl. 45. 5. **3.** Point: flake; 110 × 56 × 26 mm.; quartzite; Hsien-jên-ch'iao, I-tu hsien; AMNH 136. **4.** Point: spear-head (?); Chü-lung, K'ang-ting hsien; **26**, 6. **5.** Perforator: bi-facial; 113 × 73 × 35 mm.; quartzite; Wan-hsien; AMNH 430. **6.** Perforator: flake; 56 × 26 × 10 mm.; quartzite Lung-kai, Yüan-mou hsien; AMNH 61. **7.** Perforator: retouched; about 45 mm. long; basalt (?); Chachie-Bréi, Tao-fu Valley; **25**, Fig. 4. 4. **8.** Perforator: retouched; about 54 mm. long; basalt (?); Chachie-Bréi, Tao-fu Valley; **25**, Fig. 4. 5.

PLATE 4

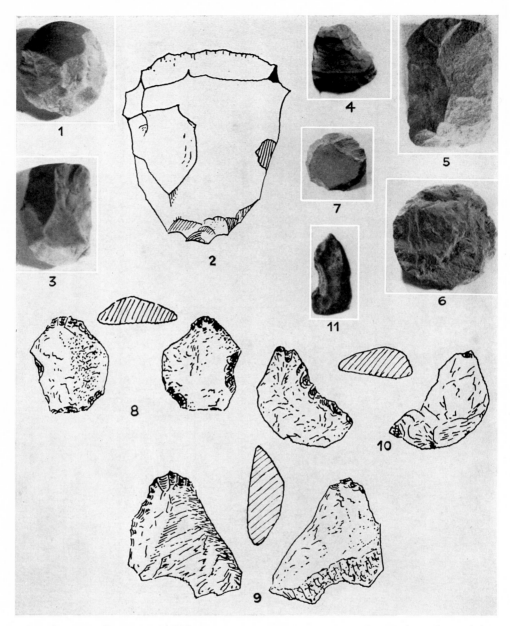

Chipped stone implements. 1. Pebble scraper: 72 × 64 × 32 mm.; quartzite; Ku-lao-pei, I-tu hsien, AMNH 88.   2. Pebble scraper: about 80 mm. long; quartzite; Tao-fu Valley; **26**, 176B; **25**, Fig. 2A; **28**, Pl. 36. 2.   3. Core scraper: 78 × 51 × 26 mm.; white quartzite; Hsien-jên-ch'iao, I-tu hsien; AMNH 137.   4. Core scraper: Hsik'ang; **28**, Pl. 45. 3.   5. Rectangular scraper: 108 × 66 × 32 mm.; quartzite; San-pa-hsi, Yün-yang hsien; AMNH 359.   6. Discoidal scraper: 73 × 13 mm.; quartzite; New Kuei-chou, Kuei-chou; AMNH 201.   7. Discoidal scraper: 50 × 15 mm.; quartzite; Ku-lao-pei, I-tu hsien; AMNH 85.   8. End scraper: about 27 mm. long; basalt (?); Chachie-Bréi, Tao-fu Valley; **25**, Fig. 5. 2.   9. Side scraper: about 40 mm. long; basalt (?); Chachie-Bréi, Tao-fu Valley; **25**, Fig. 5. 4.   10. Concave scraper: about 30 mm. long; basalt (?); Chachie-Bréi, Tao-fu Valley; **25**, Fig. 5. 1.   11. Concave scraper: with point; K'ang-ting; **20**, Pl. 40. 5.

PLATE 5

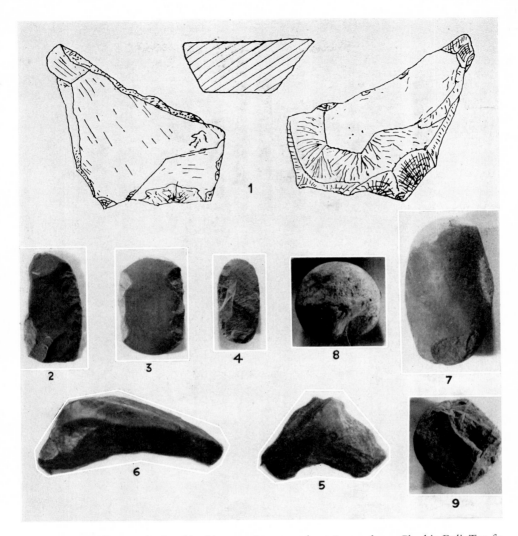

Chipped stone implements. 1. Combined borer and scraper: about 63 mm. long; Chachie-Bréi, Tao-fu Valley; **25**, Fig. 6.   2. Single-edged knife: 95 × 46 × 17 mm.; quartzite; Chi-liang-t'o, Yün-yang hsien; AMNH 399.   3. Double-edged knife: 84 × 53 × 11 mm.; quartzite; Chi-liang-t'o, Yün-yang hsien; AMNH 399.   4. Flaked knife: 61 × 28 × 9 mm.; quartzite; Chang-tso-t'an, Wan-hsien; AMNH 414.   5. Coulter-type knife: Hsik'ang; **28**, Pl. 44. 3.   6. Sicklet-ype knife: Hsik'ang; **28**, Pl. 44. 4.   7. Pebble hammerstone: 104 × 61 × 37 mm.; quartzite; Wu-shan, Wu-shan hsien; AMNH 242.   8. Hammerstone: spherical; 64 × 61 × 59 mm.; quartzite; Ku-lao-pei, I-tu hsien; AMNH 70.   9. Hammerstone: discoidal; 73 × 34 mm.; quartzite; Kuan-tu-k'ou, Kuei-chou; AMNH 203.

PLATE 6

Chipped stone implements. 1. Pitted stone: about 40 mm. long; Hsik'ang; **25**, III 13. 2. Waisted pebble: hammerstone; Wei-chou; **10**, 12. 3. Waisted pebble: 99 × 78 × 22 mm.; quartzite; Lung-kai, Yüan-mou hsien; AMNH 38. 4. Waisted pebble: 113 × 80 × 17 mm.; quartzite; Chi-liang-t'o, Yün-yang hsien; AMNH 401.

Chipped-and-polished stone implements. 5. Curved-bit axe: 225 × 85 × 38 mm.; quartzite; Site 6, I-ch'ang; AMNH 178. 6. Straight-bit axe: 129 × 59 × 17 mm.; quartzite; Ku-lao-pei, I-tu hsien; AMNH 93. 7. Stemmed axe: 144 × 92 × 42 mm.; quartzite; Chi-liang-t'o, Yün-yang hsien; AMNH 387. 8. Curved-bit adze: 121 × 50 × 23 mm.; quartzite; Chang-tso-t'an, Wan-hsien; AMNH 427. 9. Straight-bit adze: 122 × 62 × 9 mm.; quartzite; Ku-lao-pei, I-tu hsien; AMNH 112.

PLATE 7

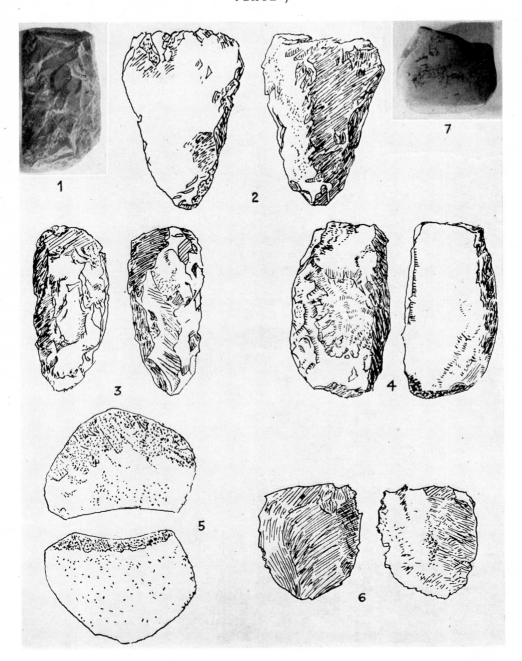

Chipped-and-polished stone implements. 1. Chisel: rectangular; 80 × 42 × 18 mm.; quartzite; Chi-liang-t'o, Yün-yang hsien; AMNH 394. 2. Pick: triangular; 145 × 52 mm.; hard sandstone; Kwan-hsien (?); **13**, Fig. 17. 3. Pick: 123 × 36 mm.; igneous rock; Kwan-hsien (?); **13**, Fig. 19. 4. Pebble knife: 128 × 48 mm.; Chengtu; **13**, Fig. 18. 5. Flake knife: 119 × 33 mm.; granite; O-mei; **13**, Fig. 12. 6. Blade: 30 × 5 mm.; Suifu; **13**, Fig. 21. 7. Polished pebble: 82 × 72 × 36 mm.; fine-grained breccia-like rock; Ta-tung-t'an, I-ch'ang; AMNH 184.

PLATE 8

Chipped-pecked-and-polished stone implements. 1. Unfinished axe: in process of being pecked into shape; 250 mm. long; quartzite; Tai-hsi, Wu-shan hsien; AMNH 308. 2. Curved-bit axe: 133 × 75 × 29 mm.; quartzite; Ku-lao-pei, I-tu hsien; AMNH 96. 3. Broad axe: 159 × 96 × 35 mm.; quartzite; Hsia-ma-t'an, Wu-shan hsien; AMNH 279. 4. Grooved axe: 268 × 167 × 53 mm.; quartzite; Site 6, I-ch'ang; AMNH 176. 5. Curved-bit adze: 178 × 73 × 40 mm.; quartzite; New Kuei-chou, Kuei-chou; AMNH 195. 6. Chisel: 86 × 45 × 20 mm.; quartzite; Ku-lao-pei, I-tu hsien; AMNH 106.

PLATE 9

Polished stone implements. 1. Axe: 131 × 76 × 26 mm.; fine grained rock; Wu-shan, Wu-shan hsien; AMNH 250.   2. Broad axe: 107 × 76 × 28 mm.; quartzite; Tai-hsi, Wu-shan hsien; AMNH 300. 3. Broad axe: rectangular; 98 × 67 × 35 mm.; sandstone (?); Wu-shan, Wu-shan hsien; AMNH 253. 4. Broad axe: short-butted; Wei-chou; **10**, Fig. 10.   5. Point-butted axe: Wei-chou; **10**, Fig. 8. 6. Vertical-grooved axe: 63 × 39 × 7 mm.; whitish jade; Lung-kai, Yüan-mou hsien; AMNH 41. 7. Curved-bit adze: 62 × 46 × 17 mm.; banded chart; Hsiao-chiang, Yün-yang hsien; AMNH 406. 8. Straight-bit adze: 52 × 51 × 10 mm.; sandstone; Ku-lao-pei, I-tu hsien; AMNH 108.   9. Flat adze: 92 × 52 × 10 mm.; sandstone; Site 6, I-ch'ang; AMNH 180.

PLATE 10

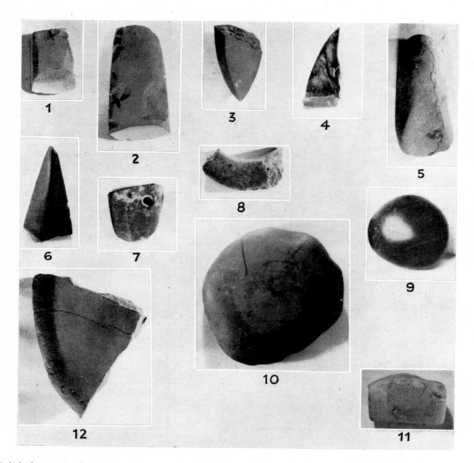

Polished stone implements. 1. Curved-bit chisel: 46 × 29 × 12 mm.; banded whitish rock; Hsien-jên-ch'iao, I-tu hsien; AMNH 139.   2. Straight-bit chisel: 64 × 32 × 9 mm.; sandstone; Ku-lao-pei, I-tu hsien; AMNH 107.   3. Narrow-bit chisel: fragment; 6·5 mm. at bit end; fine-grained rock; Tai-hsi, Wu-shan hsien; AMNH 297.   4. Punch: one-shouldered; 98 × 44 × 18 mm.; limestone; Kung-hsien; **17**, Fig. 4; **28**, P. 23. 1.   5. Gouge: pebble; 86 × 39 × 13 mm.; quartzite; Wu-shan, Wu-shan hsien; AMNH 261.   6. Spear-head: fragment; slate; Hsien-jên-ch'iao, I-tu hsien; AMNH 138.   7. Perforated knife: fragment; 37 × 7 mm.; quartzite; Lung-kai, Yüan-mou hsien; AMNH 39.   8. Stone ring: fragment; 22·5 × 11·5 × 6·5 mm.; quartzite; Tai-hsi, Wu-shan hsien; AMNH 329.   9. Polishing stone: Kung-hsien (?); **28**, Pl. 10. 7.   10. Rubbing pebble: 119 × 108 × 29 mm.; quartzite; Hsien-jên-ch'iao, I-tu hsien; AMNH 133.   11. Whetstone: 52 × 34 × 29 mm.; whitish quartzite; San-pa-hsi, Yün-yang hsien; AMNH 361.   12. Mealing stone: fragment; 13 mm. deep; sandstone; Ku-lao-pei, I-tu hsien; AMNH 127.

PLATE II

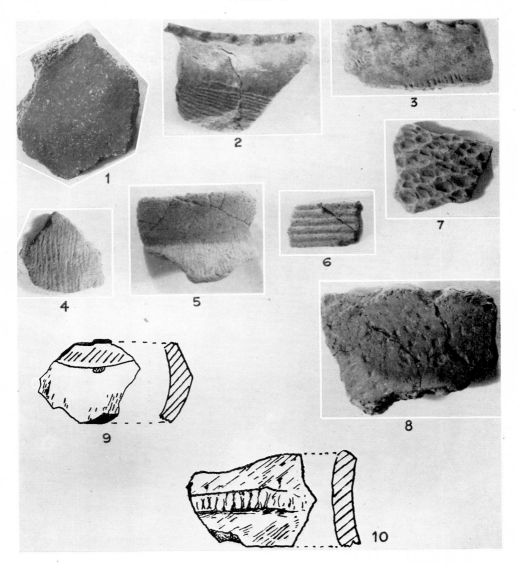

Pottery, Class A. 1. Plain coarse red ware (Type 1): medium; Tai-hsi; Wu-shan hsien; AMNH 322.
2, 3. Cord-marked coarse red ware (Type 2): thick; Hsiao-chiang, Yün-yang hsien; AMNH 404.
4. Cord-marked coarse red ware (Type 2): medium; Tai-hsi, Wu-shan hsien; AMNH 323.
5. Cord-marked coarse red ware (Type 2): thin; Ku-lao-pei, I-tu hsien; AMNH 129.   6. Grooved
coarse red ware (Type 3): medium; Ku-lao-pei, I-tu hsien; AMNH 130.   7. Stamped coarse
red ware (Type 4): thick; Lower Wushan Gorge, Wu-shan hsien; AMNH 227.   8. Stamped
coarse red ware (Type 4): thick; Kao-wei-tzŭ, K'uei-chou; AMNH 348.   9. Incised coarse
red ware (Type 5): medium; Tao-fu Valley; **25**, 12 A.   10. Appliqué coarse red ware (Type 5):
medium; Tao-fu Valley; **25**, 10 B.

PLATE 12

Pottery, Class A. 1. Cord-marked coarse black ware (Type 6): thick; Hsiang-hsia, Kuei-chou; AMNH 192 c.   2, 3. Plain coarse grey ware (Type 7): thick; Hsien-jên-ch'iao, I-tu hsien; AMNH 146.   4. Plain coarse grey ware (Type 7): medium; Hsien-jên ch'iao, I-tu hsien; AMNH 146.   5. Plain coarse grey ware (Type 7): thick; Hsiao-chiang, Yün-yang hsien; AMNH 404.   6, 7. Cord-marked coarse grey ware (Type 8): thick; Hsiao-chiang, Yün-yang hsien; AMNH 404.   8. Stamped coarse grey ware (Type 8): thick; Hsiao-chiang, Yün-yang hsien; AMNH 404.   9. Plain coarse brown ware (Type 9): thick; Lung-kai, Yüan-mou hsien; AMNH 63.   10. Cord-marked coarse brown ware (Type 10): thick; Ku-lao-pei, I-tu hsien; AMNH 129 A.

PLATE 13

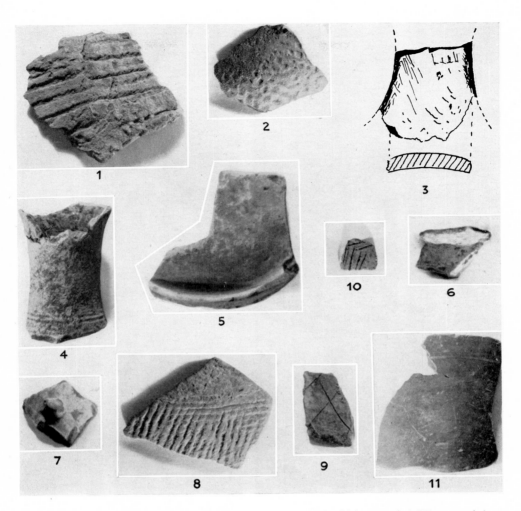

Pottery, Class A. 1. Cord-marked coarse brown ware (Type 10): thick; Lung-kai, Yüan-mou hsien; AMNH 64.   2. Stamped coarse brown ware (Type 11): medium; Hsin-t'an, Kuei-chou; AMNH 189A.

Pottery, Class B. 3. Plain fine grey ware (Type 12): medium; Tao-fu Valley, Tao-fu hsien; **25**, 13B.
4, 5. Plain fine grey ware (Type 12): medium; Hsien-jên-ch'iao, I-tu hsien; AMNH 146.
6, 7. Slipped fine grey ware (Type 12): medium; Hsien-jên-ch'iao, I-tu hsien; AMNH 146.
8. Cord-marked fine grey ware (Type 13): medium; Tai-hsi, Wu-shan hsien; AMNH 323.
9, 10. Incised fine grey ware (Type 14): medium; Lung-kai, Yüan-mou hsien; AMNH 66.
11. Incised fine grey ware (Type 14): medium; Upper Wushan Gorge, Wu-shan hsien; AMNH 270.

PLATE 14

Pottery, Class B. 1. Appliqué fine grey ware (Type 15): medium; Hsien-jên-ch'iao, I-tu hsien; AMNH 142. 2. Plain fine brown ware (Type 16): medium; Upper Wushan Gorge; Wu-shan hsien; AMNH 241. 3. Plain fine brown ware (Type 16): thin; Tai-hsi, Wu-shan hsien; AMNH 324. 4. Appliqué fine brown ware (Type 16): medium; Hsien-jên-ch'iao, I-tu hsien; AMNH 142.

Pottery, Class C. 5. Plain fine red ware (Type 17): thin; Ku-lao-pei, I-tu hsien; AMNH 128. 6. Plain fine red ware (Type 17): thin; Tai-hsi, Wu-shan hsien; AMNH 320. 7. Plain fine red ware (Type 17): medium; Hsien-jên-ch'iao, I-tu hsien; AMNH 149. 8. Slipped fine red ware (Type 17): thin; Ku-lao-pei, I-tu hsien; AMNH 123. 9. Painted fine red ware (Type 18): thin; Ku-lao-pei, I-tu hsien; AMNH 130. 10. Painted fine red ware (Type 18): thin; Wei-chou; **13**, 45. 11. Plain fine red ware (Type 17): thin; perforated; Hsien-jên-ch'iao, I-tu hsien; AMNH 149.

PLATE 15

Pottery, Class D. 1. Plain fine black ware (Type 19): thin; Hsien-jên-ch'iao, I-tu hsien; AMNH 146.

Pottery, Class E. 2. Stamped fine white ware (Type 20): thin; Site Five, I-ch'ang; AMNH 175A.

Pottery, Class F. 3, 4. Stamped fine black ware (Type 21): medium; Lower Wushan Gorge, Wu-shan hsien; AMNH 227.   5, 6. Comb-marked fine grey ware (Type 22): medium; Hsien-jên-ch'iao, I-tu hsien; AMNH 147.   7–9. Stamped fine grey ware (Type 23): medium; Hsien-jên-ch'iao, I-tu hsien; AMNH 148.   10, 11. Incised fine brown ware (Type 24): medium; Hsien-jên-ch'iao, I-tu hsien; AMNH 151.

Other pottery objects. 12. Spindle whorl: discoidal; 41 × 13 mm.; perforation incomplete; Hsien-jên-ch'iao, I-tu hsien; AMNH 152.

PLATE 16

2

1

1. Entrance to burial caves on the cliff near Lo-shan. The slanting lines are later in date as they are superimposed on the original decoration and are meant to receive the gable end of a roof. (After Bishop **349**, Fig. 146.)   2. Entrance to burial caves on another cliff near Lo-shan. (After Bishop **349**, Fig. 145.)

PLATE 17

1. Entrance to Pai-yai-tung, near Lo-shan. (After Bishop **349**, Fig. 8.)   2. Decorated walls of an entrance to the Pai-yai-tung, showing imitation of wooden architectural forms. (After Bishop **349**, Fig. 149.)   3. Entrance to Pai-yai-tung, decorated with imitation gate-towers. (After Bishop **349**, Fig. 150.)   4. A gate-tower carved in low relief at an entrance to a Pai-yai-tung cave. (After Bedford **348**.)

PLATE 18

1. Passage (Shên-tao or 'Spirit's way') leading from the entrance into the burial chamber at Pai-yai-tung. (After Bishop **349**, Fig. 151.)   2. Entrance to Pai-yai-tung. (After Bishop **349**, Fig. 144.)
3. Mutilated Buddhist carvings in the burial cave of Pai-yai-tung. (After Bishop **349**, Fig. 143.)
4. Profile of Buddhist carvings in Pai-yai-tung. (After Bedford **348**.)

PLATE 19

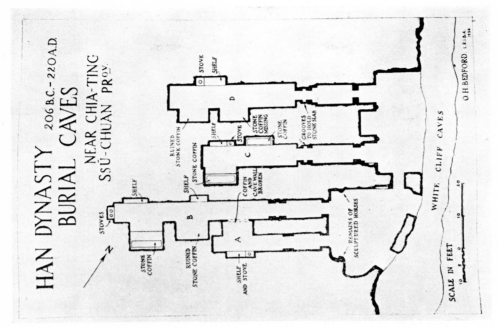

2. Cross-sections of the Pai-yai-tung caves. (After Bedford **348.**)

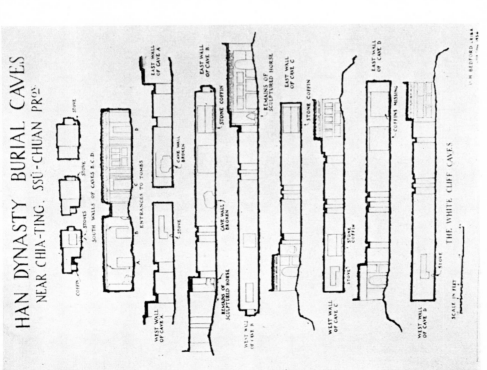

1. Horizontal plan of Pai-yai-tung. (After Bedford **348.**)

PLATE 20

1. The Fêng Huan gate-tower in Chü-hsien. (After Segalen **405**, 1, Pl. 14.)   2. The Kao Yi gate-tower at Ya-an. (After Segalen **405**, 1, Pl. 46.)   3, 4. Details of the Shên gate-tower in Chü-hsien, showing a tiger on the left and a dragon on the right in low relief. (After Segalen **405**, 1, Pl. 23.)   5. The Kao Yi stele at Ya-an. (After Segalen **405**, 1, Pl. 50.)   6–8. Detail of the Shên gate-tower and two rubbings of the scenes in low relief on the panels. (After Segalen **405**, 1, Pl. 28.)

PLATE 21

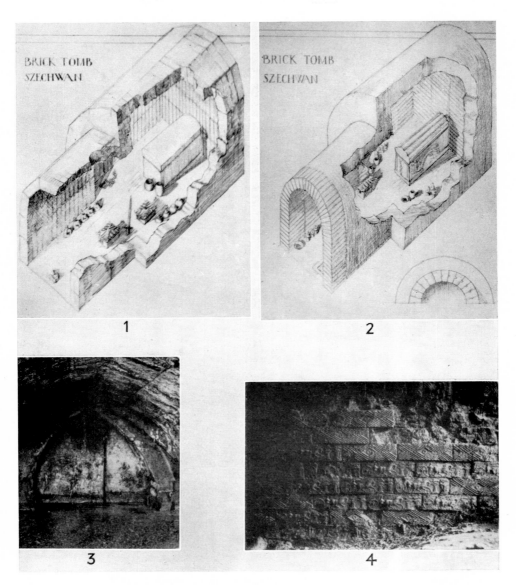

1. Sketch of a brick tomb found in Chungking. By Michael Sullivan.   2. Sketch of a brick tomb found in Lu-shan. By Michael Sullivan.   3. A 'Gothic arch' in a brick tomb in Chü-hsien. (After Segalen **405**, I, Pl. 60.)   4. Brick construction of the tomb of Pao-San-niang 鮑三娘 in Chao-hua 昭化. (After Segalen **405**, I, Pl. 58.)

PLATE 22

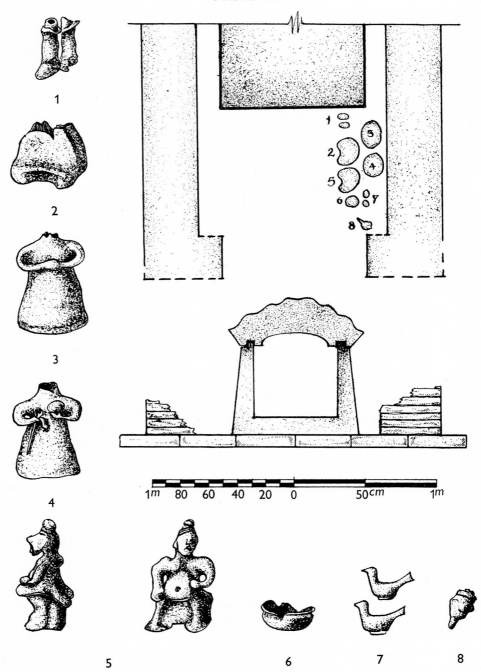

Plan and cross-section of the Wang Hui tomb 王暉 found at Lu-shan, showing the location of the stone coffin and pottery mortuary objects. By Michael Sullivan.

PLATE 23

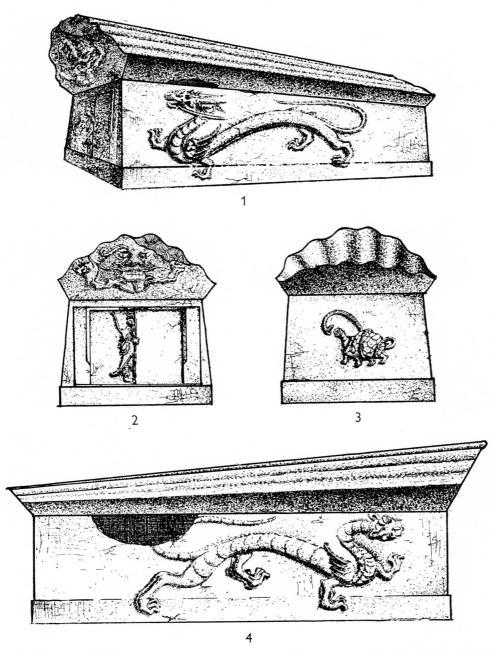

Decorations of the Wang Hui stone coffin, Lu-shan. The front (2) is decorated with a mask on the lid and a half-opened door with the figure of an attendant, the door frame bearing an inscription of 35 characters (see p. 151). A tiger is carved on the left wall (4), a dragon on the right (1), while on the end wall is a snake-and-turtle (3). Red sandstone, in low relief. By Michael Sullivan.

PLATE 24

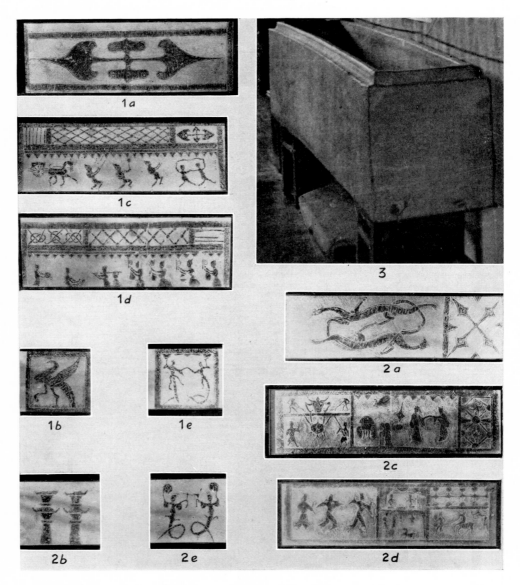

1. Rubbings from a stone coffin found in Lu-hsien: (*a*) cover, cross pattern; (*b*) front wall, the red bird; (*c*) right wall, procession of dancers and chariot and geometric designs; (*d*) left wall, procession of an orchestra and geometric designs; (*e*) rear wall, scene of the union of the 'sun' and the 'moon'. Red sandstone, in low relief. Courtesy of the Hsi-ch'êng Museum.   2. Rubbings from a stone coffin found in Lu-hsien: (*a*) cover, dragon and tiger, and the cross pattern; (*b*) front wall, a two-storied gate-tower; (*c*) left wall, scene of the tripod lifting, a meeting scene, and some geometric designs; (*d*) right wall, procession of dancers, a horse and some human figures; (*e*) rear wall, scene of the union of the 'sun' and the 'moon'. Red sandstone in low relief. (Courtesy of the Hsi-ch'êng Museum.)   3. Pottery coffin with damaged cover; plain grey ware; 6 ft. 1 in. long.

222

PLATE 25

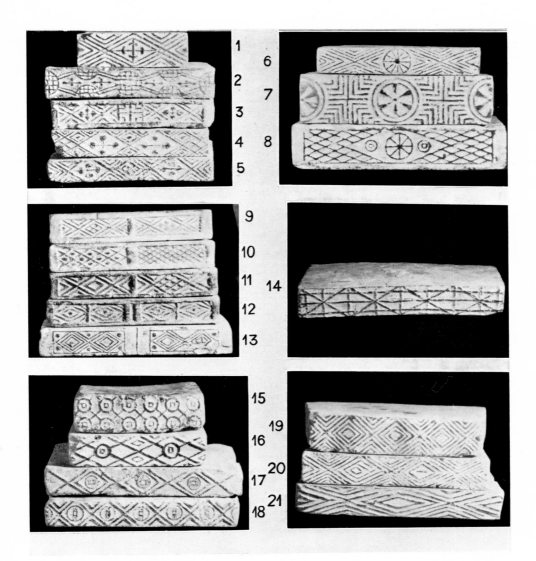

1–5. Pottery bricks with lineal decoration; grey ware; $\times \frac{1}{10}$.   6–8. Pottery bricks with lineal and wheel pattern; grey ware; $\times \frac{1}{10}$.   9–13. Pottery bricks with pearl-and-diamond pattern; grey ware; $\times \frac{1}{10}$.   14. Pottery brick with lineal decoration; grey ware; $\times \frac{1}{10}$.   15–18. Pottery bricks with coin-and-diamond pattern; grey ware; $\times \frac{1}{10}$.   19–21. Pottery bricks with diamond pattern; grey ware; $\times \frac{1}{10}$.

PLATE 26

1. Pottery brick with coin and geometric design; grey ware; $\times\frac{1}{10}$. 2. Pottery brick with disc-and-diamond pattern; grey ware; $\times\frac{1}{10}$. 3. Pottery brick with disc-and-cross design. One inscription reads *tzŭ sun* 子孫, 'sons and grandsons'. The other two characters are not clear enough to be read; grey ware; $\times\frac{1}{10}$. 4, 5. Pottery bricks with disc pattern; grey ware; $\times\frac{1}{10}$. 6, 7. Pottery bricks with floral design; grey ware; $\times\frac{1}{10}$. 8–10. Pottery bricks with lineal pattern; grey ware; $\times\frac{1}{10}$. 11. Three fragments of pottery bricks with a cart and horses in low relief; grey ware; $\times\frac{1}{10}$. 12. Fragment of a pottery brick with two seated figures in low relief; grey ware; $\times\frac{1}{10}$. 13. Fragment of a pottery brick with a phoenix in low relief; grey ware; $\times\frac{1}{10}$. 14, 15. Pottery bricks with floral pattern; grey ware; $\times\frac{1}{10}$.

PLATE 27

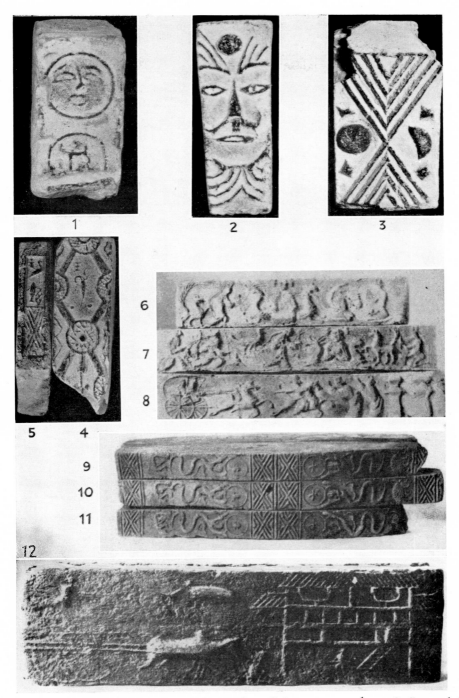

1. Pottery brick with moon-shaped mask and coin in low relief; grey ware; $\times \frac{1}{10}$. 2. Pottery brick with mask in low relief. Wedge-shaped; grey ware; $\times \frac{1}{10}$. 3. Pottery brick with sun-moon-and-stars design; grey ware; $\times \frac{1}{10}$. 4. Pottery brick with disc pattern. In one of the rhombic-shaped designs are a character *wang* 王, 'a king', a dragon-shaped animal and two dots; grey ware; $\times \frac{1}{10}$. 5. Pottery brick with decoration in two sections: a human figure, a bird and two fish in low relief on the upper part, and a lineal design on the lower; grey ware; $\times \frac{1}{10}$. 6–8. Pottery bricks with human figures, animals, chariot and gate-tower in low relief; grey ware; $\times \frac{1}{10}$. 9–11. Pottery bricks with pattern of crossed-lines, snake-bodied figures holding the sun and moon and the snake-and-turtle; grey ware; $\times \frac{1}{10}$. 12. Large pottery brick with an ox-cart coming towards a house; grey ware; $\times \frac{1}{10}$.

PLATE 28

2

1

1. Pottery brick with a flower design in the centre and a series of animal figures between the petals; grey ware; × $\frac{1}{5}$. 2. Rubbing from a pottery brick with the same design as no. 1.

PLATE 29

1. Pottery brick with a two-storied gate-tower and the red bird on the roof; grey ware. (Courtesy of the Hsi-ch'êng Museum); ×$\frac{1}{5}$.   2. Pottery brick with a horseman and horse-drawn chariot in low relief under a band of floral design; grey ware. (Courtesy of the Hsi-ch'êng Museum); ×$\frac{1}{5}$.

PLATE 30

1. Pottery brick with an acrobatic scene in low relief; grey ware. (Courtesy of the Hsi-ch'êng Museum); ×$\frac{1}{5}$.   2. Pottery brick with a 'chess'-playing scene in low relief; grey ware. (Courtesy of the Hsi-ch'êng Museum); ×$\frac{1}{4}$.

PLATE 31

1

2

1. Pottery brick with a feast scene in low relief; grey ware. (Courtesy of the Hsi-ch'êng Museum); $\times\frac{1}{5}$.   2. Pottery brick with a scene of salt manufacture against a landscape background in which two hunters are chasing and shooting at an animal; grey ware. (Courtesy of the Hsi-ch'êng Museum); $\times\frac{1}{5}$.

PLATE 32

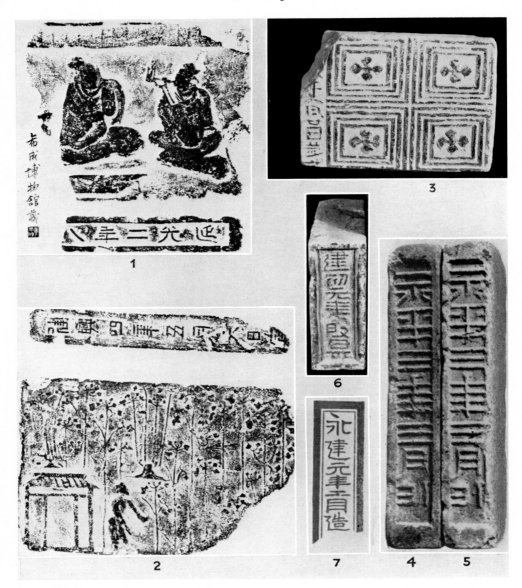

1. Rubbings of a brick fragment in the Hsi-ch'êng Museum showing a musician playing a wind instrument. Inscription: *Yên-kuang êrh nien* 延 光 二 年, 'the second year of Yên-kuang' (A.D. 123); grey ware. (Courtesy of the Ashmolean Museum, Oxford.)   2. Rubbings of a brick fragment in the Hsi-ch'êng Museum with a scene of mulberry leaf picking. Inscription: *Chien-hsing ssǔ nien wu-yüeh liu-jih tsao* 建 興 四 年 五 月 六 日 造, 'made on the sixth day of the fifth moon, in the fourth year of Chien-hsing' (A.D. 226); grey ware. (Courtesy of the Ashmolean Museum, Oxford.)   3. Pottery brick with cross-in-rectangular-frame pattern. Inscription: *Yen-p'ing yüan-nien pa-yüeh nien-jih tsao chih* 延 平 元 年 八 月 廿 日 造 之, 'it is made on the 20th day of the eighth moon in the first year of Yen-p'ing' (A.D. 106); grey ware; (cf. **372**, Fig. 19). 4, 5. Pottery bricks. Inscription: *Yung-p'ing san-nien san-yüeh i-jih* 永 平 三 年 三 月 一 日, 'the first day of the third moon in the third year of Yung-p'ing' (A.D. 60); grey ware; $\times \frac{1}{5}$. 6. Pottery brick, wedge-shaped. Inscription: *Chien-ch'u yüan nien* 建 初 元 年 閏 日 III, 'first year of Chien-ch'u' (A.D. 76); grey ware; $\times \frac{1}{4}$.   7. Inscription on a brick fragment: *Yung-chien yüan-nien êrh-yüeh tsao* 永 建 元 年 二 月 造, 'made in the second moon in the first year of Yung-chien' (A.D. 126). (After Graham **370**.)

PLATE 33

1

2

1. Painted brick of a three-legged tiger-like animal about to spring, with an inscription: *Pi hsieh* 辟 邪, 'to avoid evil'; grey ware; painting and writing in red. (Courtesy of the Hsi-ch'êng Museum); ×¼.　　2. Brick with a crouching tiger-like animal, painted in red. Inscription in red: *Ch'u hsiung* 除 凶, 'to remove evil'; grey ware. (Courtesy of the Hsi-ch'êng Museum); ×¼.

PLATE 34

1. Seated pottery figurine with a tablet in its right hand. Hand-modelled, grey ware; $\times \frac{1}{2}$.
2–4. Pottery figurines. Mould-made grey ware; $\times \frac{1}{4}$.   5, 6. Pottery warriors. Partly painted in red. Mould-made, grey ware; $\times \frac{1}{6}$.

PLATE 35

1. Pottery figurine. Mould-made, grey ware; $\times\frac{1}{4}$.   2. Pair of dancers. Mould-made, grey ware; $\times\frac{1}{4}$.   3. Figure of a dancer. Mould-made, grey ware; $\times\frac{1}{4}$.   4, 5. Pottery figurines. Mould-made, grey ware; $\times\frac{1}{4}$.   6. Pottery figurine. Mould-made, grey ware; $\times\frac{1}{2}$. 7. Pottery figurine, kneeling with left hand to ear. Mould-made, white-slipped, grey ware; $\times\frac{1}{2}$. 8. Pottery figurine in kneeling posture. Mould-modelled and scraped. White-slipped, grey ware; $\times\frac{1}{2}$.

PLATE 36

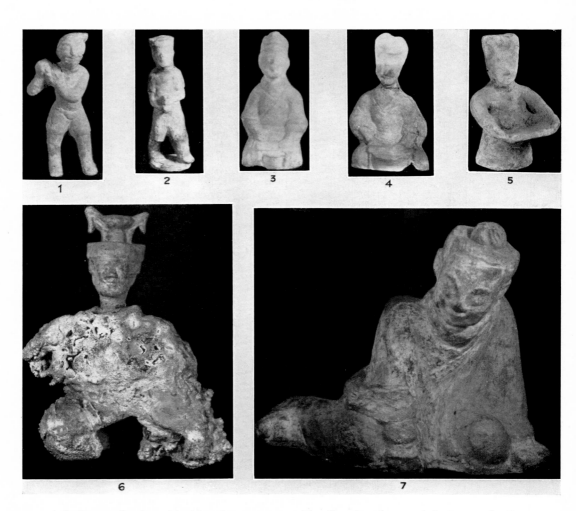

1, 2. Pottery figurines. Mould-made, grey ware; white-slipped; $\times \frac{1}{4}$. 3–5. Pottery figurines. Mould-made, grey ware; $\times \frac{1}{4}$. 6. Pottery figurine with high head-dress. Body covered with limestone encrustment. Mould-made, grey ware; $\times \frac{1}{2}$. 7. Pottery figurine with head bending forward. Modelled in a mould; white-slipped, grey ware; $\times \frac{1}{2}$.

PLATE 37

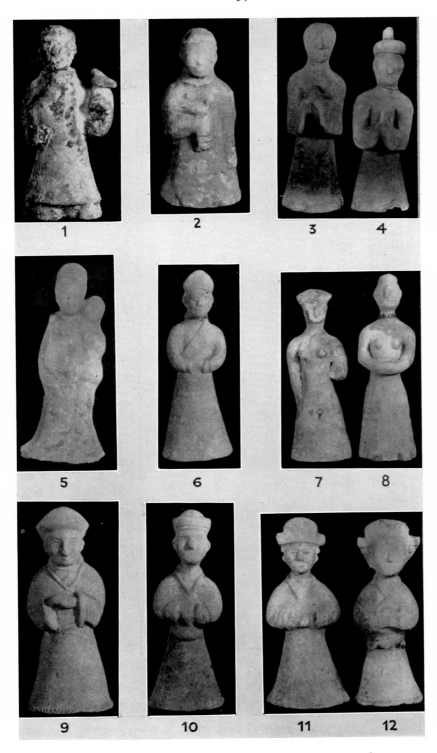

1, 2, 5, 6, 9–12. Pottery figurines. Mould-made, grey ware; × $\frac{1}{2}$.
3, 4, 7, 8. Pottery figurines. Hand-modelled, grey ware; × $\frac{1}{2}$.

PLATE 38

1, 2. Pottery owls. Hand-modelled, grey ware; ×½.   3. Pottery *p'u-shuo* 舖首 or mask. Hand-modelled, grey ware. (After Graham **369**, Pl. 8.)   4. Fragment of an animal. Hand-modelled, grey ware; ×½.   5. Pottery acrobat with tongue protruding, standing on his hands. Hand-modelled, grey ware. (After Graham **369**, Pl. 10.)   6. Leg of a pottery figurine with a sandalled foot. Mould-made, grey ware, with red surface; ×¼.   7. Pottery monkey, kneeling on one leg. Hand-modelled, grey ware; ×½.   8. Hand of a figurine. Hand-modelled, grey ware, with red surface; ×¼.   9. Pottery rabbit. Hand-modelled, grey ware; ×½.   10. Pottery bear, standing on its hind legs. Hand-modelled, grey ware; ×½.

PLATE 39

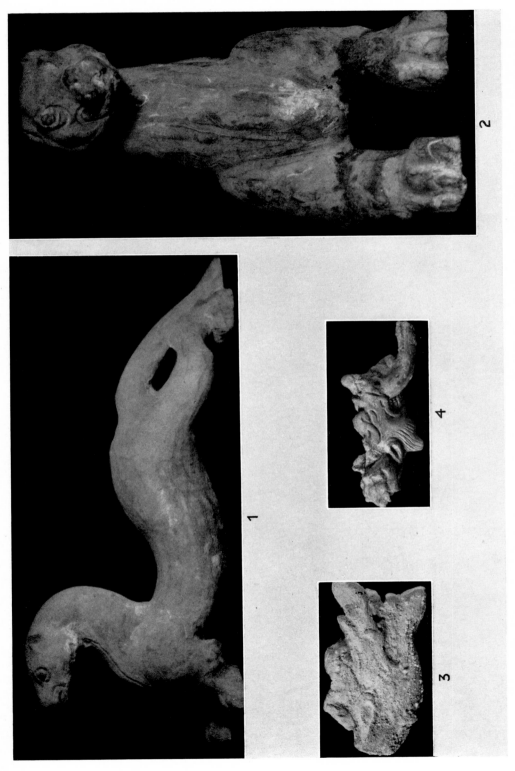

1. Pottery weasel. Hand-modelled and scraped, grey ware; $\times \frac{1}{2}$.　　2. Front view of the weasel.　　3. Head of a dragon.　Hand-modelled, grey ware.
4. Head of a dragon.　Hand-modelled, grey ware; $\times \frac{1}{2}$.
Surface covered with limestone encrustment; $\times \frac{1}{2}$.

PLATE 40

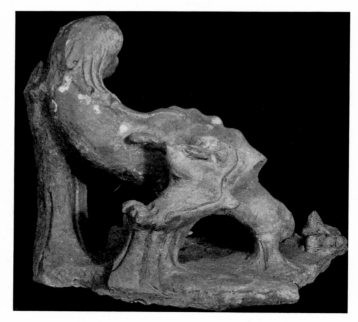

1

2

1. Body of a dragon. Hand-modelled, grey ware; $\times \frac{1}{4}$.
2. Pottery dog. Mould-made, grey ware; $\times \frac{1}{5}$.

PLATE 41

1. Pottery boar. Hand-modelled, grey ware; $\times\frac{1}{2}$.   2. Pottery boar with a perforation in its back. Hand-modelled, grey ware; $\times\frac{1}{2}$.   3. Pottery sheep. Hand-modelled, white-slipped, grey ware; $\times\frac{1}{2}$.

PLATE 42

1. Pottery dog. Hand-modelled, grey ware; $\times\frac{1}{2}$.   2, 3. Pottery horses. Mould-made, grey ware; $\times\frac{1}{2}$.   4. Pottery dog. Hand-made, grey ware; $\times\frac{1}{2}$.   5, 6. Pottery boars. Hand-made, grey ware; $\times\frac{1}{2}$.   7. Pottery dog. Mould-made, grey ware; $\times\frac{1}{2}$.   8. Pottery dog. Hand-made, grey ware; $\times\frac{1}{2}$.

PLATE 43

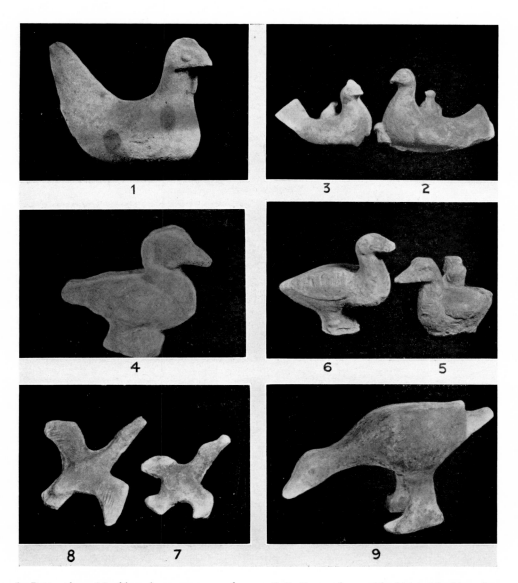

1. Pottery hen. Mould-made, grey ware; ×½.   2, 3. Pottery hens with chicks. Mould-made, grey ware; ×¼.   4. Pottery duck. Mould-made, grey ware; ×½.   5. Pottery duck with a pitcher on its back. Mould-made, grey ware; ×½.   6. Pottery duck. Mould-made, grey ware; ×½.   7, 8. Flying wild geese. Mould-made, grey ware; ×½.   9. Pottery goose. Hand-modelled and scraped, grey ware with red surface; ×½.

PLATE 44

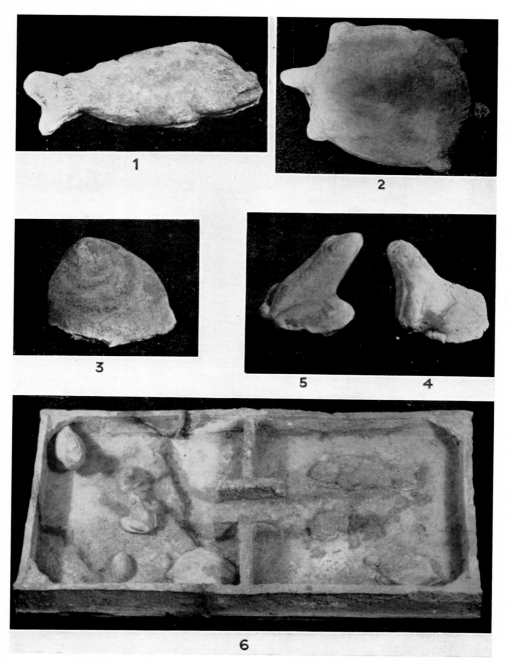

1. Pottery fish. Mould-made, grey ware; $\times\frac{1}{1}$.　　2. Pottery turtle. Mould-made, grey ware; $\times\frac{1}{1}$.　　3. Pottery snail. Mould-made, grey ware; $\times\frac{1}{1}$.　　4, 5. Pottery frogs. Mould-made, grey ware; $\times\frac{1}{1}$.　　6. Pottery pond with snails, frogs, fish and turtles. Mostly mould-made, grey ware, with part of surface red; $\times\frac{1}{4}$.

PLATE 45

1

2

1. Pottery house with two staircases, a cross-bow hanging on the central pillar and a pair of shields, one on each side of the entrance; partly mould-made and assembled; grey ware with traces of white and red paint; $\times \frac{1}{5}$.   2. Colonnaded house with a mortar on the floor. Partly mould-made and assembled, grey ware with traces of white paint; $\times \frac{1}{5}$.

PLATE 46

1. Pottery house. Partly mould-made and assembled, grey ware with greenish glaze; ×¼.
2. Pottery house. Partly mould-made and assembled, grey ware; ×¼.

PLATE 47

1. Pottery house or mortar. Mould-made and assembled, grey ware with traces of white paint; $\times\frac{1}{4}$.
2. Pottery terraced house with two staircases and railings on the roof and porch. Partly mould-made and assembled, grey ware with traces of white and red paint; $\times\frac{1}{5}$.

PLATE 48

1. Pottery *hu* 壺 or wine container, with masks and lineal decorations. Wheel-made, grey ware with traces of red paint; × $\frac{1}{5}$.   2. Axles of a wheel with perforations for spokes. Mould-made, grey ware with traces of white paint; × $\frac{1}{2}$.   3. Pottery 'banner stand' in the shape of a sheep carrying a funnel on its back. Mould-made, grey ware with red surface; × $\frac{1}{5}$.   4. Pottery 'banner stand' in the shape of a bell with two animals and a funnel on top of each other. Mould-made, grey ware with traces of white paint; × $\frac{1}{5}$.

PLATE 49

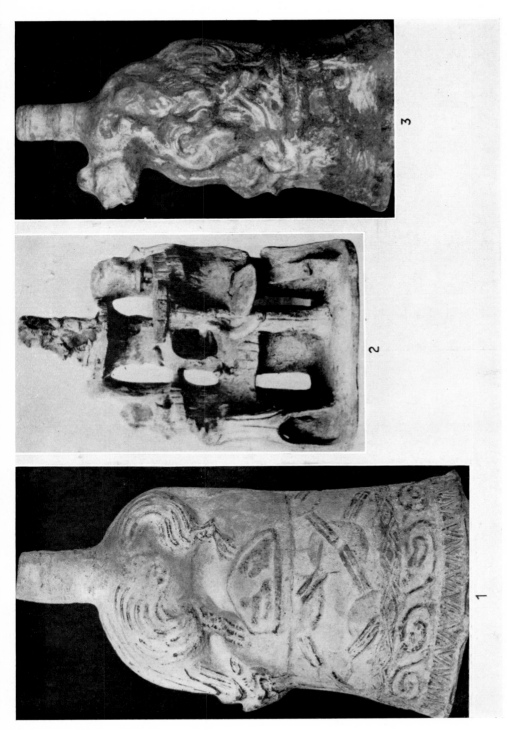

1. Pottery 'banner stand' in the shape of a bell with an animal carrying a funnel. Mould-made, grey ware with traces of white paint; ×$\frac{1}{5}$.
2. Pottery 'banner stand' in the shape of a rockery of several levels with a funnel projecting from the top. It is covered with figurines and monkeys, one of which is playing a lute. Hand-modelled, grey ware; ×$\frac{1}{10}$.   3. Pottery 'banner stand' in the shape of a bell with an animal and projecting funnel forming its upper part. Mould-made, grey ware with silvery green glaze; ×$\frac{1}{4}$.

247

PLATE 50

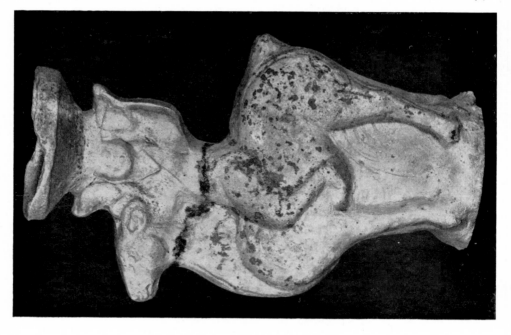

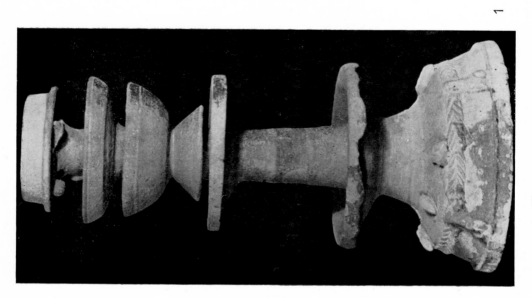

1. Pottery *têng* 燈 or lamp in five layers. Partly wheel-made and assembled, grey ware; ×⅕.   2. Pottery *têng* in the form of a horseman carrying an oil-container on his head. Partly mould-made and assembled, grey ware with red surface; ×¼.

PLATE 51

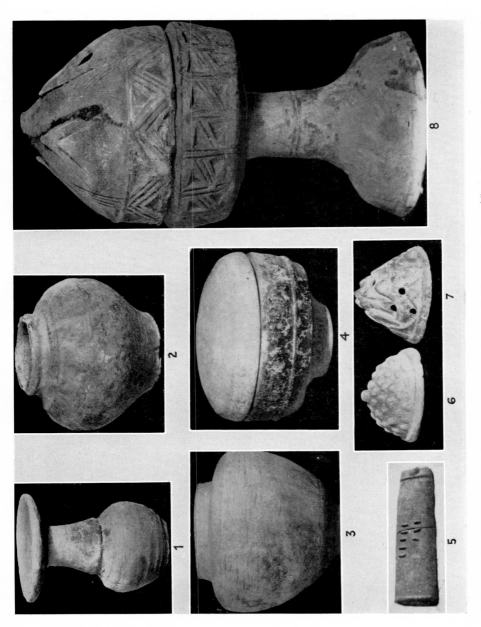

1. Pottery *p'ing* 瓶 or vase. Wheel-made, grey ware; ×½. 2. Short-necked *kuan* 罐 or jar. Wheel-made, grey ware with traces of green glaze; ×½. 3. Short-necked *t'an* 罎 or large jar, decorated with stamped ripples. Wheel-made, grey ware; ×¼. 4. Pottery *lien* 奩 or perhaps food-container. Wheel-made, grey ware with traces of white paint; ×¼. 5. Pottery *ch'in* 琴 or lute. Hand-modelled, grey ware. (After Graham 369, Pl. 9.) 6. Cover of a pottery *po shan lu* 博山爐 or incense burner. Mould-made, grey ware; ×½. 7. Cover of a *po shan lu.* Mould-made, grey ware with brownish glaze; ×½. 8. Pottery *po shan lu.* Partly mould-made, grey ware; ×½.

249

PLATE 52

1

2

1. Pottery *tsao* 灶 or cooking stove, with two holes and a chimney. Mould-made and assembled, grey ware; $\times \frac{1}{4}$.   2. Pottery tripod *lu* 鑪 or warming vessel. Wheel-made, red-slipped, grey ware; $\times \frac{1}{1}$.

PLATE 53

1. Pottery two-handled *hsüan* 鋗 or small basin. Wheel-made, grey ware; × ½.
2. Pottery two-handled *hsüan* or small basin. Wheel-made, white-slipped, grey ware; × ½.

PLATE 54

1. Pottery *yü-shang* 羽觴 or oval cup. Hand-made, hard grey ware with brownish-green glaze; × ½.
2. Pottery *yü-shang*. Hand-made, grey ware; × ⅓.　　　3. Pottery *yü-shang*. Made by scraping out a lump of clay, grey ware; × ⅓.　　　4, 5. Pottery *kuo* 鍋 or cooking vessels. Wheel-made, cord-marked, grey ware; × ¼.　　　6. Pottery chicken on a *tsu* 俎 or stand. Partly mould-made and assembled, grey ware with partly red surface; × ⅕.　　　7. Pottery handled *kuo*. Wheel-made, grey ware; × ⅓.

PLATE 55

Bronze two-handled *kuo* on a three-legged pottery 'stove'. The stove is similar to the iron ones still in use among the Ch'iang 羌 people in the Li-fan region. Mould-made and assembled, grey ware; ×¼.

253

PLATE 56

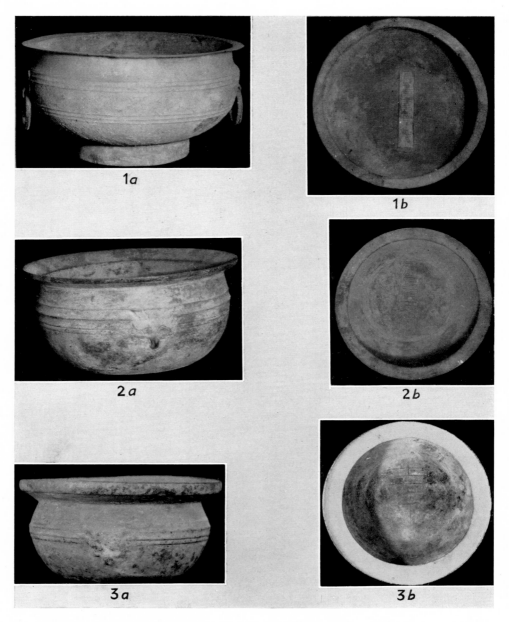

1*a*. Bronze two-handled *hsüan* or basin with horizontal lineal decoration. An inscription cast in the bottom of the vessel (*b*) reads: *Fu kuei ch'ang, yi hou wang* 富貴昌宜侯王, 'You deserve wealth, honour and prosperity, and are fit to become a marquis or a prince'; × ⅕. 2*a*. Bronze *hsi* 洗 or basin decorated with a pair of masks and horizontal lines. In the bottom of the vessel is a design in low relief of two fish and an inscription (*b*) which reads: *Chün yi hou wang, pao yung* 君宜侯王寶用 'Your excellency is fit to become a marquis or a prince, treasure and use this vessel'; × ⅕. 3*a*. Bronze *hsi* decorated with a pair of masks and horizontal lines. The inscription (*b*) reads: *Chi hsiang* 吉羊, 'May you have good fortune'; × ⅕.

PLATE 57

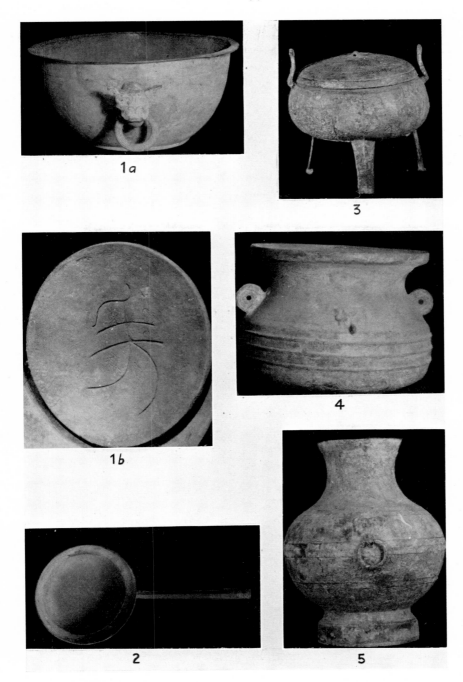

1 *a*. Bronze one-handled *hsiian* or large basin. Under the vessel at the base is an inscription, three fish and one bird (*b*). The inscription may be read as *Ch'ien wan* 千 萬, and with the figures, it may mean that the vessel is to contain thousands of fish and birds; ×$\frac{1}{5}$. 2. Bronze *yun tou* 熨 斗 or iron with a long handle; ×$\frac{1}{5}$. 3. Bronze *ting* 鼎 or tripod. The cover is decorated with rope and lineal patterns: ×$\frac{1}{2}$. 4. Bronze two-handled *hsiian* or *kuo* with two masks and some lineal decoration; ×$\frac{1}{5}$ 5. Bronze two-handled *hu* with lineal decoration; ×$\frac{1}{5}$.

255

PLATE 58

1a

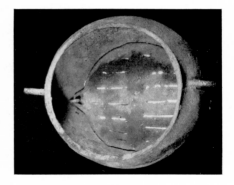

1b

2

1. Bronze two-handled *tsêng* 甑 or steaming vessel. The bottom is of a separate sheet and is perforated in horizontal lines; ×⅕. 　　2. Bronze *wên-lu* 溫 鑪 or charcoal burner. The oval-shaped frame on the top of the vessel is meant to hold a *yü-hsiang* cup; a rectangular opening at its base is possibly a socket for a wooden handle; ×⅟₁.

PLATE 59

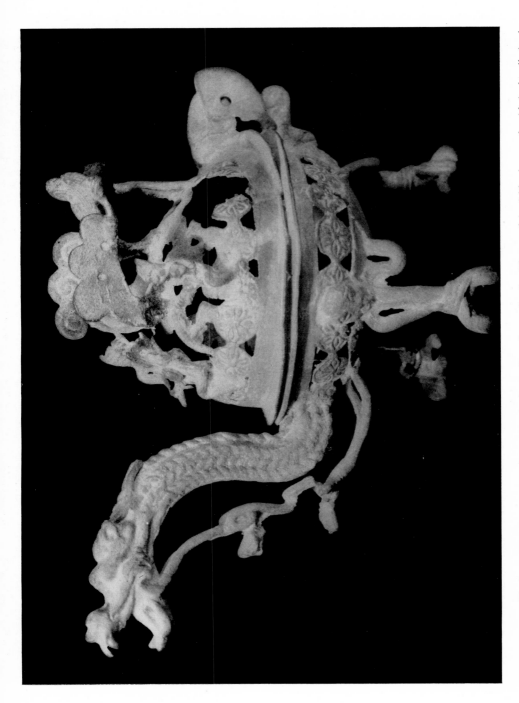

Bronze *chiao-tou* 鐎斗 or warming vessel with a cover similar to that of a *po shan lu*. The vessel is richly decorated, with its handle in the shape of a dragon, from whose mouth is suspended a string of three acrobats, holding each other by the feet. The body of the vessel has some open-work floral designs. Three human figures forming a tripod support the vessel. The cover also has a filigree pattern of flowers, hills and floating clouds with a group of 'fairies' riding on them. The casting is crude yet elaborate, similar to some of the Indo-Chinese bronzes **482**; × $\frac{1}{1}$.

PLATE 60

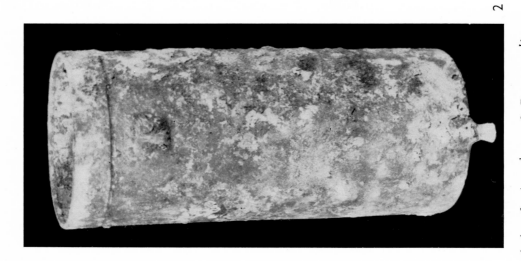

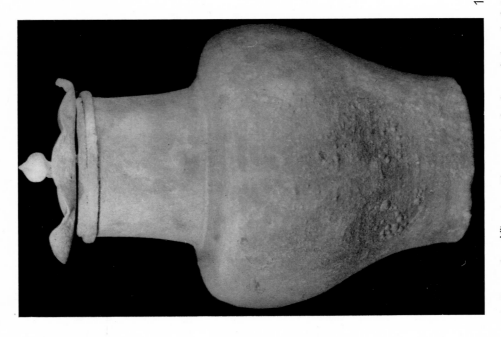

1. Pewter *kuan* 罐 or jar with a cover in the shape of a lotus leaf. It contained ashes of grain; × 1/1.　　2. Bronze *yu* 卣 or cylindrical container with two masks under the rim and three short legs. (Courtesy of the Hsi-ch'êng Museum); × 1/2.

PLATE 61

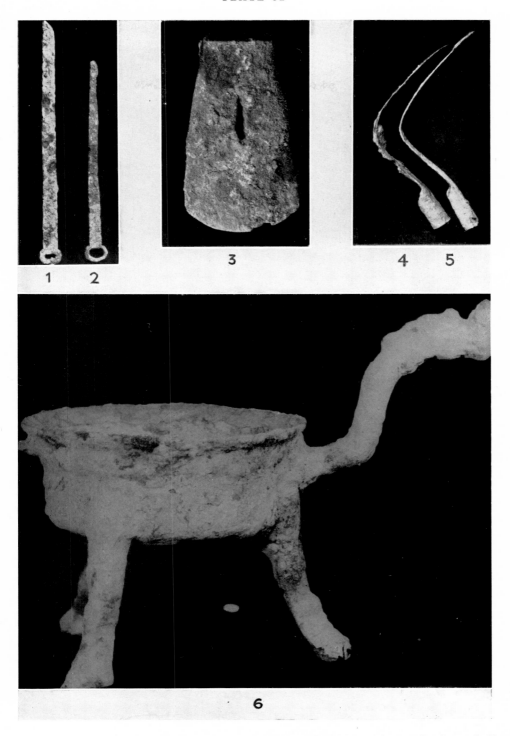

1–2. Iron knives with loop handles; $\times\frac{1}{4}$.   3. Iron socketed hoe with a perforation to hold a cross-bar to keep the handle in position; $\times\frac{1}{2}$.   4–5. Iron socketed scythes; $\times\frac{1}{4}$.   6. Iron *chiao tou* or warming vessel with a handle in the shape of a dragon; $\times\frac{1}{1}$.

PLATE 62

1

2

1. Bronze mirror with seal-and-animal design; ×½.　　2. Bronze mirror with seal-and-animal design and a long handle. It is partly covered with iron rust showing the presence of iron in the alloy; ×½.

PLATE 63

1. Bronze mirror with dragon design; $\times \frac{1}{1}$.   2. Bronze mirror with bird design; $\times \frac{1}{1}$.

PLATE 64

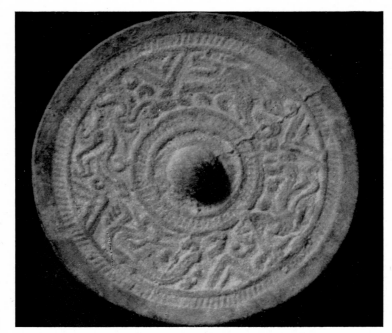

1. Bronze mirror with dragon-and-square design; $\times \frac{1}{1}$.
2. Bronze mirror with nipple-and-lineal design; $\times \frac{1}{1}$.

PLATE 65

1a

1b

2

1. Bronze cormorant with a basket on its back and a fish in its beak; *a*, front view; *b*, side view.
(Courtesy of Pi-chia-shan-chuang); ×⅓.   2. Bronze bird probably the trunk of a 'coin-tree'
as a fragment of a coin is still attached to its breast. The base is cast into a socket for fitting into a stand
of some kind; slightly enlarged.

PLATE 66

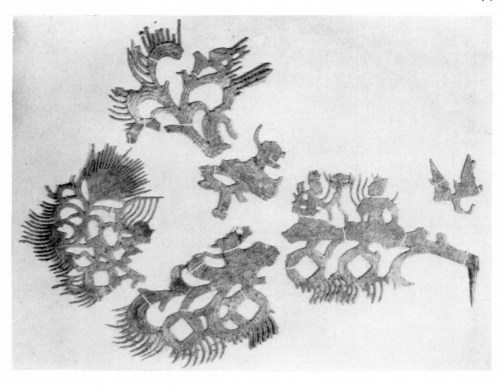

1. Fragments of a bronze *ch'ien shu* 錢 樹 or 'coin-tree' with three big *pi*-shaped discs and two small coins among the leaves and branches; ×¼.

2. Fragments of a bronze 'coin-tree' with a branch bearing a series of coins; ×¼.

PLATE 67

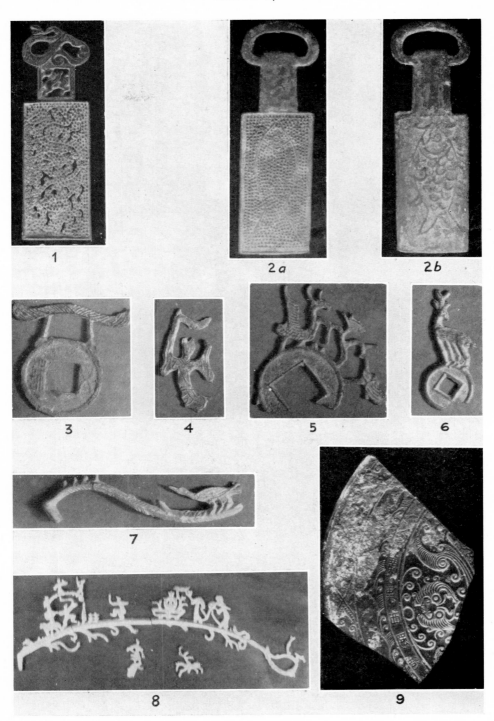

1. Bronze *ya-shêng ch'ien* 壓 勝 錢 or coin to ward off evil influence; dragon design; ×½.
2. Bronze *ya-shêng ch'ien*; fish design; ×½.   3–8. Fragments of a bronze 'coin-tree' showing coins as well as human figures and animals; ×1.   9. Fragment of a bronze mirror with a mask design and part of an inscription which reads: *Kuang-han hsi Shu tsao* 廣 漢 西 蜀 造, 'made in Kuang-han, western Shu'; ×1.

PLATE 68

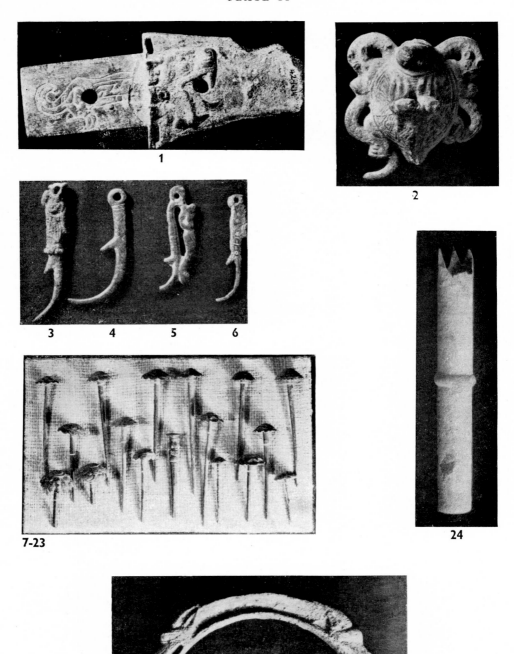

1. Fragment of a decorated *ko* 戈 or weapon with perforations for haft; ×½. 2. Base of a vessel in the form of a turtle and two dragons. The legs of the vessel still remain on the turtle's back; ×½. 3–6. A series of bronze *hsi* 觿 or knot-undoers; ×⅓. 7–23. A series of bronze *tsan* 簪 hair-pins; ×½. 24. Bronze finial of a staff or weapon; ×½. 25. Bronze handle in the shape of two dragons' heads for suspending a sacrificial vessel; ×⅓.

266

PLATE 69

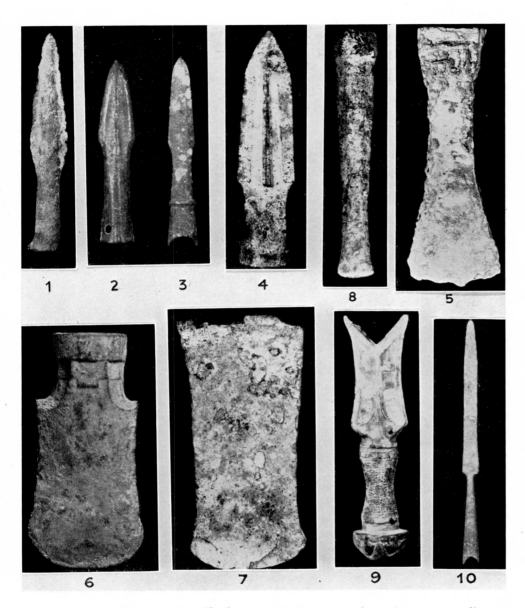

1–4, 10. A series of bronze *mao shou* 矛首 or socketed spear heads; × ½.　　　5–7. A series of bronze *ch'u shou* 鋤首 or socketed celts or hoes; × ½.　　　8. Bronze *tso* 鑿 or socketed chisel; × ⅟₁. 9. Bronze *chien ping* 劍柄 or hilt of a sword; × ½.

PLATE 70

1. Inscription on the stone door of a burial cave in Hsin-tsin: *Chang shih ch'ung chih* 張氏家幖 'a sign for the tomb of Chang Shih'.　　2. Stone door of a burial cave decorated with the phoenix-and-knocker design. Red sandstone; $\times \frac{1}{20}$.　　3. Stone beam of a burial cave with a racing dragon in low relief. From Hsin-tsin. Red sandstone; $\times \frac{1}{20}$.　　4. Stone beam of a burial cave from Hsin-tsin, with a galloping tiger in low relief. Red sandstone; $\times \frac{1}{20}$.

268

PLATE 71

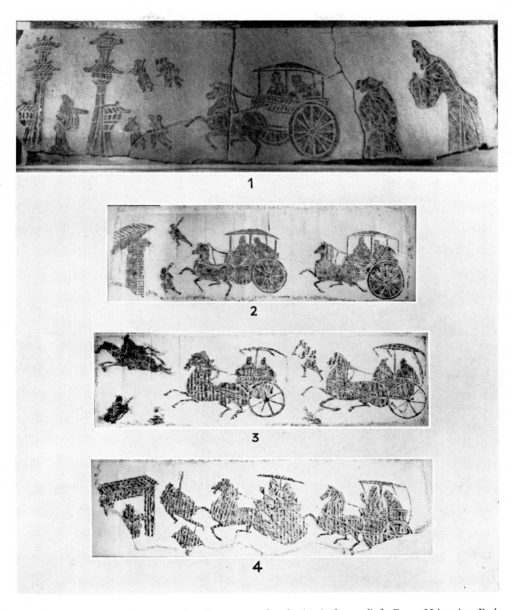

1. Stone panel from a cave-burial with a scene of a chariot in low relief. From Hsin-tsin. Red sandstone; $\times \frac{1}{20}$.   2–4. Rubbings of stone panels with chariot scenes. Originals in the Szechwan Museum. (Courtesy of Dr L. Picken.)

PLATE 72

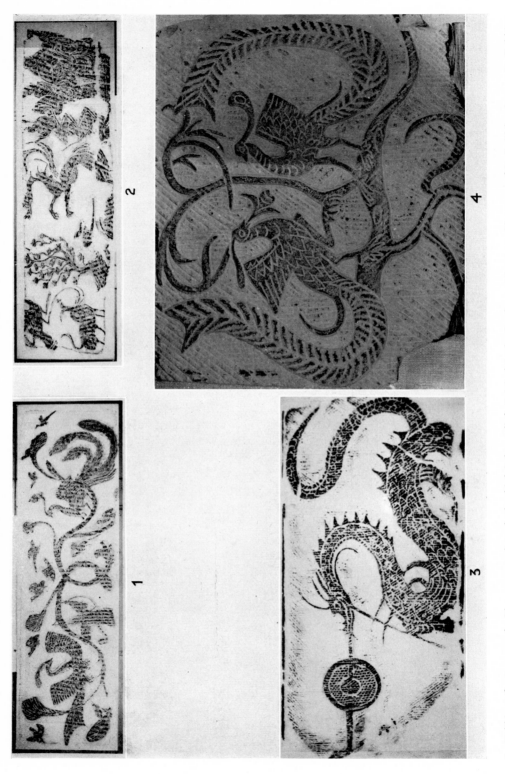

1. Rubbing of a stone panel with two peacocks and other birds in low relief. Original in the Szechwan Museum. (Courtesy of Dr L. Picken.)   2. Rubbing of a stone panel with an attacking winged dragon and other scenes in low relief. Original in the Szechwan Museum. (Courtesy of Dr L. Picken.)   3. Rubbing of a stone panel with a dragon pulling a cord and a *pi* disc. Original in the Szechwan Museum. (Courtesy of Dr L. Picken.)   4. Stone panel from a burial cave in Hsin-tsin with a pair of peacocks in low relief; × $\frac{1}{10}$.

PLATE 73

1, 2. Rubbings of stone panels with peacocks in low relief. Originals in the Szechwan Museum. (Courtesy of Dr L. Picken.)   3. Rubbing of stone panel with human figures in low relief. Original in the Szechwan Museum. (Courtesy of Dr L. Picken.)

PLATE 74

1   2

3

1, 2. Rubbings of stone panels with the crossing of the 'sun' and 'moon' in low relief. Originals in the Szechwan Museum. (Courtesy of Dr L. Picken.)   3. Rubbing of stone panel with human figures in low relief. Original in the Szechwan Museum. (Courtesy of Dr L. Picken.)

PLATE 75

1

2

1. Stone panel from a burial cave in Hsin-tsin with a scene in low relief of a horseman entering a gate. Red sandstone; $\times \frac{1}{10}$.　　2. Stone from a burial cave in Hsin-tsin with two fairies playing a game of 'chess' in low relief. Red sandstone; $\times \frac{1}{10}$.

PLATE 76

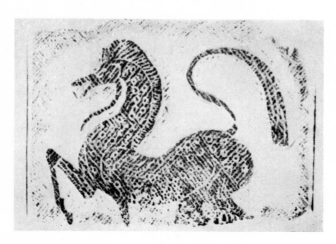

Rubbings of stone panels with horses in low relief. Originals in the Szechwan Museum.
(Courtesy of Dr L. Picken.)

PLATE 77

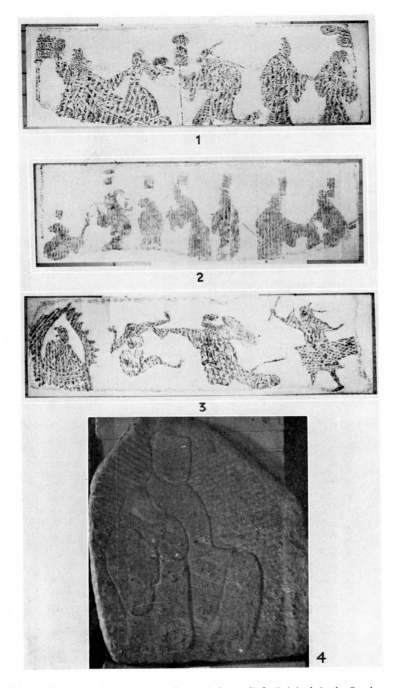

1, 2. Rubbings of stone panels with human figures in low relief. Originals in the Szechwan Museum. (Courtesy of Dr L. Picken.)   3. Rubbing of a stone panel with a scene of the 'monkey show' in low relief. Original in the Szechwan Museum. (Courtesy of Dr L. Picken.)   4. Stone panel from a cave in Hsin-tsin with human figure in low relief. Red sandstone; $\times \frac{1}{10}$.

PLATE 78

2

1

1. Stone panel from a burial cave in Hsin-tsin with a human figure in low relief. Red sandstone; ×$\frac{1}{10}$. 2. Stone panel from a cave in Hsin-tsin with two servant; coming out of the 'kitchen', in low relief. Red sandstone; ×$\frac{1}{10}$.

PLATE 79

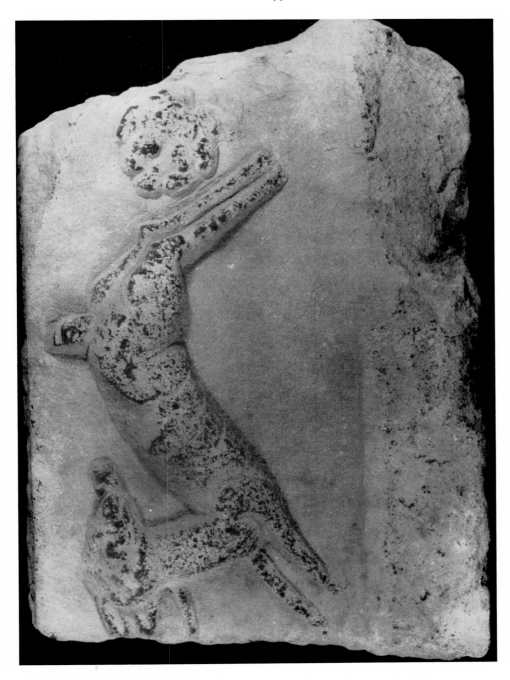

Stone panel from a cave in Hsin-tsin with a galloping doe in high relief.
Red sandstone; $\times \frac{1}{4}$.

PLATE 80

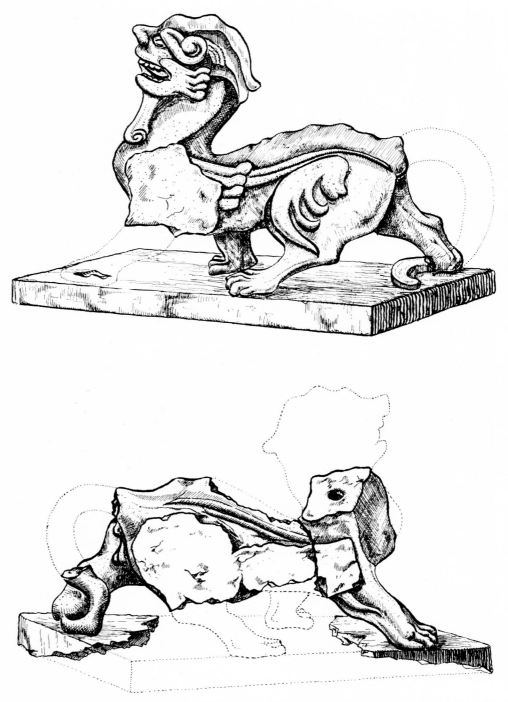

Drawings of two badly damaged stone animals found in Lu-shan. By Michael Sullivan.

PLATE 81

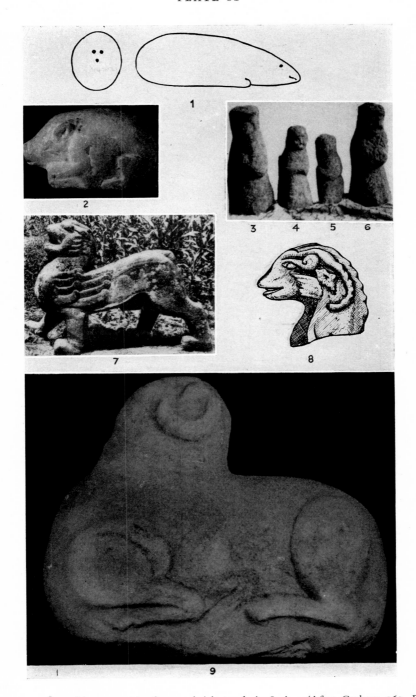

1. Drawing of a white stone pig from a brick tomb in I-pin. (After Graham **369**, Fig. 11.)
2. White stone pig; $\times \frac{1}{2}$.   3–6. A series of stone figurines from a brick tomb in I-pin. Red sandstone. (After Graham **369**, Pl. 7.)   7. Winged lion from the Kao Yi tomb. (After Segalen **405**, 1, Pl. 54.)   8. Drawing of a stone goat's head found in Lu-shan. By Michael Sullivan.
9. Stone ram with damaged head. Red sandstone; $\times \frac{1}{2}$.

PLATE 82

1. Stone head of a figurine. Red sandstone; slightly reduced.　　2. Profile of the stone head.

PLATE 83

1

2

1. Ch'iung-lai kiln site as viewed from the eastern bank of Ta-nan Ho.   2. The Taoist temple, Shih-fang-t'ang 什仿堂 on a steep mound at the Ch'iung-lai kiln site.

PLATE 84

Ch'iung-lai pottery. 1. Pitcher of white-slipped ware with small spout and tall handle; $\times \frac{1}{2}$. 2. Pitcher of white-slipped ware with small spout, tall and small handles; $\times \frac{1}{2}$. 3. Five-legged vessel of white-slipped ware. The legs are moulded with a mask in relief; $\times \frac{1}{2}$. 4. Globular jar with handle in the shape of a dragon. Partly slipped and glazed. Most of the glaze had flaked off except the thicker part at the edge of the glaze; $\times \frac{1}{4}$. 5. Semi-globular bowl of white-slipped ware; $\times \frac{1}{2}$. 6. Spittoon of white-slipped ware; $\times \frac{1}{4}$.

PLATE 85

Ch'iung-lai pottery. 1. Jar of pale yellowish glazed ware with four small handles; ×⅙. 2. Flask of green glazed ware with small spout on the shoulder and ringed neck and contracted mouth; ×½. 3. Vase of greyish-green glazed ware with two small handles and cover; ×½. 4. Flask of crackled, greyish glazed ware with six small handles; ×⅓. 5. Pitcher of greyish glazed ware with long spout, and small and large handles; ×⅓. 6. Jar of olive green glazed ware with small handles; ×½.

PLATE 86

Ch'iung-lai pottery. 1. Lamp of greyish-green glazed ware with spout and handle; $\times \frac{1}{2}$.   2. Lamp of greyish-green glazed ware with handle; $\times \frac{1}{2}$.   3. Lamp of green and brown glazed ware with handle projecting from the rim; $\times \frac{1}{2}$.   4. Lamp of green and brown glazed ware; $\times \frac{1}{2}$. 5. Box of greenish-grey glazed ware with dragon design in low relief under the glaze; $\times \frac{1}{1}$. 6. Box of greenish-grey glazed ware with cover in the shape of a flower; $\times \frac{1}{1}$.   7. Bowl of greenish-grey glazed ware decorated with pie-rim pattern on the shoulder; $\times \frac{1}{2}$.   8. Vase of green glazed ware; $\times \frac{1}{3}$.   9. Four legged basin of greenish-grey glazed ware decorated with masks in relief on the four sides above the legs. Repaired parts in brown; $\times \frac{1}{4}$.

PLATE 87

Ch'iung-lai pottery. 1. Vase of white-slipped ware painted with floral design in brown. Four pairs of handles round the neck; $\times\frac{1}{4}$.   2. Cup of white-slipped ware painted with grass design in brown. Loop handle. Repair at rim; $\times\frac{1}{2}$.   3. Vase of light green glazed ware decorated with deep green patches. Small spout and handles on the shoulder; $\times\frac{1}{3}$.   4. Vase of light green glazed ware decorated with brown patches. Four spouts around the shoulder; $\times\frac{1}{3}$.   5. Vase of light green glazed ware painted with grass pattern in brown. Handles just under the neck; $\times\frac{1}{4}$. 6. Vase of yellowish-green glazed ware with brown and dark green patches. Beaked spout on the shoulder; $\times\frac{1}{4}$.

PLATE 88

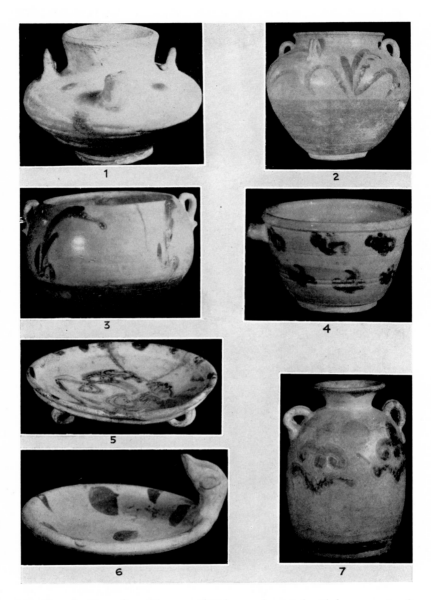

Ch'iung-lai pottery. 1. Vase of greyish-green glazed ware decorated with brown spots. Spout and handles on the shoulder; $\times\frac{1}{2}$. 2. Jar of greyish-green glazed ware with grass pattern in brown. Four handles on the shoulder; $\times\frac{1}{4}$. 3. Jar of greyish-green glazed ware with grass pattern in brown. Handles near the mouth-rim; $\times\frac{1}{4}$. 4. Deep basin of greyish-green glazed ware painted with brown patches. Spout just under the rim; $\times\frac{1}{4}$. 5. Three-legged dish of greyish-green glazed ware with decorative design in brown and yellow. Legs in the shape of a ring; $\times\frac{1}{5}$. 6. Lamp of white-slipped ware with brown patches. Handle projects from the rim in the shape of a duck; $\times\frac{1}{2}$. 7. Vase of greyish-green glazed ware with decorative design in brown. Handles on the shoulder; $\times\frac{1}{5}$.

286

PLATE 89

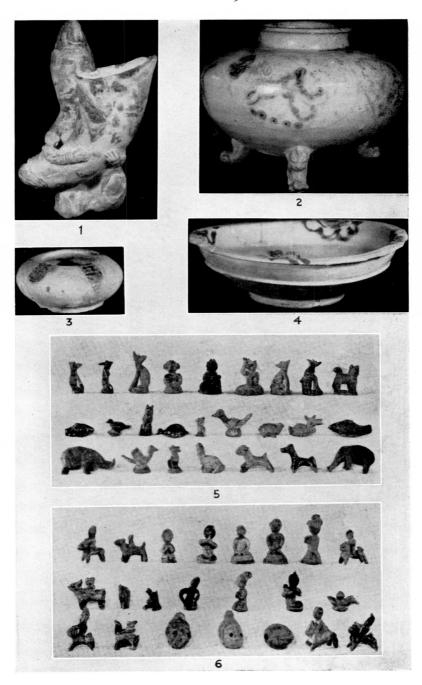

Ch'iung-lai pottery. 1. The T'ang poet, Li Po 李白, holding his cup of greyish-green glazed ware decorated with brown patches; × ½.   2. Three-legged jar of greyish-green glazed ware with decorated design in greenish-brown. Legs moulded with masks in relief; × ⅕.   3. Water vessel of greyish-green glazed ware with brown-green patches as decoration; × ⅟₁.   4. Basin of greyish-green glazed ware with decorative pattern in green and brown; × ⅕.   5. Toys in the shape of birds and animals of green, brown and grey glazed ware; × ½.   6. Toys in the shape of human figures of green, brown and grey glazed ware; × ½.

287

PLATE 90

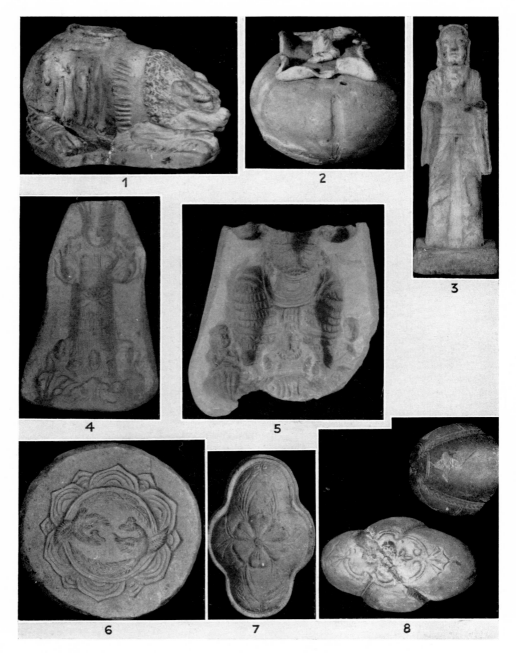

Ch'iung-lai pottery. 1. Water vessel in the shape of a lion of white-slipped ware; ×½.
2. Persimmon of white-slipped ware. Hand-modelled. Pi-chia-shan-chuang collection; slightly
reduced.   3. Buddhist figurine of white-slipped ware; ×¼.   4. Pottery mould of a
Lokapala of hard-baked terra-cotta ware; ×⅓.   5. Fragment of a Lokapala mould of hard-
baked terra-cotta ware; ×⅓.   6. Mould of a bowl of hard-baked terra-cotta ware. Design of
a pair of phoenix over lotus petals in low relief; ×¼.   7–9. Moulds of 'oval-shaped' cups of
hard-baked terra-cotta ware. Carved floral patterns; ×½.

PLATE 91

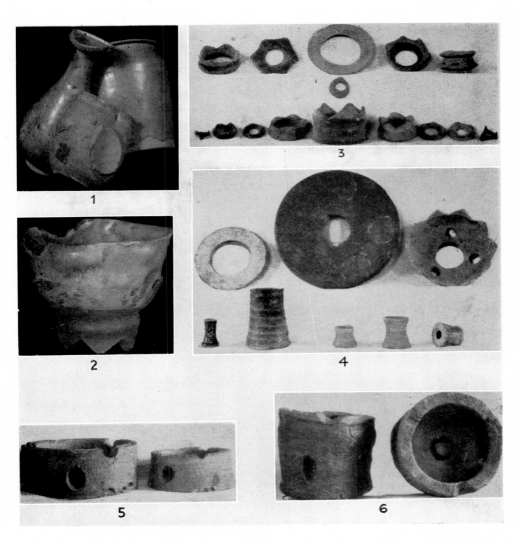

Ch'iung-lai pottery. 1. Kiln reject. Three deformed jars stuck together; ×¼. 2. Kiln reject. Deformed and broken cup attached to a firing stand or 'separator'; ×¼. 3–4. Groups of firing stands or 'separators' of hard-baked terra-cotta ware; ×½–¹⁄₁₀. 5–6. Saggars of hard-baked coarse terra-cotta ware; ×⅕.

PLATE 92

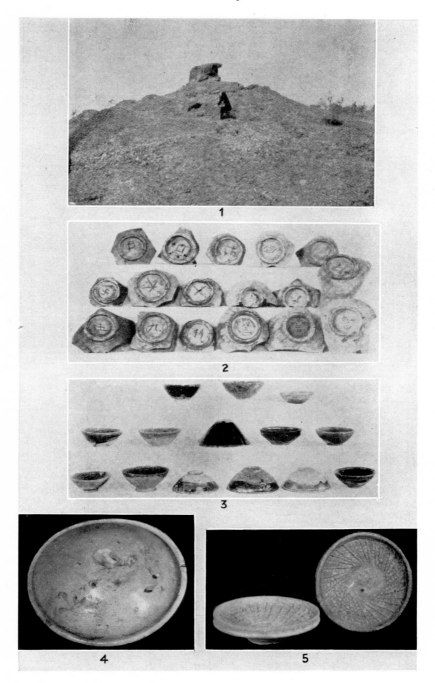

Liu-li-ch'ang pottery. 1. One of the refuse heaps at Liu-li-ch'ang. 2. Base fragments showing various types of potter's marks; $\times \frac{1}{4}$. 3. Conical-shaped bowls of brown and green glazed ware; $\times \frac{1}{4}$. 4. Bowl of greyish-green glazed ware with light brown decorative pattern. A loop handle at the bottom inside; $\times \frac{1}{2}$. 5. Graters of hard-baked terra-cotta ware; $\times \frac{1}{2}$.

PLATE 93

Liu-li-ch'ang pottery. 1. Jar of brownish glazed ware; $\times \frac{1}{4}$. 2. Vase of brownish glazed ware. Handles on the shoulder; $\times \frac{1}{5}$. 3. Vase of brownish glazed ware. Handles on the shoulder; $\times \frac{1}{10}$. 4. Tripod incense-burner of brownish glazed ware with metal-shaped handles; $\times \frac{1}{4}$. 5. Vase of brownish glazed ware with two loop handles; $\times \frac{1}{2}$. 6. Pitcher of greyish glazed ware with spout and handles on the shoulder; $\times \frac{1}{2}$. 7. Flat disc-shaped flask of greyish glazed ware with handles on the shoulder; $\times \frac{1}{2}$.

PLATE 94

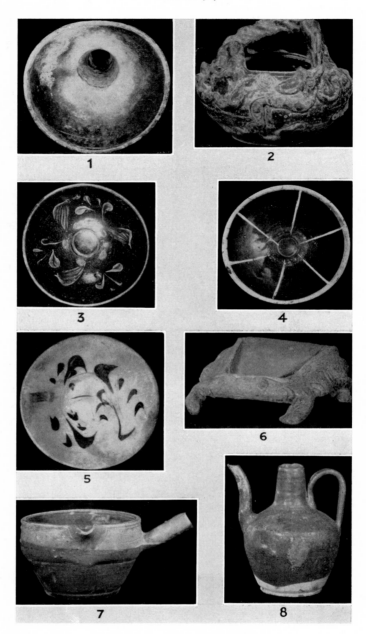

Liu-li-ch'ang pottery. 1. Funnel of hard-baked terra-cotta ware; ×⅓. 2. Water bucket of brown glazed ware with handle in the shape of a dragon whose head is missing; ×⅓. 3. Shallow bowl of brown glazed ware with painted design in white glaze; ×⅓. 4. Bowl of brown glazed ware with painted design in white glaze; ×⅓. 5. Bowl of yellowish glazed ware with painted design in green glaze; ×¼. 6. Ink-slab in the shape of a frog of light brown glazed ware; ×¼. 7. Cauldron of yellowish glazed ware with beak at the mouth-rim and socketed handle at the side; ×¼. 8. Pitcher of brown glazed ware with tall spout and handle; ×¼.

PLATE 95

Liu-li-ch'ang pottery. 1. Pitcher of yellowish-green glazed ware with tall spout and handles, and dark green glazed design; × $\frac{1}{4}$. 2. Pitcher of yellowish-green glazed ware with spout on the shoulder and handles between shoulder and neck. Cloud pattern painted in dark green glaze; × $\frac{1}{4}$. 3. Vase of yellowish-green glazed ware with handles on the shoulder. Cloud pattern painted in dark green glaze; × $\frac{1}{8}$. 4. Vase of yellowish-green glazed ware with six handles. Painted design done in green glaze; × $\frac{1}{8}$. 5. Cup of white glazed ware with four handles; × $\frac{1}{2}$. 6. Basin of yellowish-green glazed ware with incised floral design painted in various shades of green and yellow glaze; × $\frac{1}{8}$.

PLATE 96

SUNG STONE TOMB

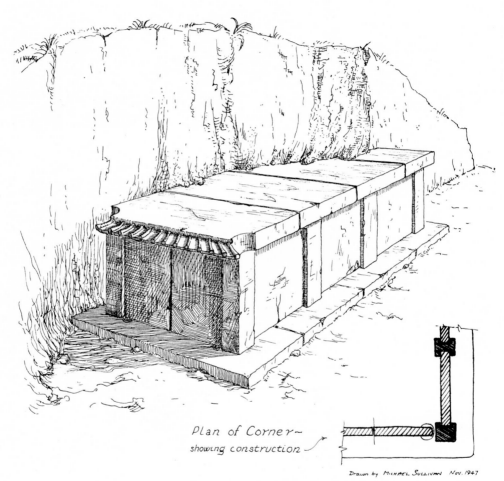

Plan of Corner~
showing construction

Drawn by Michael Sullivan Nov. 1947

Sketch of a Sung stone tomb near Chengtu. By Michael Sullivan.

294

PLATE 97

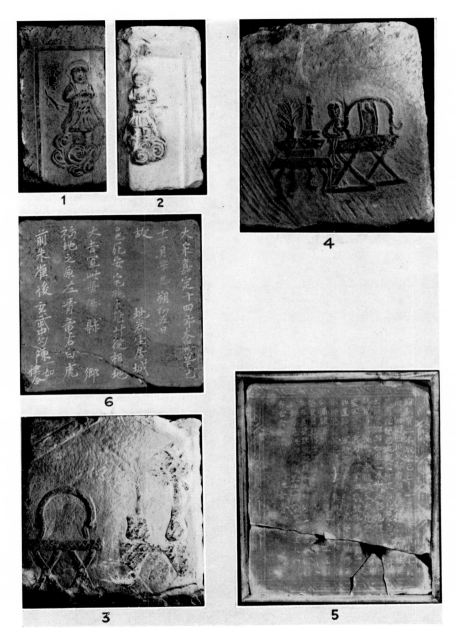

1–2. Decorated stone columns from a Sung tomb in Chengtu. Red sandstone; $\times\frac{1}{10}$. 3–4. Decorated stone wall panels from a Sung tomb in Chengtu. Red sandstone; $\times\frac{1}{10}$. 5. Inscribed tombstone dated A.D. 969. Red sandstone; $\times\frac{1}{8}$. 6. Inscribed tombstone dated A.D. 1221. Excavated on the University campus. Red sandstone; $\times\frac{1}{4}$.

PLATE 98

SUNG BRICK TOMB

Drawn by Michael Sullivan Nov 1947.

Sketch of a Sung brick tomb in Chengtu. By Michael Sullivan.

PLATE 99

1. Contents of a small brick burial excavated by Dr David C. Graham in 1934 on the West China Union University campus.　　2. Green-glazed drum-shaped container. Terra-cotta soft ware; $\times \frac{1}{2}$.　　3. Green-glazed three-legged *lu* or container. Terra-cotta soft ware; $\times \frac{1}{3}$.　　4. Brown glazed two-handled jar. Terra-cotta hard ware; $\times \frac{1}{2}$.　　5. Brown-glazed small bowl. Terra-cotta hard ware; $\times \frac{1}{2}$.

PLATE 100

1. Pottery warrior. White-slipped grey ware; ×¼.   2, 3. Heads of pottery warriors.
Painted and glazed, red soft ware; ×½.

PLATE 101

1–3. Pottery warriors. Tri-coloured glazed, red soft ware; ×$\frac{1}{2}$–$\frac{1}{4}$.
White-slipped, terra-cotta ware; ×$\frac{1}{3}$.

4. Pottery warrior.

PLATE 102

1, 2. Pottery warriors. Tri-coloured glazed, red soft ware; $\times \frac{1}{3}$.
3–5. Pottery warriors. Yellow-glazed, terra-cotta ware; $\times \frac{1}{3}$.

PLATE 103

1–5. Pottery male figurines. Tri-coloured glazed, red soft ware; × ½.
6. Pottery male figurine. Yellow-slipped, red soft ware; × ½.

PLATE 104

1, 2, 4. Pottery female figurines. Tri-coloured glazed, red soft ware; $\times\frac{1}{2}$.
3. Pottery female figurine. Yellow-slipped, red soft ware; $\times\frac{1}{3}$.

PLATE 105

1–4. Pottery kneeling figurines. Tri-coloured glazed, red soft ware; $\times \frac{1}{2} - \frac{1}{3}$.

PLATE 106

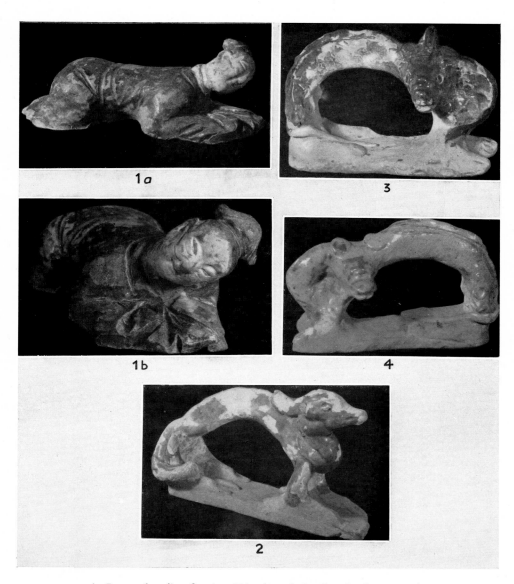

1a

1b

3

4

2

1. Pottery kneeling figurine. Tri-coloured glazed, red soft ware; ×½.
2–4. Pottery dragons. Green- or yellow-glazed, red soft ware; ×½.

PLATE 107

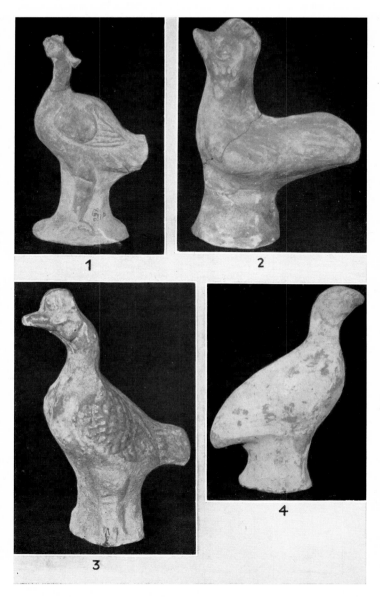

1–3. Pottery roosters. Red- or yellow-glazed, red soft ware; × ½.
4. Pottery rooster. Yellow-slipped, red soft ware; × ½.

PLATE 108

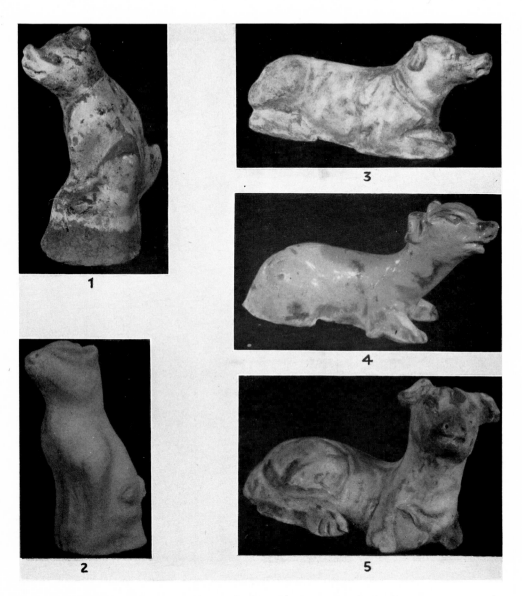

1, 3–5. Pottery dogs. Yellow-glazed, red soft ware; × ½.   2. Pottery dog. Terra-cotta ware; × ½.

PLATE 109

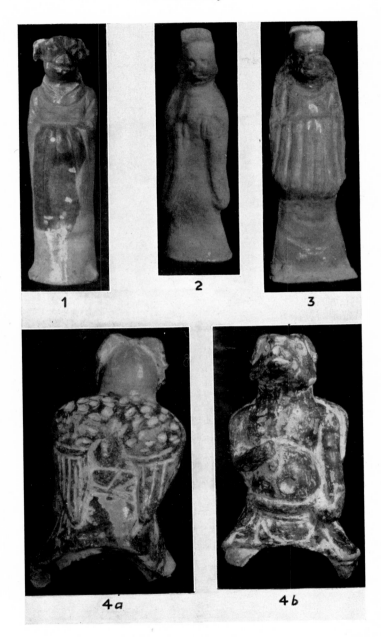

1. Pottery cow with human body. Tri-coloured glazed, red soft ware; ×½.　　2. Pottery monkey with human body. Terra-cotta ware; ×½.　　3. Pottery monkey with human body. Tri-coloured glazed, red soft ware; ×½.　　4. Pottery pig with wings. Red-glazed, red soft ware; ×½.

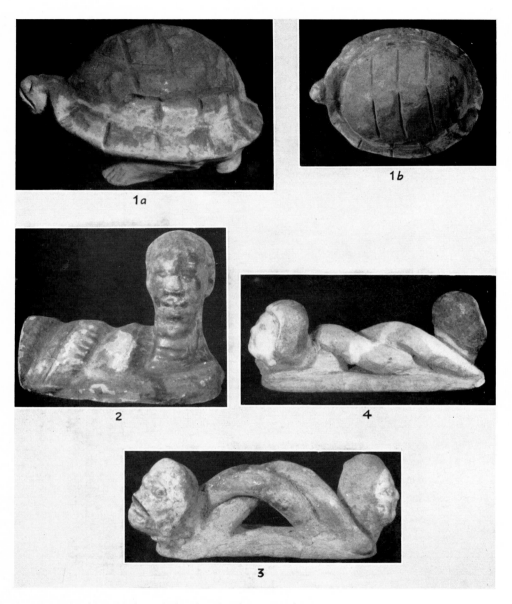

1a

1b

2

4

3

1. Pottery turtle. Tri-coloured glazed, red soft ware; ×½.   2–4. Pottery snakes with human head. Painted and glazed, red soft ware; ×½.

PLATE III

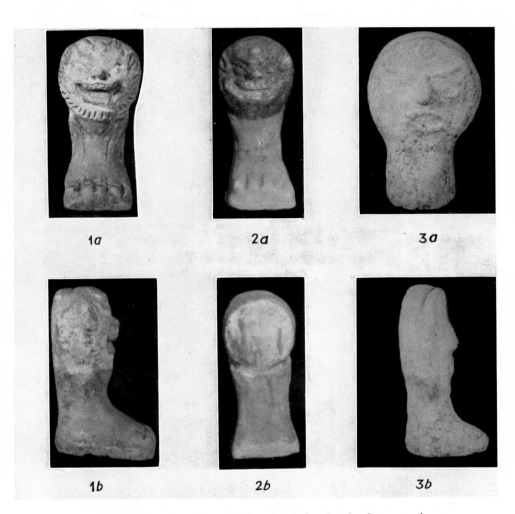

1, 2. Pottery masks with legs. Slipped and glazed, red soft ware; ×½.
3. Pottery mask with legs. Terra-cotta ware; ×½.

PLATE 112

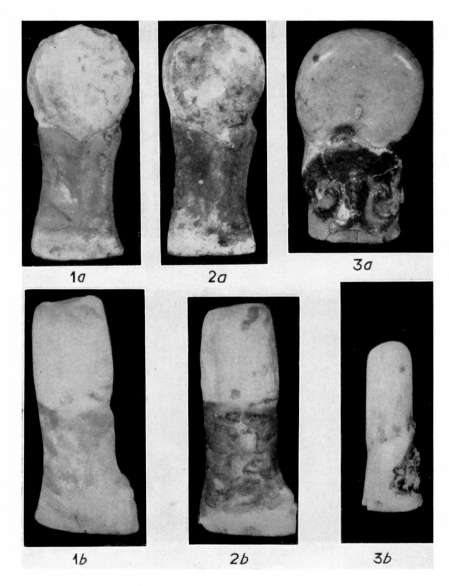

1. Pottery drum on stand. Yellow- and red-glazed, red soft ware; ×½.
2, 3. Pottery discs with pedestal. Yellow-glazed, red soft ware; ×½.

PLATE 113

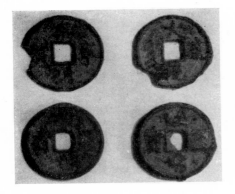

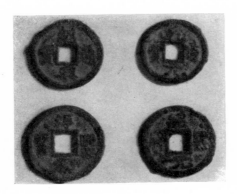

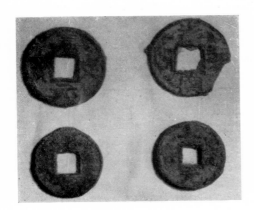
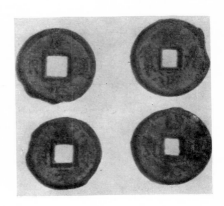

A series of iron coins (slightly smaller than the originals).

PLATE 114

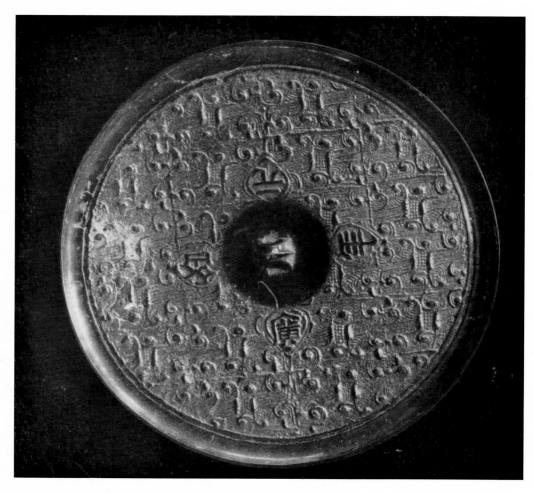

Kuang-chêng mirror with comma pattern. Bronze; $\times \frac{1}{1}$.

PLATE 115

1. *Ch'ien-tê* mirror. Iron; $\times \frac{1}{2}$. 2. *Chun yi kuan wei* mirror. Iron; $\times \frac{1}{2}$.
3. *Ch'êng-an* mirror. Bronze; $\times \frac{1}{2}$. 4–6. *Hu-chou* mirrors. Bronze; $\times \frac{1}{2}$.

PLATE 116

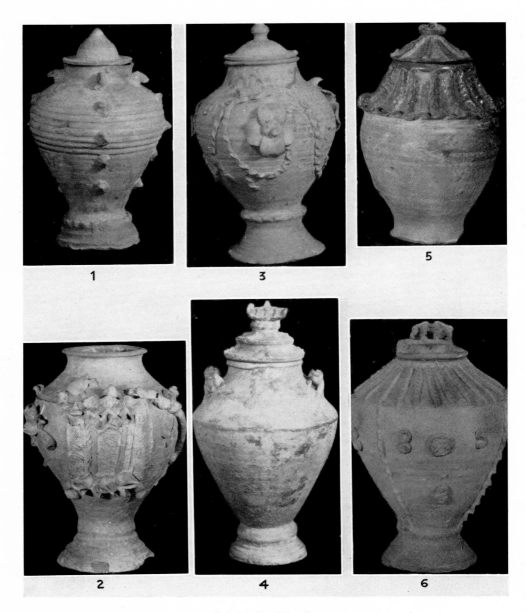

Pottery grave-jars. Slightly glazed, hard terra-cotta ware; $\times \frac{1}{4}$.

PLATE 117

1–3, 5–6. Pottery grave-jars. Terra-cotta ware (1, with yellow slip); $\times\frac{1}{4}$.
4. Pottery two-handled jar. Cord-marked, terra-cotta ware; $\times\frac{1}{4}$.

PLATE 118

1*a*
2*a*
3*a*

1*b*
2*b*
3*b*

1. Pottery *Pi-hsieh* from Shensi. Yellow-glazed, white ware; $\times \frac{1}{3}$. 2. Pottery *Pi-hsieh* from Shensi. Painted red soft ware; $\times \frac{1}{2}$. 3. Bronze *Pi-hsieh* from Shensi; $\times \frac{1}{2}$.

INDEX